Improving Schools,
Developing Inclusion

D1386107

Despite the efforts that have been made to bring about improvements in schools, some children and young people remain marginalised by current arrangements. The development of more inclusive schools remains one of the biggest challenges facing education systems throughout the world. However, inclusion remains a complex and controversial issue, and the development of inclusive practices in schools is not well understood.

Improving Schools, Developing Inclusion uses evidence from in-depth research to provide new insights as to how this important agenda should be addressed. The authors challenge many existing assumptions about school improvement and educational reform, and propose that the development of inclusive practices will only be achieved by engaging in dialogue about the deeply held beliefs of teachers and policy makers. In so doing, they provide a new way of thinking about how schools can be made more inclusive.

The approach to inclusive development recommended in the book has major implications for policy and practice in the field. It looks at:

- Implications for the work of school leaders
- How staff teams can work together in order to address barriers to participation and learning
- How schools can collect and use evidence in order to strengthen their practices
- The critical and alternative perspectives to which schools need access
- The implications for relationships between schools, local authorities and researchers

At a time when policy-makers and practitioners are searching for more effective ways of responding to student diversity, this challenging book offers powerful messages as to what needs to be done to move schools in a more inclusive direction.

Mel Ainscow, School of Education, University of Manchester, UK.
Tony Booth, Canterbury Christ Church University, UK.
Alan Dyson, School of Education, University of Manchester, UK.

Improving Learning TLRP

Series Editor: Andrew Pollard, Director of the ESRC Teaching and Learning Programme

Improving Schools, Developing Inclusion

Mel Ainscow, Tony Booth and Alan Dyson

with Peter Farrell, Jo Frankham, Francis Gallannaugh, Andy Howes and Roy Smith

Routledge
Taylor & Francis Group

LONDON AND NEW YORK

First published 2006
by Routledge
2 Park Square, Milton Park, Abingdon, Oxon OX14 4RN

Simultaneously published in the USA and Canada
by Routledge
270 Madison Ave, New York, NY 10016

Routledge is an imprint of the Taylor & Francis Group, an informa business

Transferred to Digital Printing 2007

Typeset in Charter ITC and StoneSans by
Keystroke, 28 High Street, Tettenhall, Wolverhampton
Printed and bound in Great Britain by
Cpod, Trowbridge, Wiltshire

British Library Cataloguing in Publication Data
A catalogue record for this book is available from the British Library

Library of Congress Cataloging in Publication Data
Ainscow, Mel.
Improving schools, developing inclusion / Mel Ainscow, Alan Dyson
and Tony Booth.
    p. cm.
Includes bibliographical references.
ISBN 0–415–37236–4 (hardback) – ISBN 0–415–37279–8 (pbk.)
1. Inclusive Education—England. I. Dyson, Alan.
II. Booth, Tony, 1944– III. Title.
LC1203. E54A56 2006
371.9′046—dc22   2006006405

ISBN10: 0–415–37236–4 (hbk)
ISBN10: 0–415–37279–8 (pbk)
ISBN10: 0–203–96715–8 (ebk)

ISBN13: 978–0–415–37236–7 (hbk)
ISBN13: 978–0–415–37279–4 (pbk)
ISBN13: 978–0–203–96715–7 (ebk)

Contents

Appendix

Series editor's preface

The Improving Learning series showcases findings from projects within ESRC's Teaching and Learning Research Programme (TLRP) – the UK's largest ever coordinated educational research initiative.

Books in the Improving Learning series are explicitly designed to support 'evidence-informed' decisions in educational practice and policy-making. In particular, they combine rigorous social and educational science with high awareness of the significance of the issues being researched.

Working closely with practitioners, organisations and agencies covering all educational sectors, the Programme has supported many of the UK's best researchers to work on the direct improvement of policy and practice to support learning. Over sixty projects have been supported, covering many issues across the life course. We are proud to present the results of this work through books in the Improving Learning series.

Each book provides a concise, accessible and definitive overview of innovative findings from a TLRP investment. If more advanced information is required, the books may be used as a gateway to academic journals, monographs, websites and so on. On the other hand, shorter summaries and research briefings on key findings are also available via the Programme's website at www.tlrp.org.

We hope that you will find the analysis and findings presented in this book helpful to you in your work on improving outcomes for learners.

Andrew Pollard
Director, Teaching and Learning Research Programme
Institute of Education, University of London

Acknowledgements

A key theme of this book is that of learning from difference. Our experience has been that knowledge about how schools can become more inclusive arises when we make use of the different views of those involved. It follows that the ideas that we develop in the book have been influenced by many people and that it is impossible to list them all by name.

We must thank our partners in the schools and LEAs who worked with us in the research network 'Understanding and Developing Inclusive Practices in Schools' and allowed us to join them as they strived to develop more inclusive practices. We hope that our accounts of their efforts provide at least a flavour of their commitment and dedication.

Two colleagues in particular, Alan Millward at Newcastle and Carrie Weston at Canterbury, made important contributions to the development of the network but are not listed in the authorship of this book. We must also thank our colleagues in the Teaching and Learning Research Programme for their support, particularly Judy Sebba who acted as our critical friend. Finally, we thank Averil Gould who became the communication hub for the network and also assisted in the production of the final text of the book.

Introduction

This book attempts to increase understanding of inclusion in education by engaging with the experiences of twenty-five schools as they sought to develop aspects of their cultures, policies and practices. In so doing it challenges many assumptions about school improvement and educational reform. It is, if you like, about 'school improvement with attitude'.

Most work on school effectiveness and improvement assumes that agreement about what constitutes a good school is possible and does not require discussion of fundamental questions of value (Morley and Rassool, 1999; Slee *et al.*, 1998; Thrupp 1999). Injecting 'attitude' into school improvement means forgoing this pretence at value neutrality. It reminds us that schools are concerned with how people learn together, how they treat one another and how they learn to live within a common world. So, school improvement becomes far more than a technical process of raising the capacity of schools to generate particular measurable outcomes. It involves dialogues about ethical principles and how these can be related to curricula, approaches to teaching and learning, and the building of relationships within and beyond schools. Discussions about school improvement must make explicit the values that underlie the changes seen to 'improve' them.

However, our version of improvement also involves challenging the separation of schools from their roles within communities and society. For us, educational policy should be concerned with the provision of 'good' local schools that encourage the participation of all within their communities. The development of such schools should be integrated with aspirations for the development of decent neighbourhoods for everyone. We see schools as having a mutually sustaining relationship with their communities, in which they recognise their role as a support to the education of communities, rather than as the sole source of educational opportunity. In Chapter 2 we discuss further how government policies both support and oppose such ideas.

We see inclusion as involving a principled approach to education and make explicit the values constituting this approach in Chapter 1. For us, then, an improved school is inevitably a more inclusive school. Our position is that schools should seek to put into practice, and so contribute to the development of a society more fully based on, inclusive values. Concerns with raising the attainment of children and young people can contribute to the enactment of these values. However, an exclusive focus on measured attainment reduces the possibilities of schools for realising their wider social purposes.

An exploration of inclusion requires us to make explicit the particular values, their meanings and implications, that we wish to see enacted through education. It starts from the belief that education is a basic human right and the foundation for a more just society. For many people, inclusion in education is thought of only as an approach to serving children with disabilities within general education settings. Internationally, however, it is increasingly seen more broadly as a reform that supports and welcomes diversity among all learners (UNESCO, 2001). The argument developed in this book adopts this broader formulation. It asserts that the aim of inclusion is to reduce exclusion and discriminatory attitudes, including those in relation to age, social class, ethnicity, religion, gender and attainment. It does not focus only on a response to individuals but on how settings, policies, cultures and structures can recognise and value diversity.

One of the advantages of working within the framework of inclusion is that it gives us access to a growing body of literature which articulates principles, undertakes critical analysis of current policy and practice, and offers examples of classrooms, schools and systems which to some extent enact the values in which we are interested. However, it would be a mistake to assume that this framework of values is uncontested and allows unequivocal translation into practice. There are at least three areas of uncertainty:

1. *The principles of inclusion.* Although we think it is important to make explicit the values on which our own work is based, simple assertion does not take those values beyond debate, as we discuss further in Chapter 1. We are aware that values are both historically and culturally located, and that other people, at other times and in other places, articulate different values. Even those who broadly support our approach to inclusion may wish to discuss their concerns using different terms and emphasising different issues. For us inclusion and its constituent values are meant to have

clear practical implications. We are aware that people may be happy to agree on values, say, those concerned with equity and participation, until they start to look in detail at their implications for practice.

2. *Enactment in context*. We are also aware that values and principles have to be enacted in particular institutional contexts, nested within particular local and national policy circumstances, and that this can make it far from obvious how they should be put into practice. However clearly we articulate values and principles, we still do not know everything about what they imply for actions in particular schools and classrooms; apparently similar actions may have different meanings in different contexts. The meaning of actions depends on how they are interpreted within a particular community and its cultures. Further, there can be conflicts over the implication of values for upholding the rights of different individuals; for example, when the participation of one interferes with the participation of another. Members of our team had previously set out in considerable detail what inclusion might mean for what happens in schools in the form of the 'Index for Inclusion' (Booth and Ainscow, 2002). It is argued in the Index that barriers to learning and participation, and the resources available to support learning and participation, have to be explored in any particular setting. This underlines the view that there can be no approach to development which does not involve a detailed exploration of a particular setting, drawing on the deep knowledge of its participants.

3. *Developing inclusive practices*. Even if we know a considerable amount about the implications of inclusive values for any particular context, we still do not know how best to put them into action, since making sustained principled changes within schools is notoriously difficult. How are schools developed? What should be the priorities for development within any particular setting and how should they be derived? How, precisely, do schools become more inclusive and sustain their development? What conditions make this most likely and what support do they need? What policies promote inclusion and what policies undermine it?

The purpose of this book is to shed further light on these areas of uncertainty. In particular, it explores what inclusion means and how it can be developed. Moreover, it addresses these issues in a very particular and challenging context.

Since 1988, different governments in England have introduced a series of much publicised policy changes in order to foster 'improvements' in state education. This massive 'reform' agenda has led American researchers to describe England as 'a laboratory where the effects of market-like mechanisms are more clearly visible than they are in the United States' (Finkelstein and Grubb, 2000, p. 602). Within this context, the notion of improvement has been narrowly defined. Consequently, while the government boasts of increases in national test and examination results, there is evidence that many students still feel marginalised. So, for example, following the publication of national examination results in 2004, it was reported that some 30,000 youngsters had left school without any qualifications at all, including disproportionate numbers from economically deprived areas and from certain minority ethnic groups (Machin *et al.*, 2005). At the same time, teachers report high levels of stress and there are particular problems of teacher retention in urban areas.

The national policy context is not entirely supportive of inclusion as we have defined it. However, it is not enough to wish away these negative features, nor even simply to berate government for its failures. The policy contexts within which inclusive values and principles have to be enacted are always likely to be complex, contradictory and, in some respects at least, inimical to inclusion. So too are institutions and classrooms, where multiple priorities, competing values, practical difficulties and personal relations interact. What matters, therefore, is that we understand what happens to inclusive values and principles in such hostile environments and how best to promote the growth of inclusion in circumstances with are always likely to be less than ideal.

This means that there is a tension at the heart of this book. It is a tension between the attempts to put values and principles into action, and the complexities of schools and education systems. The book is about engaging with the current realities of schools and exploring ways in which they might become more inclusive. Some may say that the tensions we explore lead us to compromise the very values we claim to be advocating. In our team meetings, we have confronted each other with this challenge many times. However, we prefer to say that our concern is not only with advocating the values of inclusion but also with finding ways of enacting them – and that enactment is always about messy complexities. If, therefore, this book is about school improvement with attitude, it is also about inclusion which is not afraid to get its hands dirty.

The research network

The research we present arises from the work of one of four national networks set up as the first phase of the Economic and Social Research Council's Teaching and Learning Research Programme (TLRP), the largest ever research initiative in education in the United Kingdom. The network called 'Understanding and Developing Inclusive Practices in Schools' involved teams of researchers from three higher education institutions (Manchester, Newcastle and Canterbury Christ Church Universities), each working with schools in one Local Education Authority (LEA). We wished to understand how, and how far, those schools set about developing inclusive practices, particularly in the context of a national policy environment that seemed indifferent if not downright hostile towards such development.

There is no shortage of books and articles that have extolled the value of inclusive education. These have provided a whole range of accounts of what we prefer to call 'instructive practice', since, unlike notions of 'good practice', such accounts invite the reader to retain a critical perspective and learn from the ideas, including the mistakes of others. However, despite these developments, inclusion remains a complex and controversial issue, and the development of inclusive practices in schools is not well understood. This study differed significantly from much of the existing literature on inclusion in education in the following ways:

- It defined inclusion as an *approach* to education embodying particular values. It was therefore concerned with all learners and with overcoming barriers to all forms of marginalisation, exclusion and underachievement. The great majority of previous studies take a much narrower view of inclusion as concerned with children with impairments, or otherwise categorised as 'having special educational needs'.
- Its scrutiny of developments in twenty-five schools, in three local education authorities, over three years, contrasts with shorter-term studies of individual schools.
- It was based in schools that thought about inclusion in different ways and varied in their commitment to the inclusive development of their cultures, policies and practices. Schools were not selected because they were thought to represent 'advanced' practice.
- It included some schools that the national system of inspection had rated as 'requiring special measures', or as 'having serious

weaknesses' as well as those seen to be successful. As a result, the findings of the study may be seen to be broadly relevant to schools.

• Its analysis of the development of practice in the context of classroom, institutional and systemic factors contrasts with research that explores only one of these levels.

• It made use of the different theoretical perspectives of a large team of researchers to analyse the findings of the study, rather than relying on a single viewpoint or conceptual framework.

The arguments presented are aimed at a wide range of readers interested in widening the participation, and improving the educational achievement, of children and young people, both in this country and overseas.

Outline of the book

The book has three parts. Following this introduction, Part I consists of three chapters that outline the context and agenda for the research that is reported. Chapter 1 explains what the three university groups brought to the work, explores the variety of approaches to inclusion and sets out the particular approach of the research team. Chapter 2 focuses more specifically on the English policy context, and reflects upon the implications of inclusion for approaches to school development and government educational policy. It stresses the significance of the English case as a context for researching the development of inclusion in schools, and analyses the barriers and resources for the development of inclusion located within government education policy. Chapter 3 explains how the network was set up in the three local authorities and describes the collaborative action research approach that was used.

There are three chapters in Part II, each of which draws on evidence from the three interconnected studies. These chapters analyse how barriers to participation are created within the English education system, the attempts of practitioners in schools to address these barriers and the possibilities for those working within higher education to contribute to school development. Each of these chapters is focused on one local authority, its schools and classrooms, and the impact of local and national policies on them.

Part III consists of two chapters that draw out the implications of the research. Chapter 7 compares and contrasts the findings of the three studies, focusing on both their process and outcomes, in order to synthesise the findings of the network's programme of research. It analyses the different ways in which the three university groups chose to interpret their common task and uses these differences as a resource to deepen the analysis of what happened in each case. It draws together the explanations of the barriers to participation and learning experienced by students in English schools and how such barriers might be addressed. It argues that current efforts to raise standards are themselves creating barriers for some groups. Nevertheless, the three studies point to strategies for inclusive development that may be applied within the existing policy environment and consideration is given to the impact of such approaches on the learning of all members of a school's communities. Here the emphasis on 'levels' that is evident in each of the accounts provides a means of illuminating the complex interaction of a range of factors.

The final chapter addresses the strategic implications of the findings, focusing once again on different levels in the education system. It is suggested that substantial progress towards a more inclusive education system will depend on: a clearer conceptualisation of the term 'inclusion' among all stakeholders; less fragmentation of efforts among support and regulatory agencies; and a reform of the criteria used to measure student progress and school effectiveness. It is argued that the development of inclusive practices, particularly on a wide, national basis, can only be achieved by engaging in dialogue about the deeply held beliefs of teachers and policy makers rather than through sudden transformations imposed from outside. This has implications for the roles of headteachers, for how staff teams work together, and for how schools collect and use evidence about their practice. It also has implications for the sorts of critical and alternative perspectives to which schools have access and therefore for their relationships with other schools, LEAs and researchers. Finally, this has clear implications for the national policy framework.

Part I

What is the issue?

Chapter 1

Improving schools, developing inclusion?

In this chapter we examine what we brought to the research from our own knowledge and experience, and from examining the thinking of others. In so doing, we explore the ways in which inclusion has been and should be understood before beginning, in the next chapter, the process of analysing the resources for, and barriers to, the development of inclusion within government education policies. Within this overall context, we define the main agenda for the book, namely that of determining ways in which inclusive school development can be encouraged.

The title of this book is intended to provoke thinking about two questions: When and how do improvements in schools become inclusive development? How can inclusive school development be best supported? In so doing, we draw attention to the highly contentious nature of improvement in schools. One person's view of an improving institution may be another's vision of educational hell. This means that we cannot understand improvement in education without considering the values underlying the changes we would like to take place. For us, inclusion is fundamentally about the specification of those values and how they can be put into action.

The English educational policy context makes the study of inclusion particularly interesting. Since 1988, both Conservative and Labour governments have introduced a series of policy changes which have encouraged competition and accountability regimes as the means for driving up 'standards' in state education (Ball, 2001). Yet since the Labour government came to power in 1997, this agenda has been combined with an unprecedented emphasis on inclusion.

On the face of it, inclusion and the standards agenda are in conflict because they imply different views of what makes an improved school, different ways of thinking about achievements and different routes for raising them. How would schools in this period make sense of such competing pressures? The research we report also attempts to provide some answers to this further question.

Building on experience

The three co-directors of the network brought with them many years of experience in studying the issues of inclusion and exclusion in education. Alan Dyson had previously carried out a series of detailed studies of processes of inclusion in schools. Some of his early work was based on what he has referred to as an 'optimistic view', in which radical change to education seemed possible, particularly in terms of over-throwing established and discredited categorical approaches to children who experienced difficulties in schools (Dyson, 1990a, 1990b, 1991). Together with his colleagues, Dyson spent some time working with schools which reconstructed their 'special educational needs' systems in favour of more flexible, non-categorical responses to a much wider range of student diversity (Clark et al., 1995a; Dyson et al., 1994). They noted that these schools seemed to be bucking the trend of how schools understood and responded to students who experienced difficulties, to be locating the source of those difficulties in their own systems, structures and practices and, to that extent, to be pointing the way towards an unequivocally more inclusive future. However, as they studied these schools more closely, they came to the conclusion that all was not as it seemed (Clark et al., 1995b, 1997, 1998, 1999; Dyson and Millward, 2000, 2001). Developments in these schools, they concluded, were full of contradictions: the rhetoric of radical approaches was not shared by some – or, in some cases, by most – of their teachers; radical aspects of practice and provision were commonly accompanied by other aspects that were far less radical and some way from being 'inclusive'; and even the radical policies which they espoused were ambiguous and contradictory.

Much of Mel Ainscow's previous work, too, had focused on processes of inclusive development within educational systems. This had also shown that such changes are far from straightforward, not least because they challenge so much of existing attitudes and practice, and the current use of resources (Ainscow, 1999). Other research had focused on classroom processes (e.g. Ainscow, 1999, 2000; Ainscow and Brown,

2000), school development (e.g. Ainscow, 1995; Ainscow *et al.*, 1998; Hopkins *et al.*, 1994, 1997a, b), teacher development (e.g. Ainscow, 1994), and systemic change (e.g. Ainscow and Haile-Giorgis, 1999; Ainscow *et al.*, 2000), particularly in respect to the role of LEAs (e.g. Ainscow and Howes, 2001; Ainscow and Tweddle, 2003). Members of the Manchester group had also carried out a series of research reviews in relation to the research described in this book (e.g. Ainscow, Fox and O'Kane, 2003; Howes *et al.*, 2002). Much of their earlier research had been influenced by Kurt Lewin's dictum that 'you cannot understand an organisation until you try to change it' (Lewin, 1946; Schein, 1992), and so it had led the Manchester group to position themselves as agents for development alongside their partners in the field.

Tony Booth came to the research with an involvement in developing ideas about inclusion since the 1970s (Booth, 1981a; Booth and Potts, 1983). While some people now wish to draw a clear line between the meanings of integration and inclusion, Booth and his colleagues always saw the notion of integration as carrying an approach to school and social reform (Booth, 1988, 1999). Views of integration and then inclusion were linked to a notion of comprehensive community education from nursery, through the years of compulsory education to higher or lifelong education (Booth, 1983, 1996a). Inclusion was connected to a principle of equality of value of all students and staff within education (Booth, 1981b). Inclusion was seen to involve schools in recognising and valuing the diversity of their students and thus arranging for them to learn together in mixed collaborating groups. The process of inclusion involved schools in extending this diversity to include all students within their communities and to counter all forms of selection and exclusion (Booth, 1996b, 2003a and 2003b). From early on, accounts were gathered about the implications of an inclusive approach to the development of practice and policy within education systems (Booth and Coulby, 1987; Booth and Swann, 1987; Booth *et al.*, 1987, 1992a, 1992b). Such implications were set out in most precise detail, for schools, and for early years and childcare settings, within versions of the Index for Inclusion (Booth and Ainscow, 2002; Booth *et al.*, 2004). These placed a new emphasis on the role of cultures in creating and sustaining development.

Some previous work had involved the three senior authors in working together. In what turned out to have been a pilot for this book, in the mid-1990s they carried out a series of studies of processes of inclusion and exclusion in an urban secondary school (Ainscow *et al.*, 1999; Booth *et al.*, 1997, 1998; Dyson *et al.*, 1999). The experience of working collaboratively in the context of that school pointed to the benefits of researchers with different points of view exploring a common context. It also drew attention to the value of working in partnership with practitioners in order to make sense of such experiences.

In researching areas in which we had already done a considerable amount of work, there was the obvious danger that we would look for, and then find, only what supported our preconceptions. In the event, we set out to challenge our previous ideas, not least by challenging one other. We added to the theoretical resources available by creating teams of researchers in each of the participating universities, the members of which also brought their own experiences and perspectives. In addition, we were helped considerably by the astute questioning from those with whom we researched in schools and LEAs.

Defining inclusion

Inclusion may be defined in a variety of ways. Often, however, explicit definitions of the term are omitted from publications, leaving readers to infer the meanings it is being given for themselves. Definitions can be descriptive or prescriptive. A descriptive definition of inclusion reports on the variety of ways 'inclusion' is used in practice, whereas a prescriptive definition indicates the way we intend to use the concept and would like it to be used by others. Both kinds of definition are important to us.

Experience had taught us that many different views of inclusion exist in the field (Ainscow *et al.*, 2000) and that there is no one perspective on inclusion within a single country or school (Booth, 1995; Booth and Ainscow, 1998). Consequently, we felt it was important within our research to find out more about how policy makers, local authority staff and teachers in schools talked about inclusion. However, in order to be able to assess and comment on the extent to which 'inclusion' was occurring in the schools we had to decide how we thought the term should be used.

While we were keen to bring a degree of coherence to our own thinking, we also felt it important to map the complexity of the contexts in which we were to work. In particular, we wanted to be clear about the strands of thinking about inclusion within government policies, not least because we assumed that these influenced schools and LEAs which we set out to understand. Indeed, our previous work had led us to anticipate that such separate strands might in themselves act as barriers to the development of coherent change.

With this in mind, we developed a typology of six ways of ways of thinking about inclusion:

1. Inclusion as a concern with disabled students and others categorised as 'having special educational needs'.
2. Inclusion as a response to disciplinary exclusion.
3. Inclusion in relation to all groups seen as being vulnerable to exclusion.
4. Inclusion as developing the school for all.
5. Inclusion as 'Education for All'.
6. Inclusion as a principled approach to education and society.

In what follows we outline these six approaches and offer a commentary on them.

Inclusion as concerned with disability and 'special educational needs'

There is a common assumption that inclusion is primarily about educating disabled students, or those categorised as 'having special educational needs', in mainstream schools. Inevitably many of the participants in the research started out with such an assumption. This is also true of several government documents. Thus, for example, the government's programme for action on special educational needs referred to inclusion as 'the keystone' of its educational policy (DfEE, 1998b). Yet this was a reference not to general educational policy but to policy concerned with children categorised as 'having special educational needs':

> We want to see more pupils with SEN included within mainstream primary and secondary schools. We support the United Nations Educational, Scientific and Cultural Organisation (UNESCO) Salamanca World Statement on Special Needs Education 1994. This calls on governments to adopt the principle of inclusive education, enrolling all children in regular schools, unless there are compelling reasons for doing otherwise. That implies the progressive extension of the capacity of mainstream schools to provide for children with a wide range of needs.
>
> (DfEE, 1997, p. 44)

We question the usefulness of an approach to inclusion that, in attempting to increase the participation of students, focuses on a 'disabled' or 'special needs' part of them and ignores all the other ways in which participation for any student may be impeded or enhanced. The Index for Inclusion dispensed with the use of the notion of 'special educational needs' to account for educational difficulties. Specifically, it proposed the replacement of notions of 'special educational need' and 'special educational provision' with those of 'barriers to learning and participation' and 'resources to support learning and participation'. In this context, support was seen as all activities, which increase the capacity of schools to respond to diversity (Booth and Ainscow, 2002). Such a shift complements the ideas of others, such as Susan Hart in her 'innovative thinking' (Hart, 1996, 2000), and in 'learning without limits' (Hart *et al.*, 2004).

Yet in rejecting a 'special educational needs' view of inclusion, we would not wish to deflect attention from the continued segregation of disabled students, or, indeed, students otherwise categorised as 'having special educational needs'. Inclusion may be seen to involve the assertion of the rights of disabled young people to a local mainstream education, a view propounded vociferously by sections of the disabled people's movement (see e.g. Lipsky and Gartner, 1997; Peters, 2003). Where people see placement in special schools as a neutral response to 'need' they may argue that some children are best served in special settings. However, a rights perspective invalidates such arguments. Thus, compulsory segregation is seen to contribute to the oppression of disabled people (Abberley, 1987), just as other practices marginalise groups on the basis of race, gender or sexual orientation (Corbett, 1995).

We are also concerned about the significant effect that categorisation has on the education system as a whole. The practice of segregation within special schools involves a relatively small number of students (approximately 1.3 per cent in England – Norwich, 2002), yet it exerts a disproportionate influence within the education system. It perpetuates a view that some students 'need' to be segregated *because* of their deficiency or defect. In this way it legitimates a ladder of increasingly specialised support within the mainstream for children seen to 'have special educational needs', which may lead eventually to special school placement. It also reinforces a mistaken connection between special provision and special placement.

The conception of children as 'having special educational needs', backed up by the revised Special Educational Needs Code of Practice (DfES, 2001a), undermines a transformative view of inclusion, in which diversity is seen as making a positive contribution to the creation of responsive educational settings. At the same time, it limits notions of 'support' to work with particular categorised students, rather than the inclusive development of all aspects of a school.

The special educational needs view of educational difficulty is deeply entrenched within English national and local educational policies, and practices in schools. It also remains the dominant perspective in many other countries (Mittler, 2000). It absorbs difficulties that arise in education for a wide variety of reasons within the frame of individual defect. When, as is sometimes the case in England, 40 per cent or more of students may be thought, in a particular school, to 'have special educational needs', this weights discussion of inclusion through force of numbers, dragging it away from a broad conception concerned with developing schools for all students and staff, to a narrower view. It is hardly surprising, therefore, that many see inclusion through this lens.

Such a view is further reinforced when the deployment of additional resources, particularly the allocation of teaching assistants, is related to the categorisation of students. This growing body of support staff, who are usually drawn from their surrounding communities, and may move on from a school less frequently than teachers, may carry in the school cultures the default position on inclusion. Hence, they may convey a view of educational difficulties as created through student deficits to new members of staff, and to children and their families, even where this is countered by the perspectives of some teachers.

It is our view that categorisation processes, and the practices and language associated with them, act as barriers to the development of a broader view of inclusion. Understanding these processes, their effects, and ways of replacing them with alternative responses to educational difficulties, are of critical importance to research on inclusion. We note, for example, that there remains a massive over-representation of working-class boys in those categorised as having special educational needs, and a particular over-preponderance of African-Caribbean boys in those categorised as 'having emotional and behavioural difficulties' and in those subjected to disciplinary exclusion (Blair, 2001).

The legacy of such categorisation, and the way the term 'special educational needs' obscures such over-representation, means we still have limited understanding of how perceptions and constructions of gender, class and ethnicity contribute to the difficulties children and young people experience in schools. Yet it is more productive to explore the barriers to learning and participation that arise in education as a result of the way boys and girls, or children from different class and ethnic groups, are treated within and outside schools, than to categorise them and then explore their 'special educational needs' (see e.g. Epstein *et al.*, 1998).

Inclusion as a response to disciplinary exclusions

If inclusion is most commonly seen as associated with children categorised as 'having special educational needs', then its connection to 'bad behaviour' comes a close second. This arises in part because of the particular meaning given to exclusion within the 1986 Education Act, which used the term to refer to the temporary or permanent exclusion of children from school premises for disciplinary reasons. Thus, at the mention of the word 'inclusion', some within schools become fearful that it means they are to be immediately asked to take on disproportionate numbers of behaviourally 'difficult' students.

Although the number of students permanently excluded from schools for disciplinary reasons in England may be high by European standards (currently running at about 9,000 nationally), this is very few in any one area (there are 15,000 schools in England). We draw attention to this fact in response to commentators such as Garner and Gains (2001), who appear to exaggerate the numbers of children viewed as having difficulties in behaviour who are currently outside mainstream schools as a way of encouraging opposition to inclusion.

Just as in the case of 'inclusion', we prefer to define 'exclusion' for ourselves rather than follow a definition in a government document, and to see the two terms as inextricably linked. Inclusion involves the overcoming of exclusionary pressures; reducing exclusion involves finding ways to increase participation. Instead of seeing exclusion as a state of being barred from a school, we see it as concerned with all the discriminatory, devaluing as well as self-protective processes that go on within schools and society. Exclusion in this broader sense is pervasive and elusive, permeating our cultures and society, the institutions in which we work, and the aspirations which shape our identities. It can involve discrimination that may be personal or institutional, both local and global. Thus, inclusion may be viewed as being about reducing discrimination on the basis of gender, class, disability, sexual orientation, ethnicity, faith and family background.

Disciplinary exclusion itself cannot be understood without being connected with the events and interactions that precede it, the nature of relationships, and the approaches to teaching and learning in a school. Even at the level of simple measurement, the figures for formal disciplinary exclusion mean little when separated from numbers for informal disciplinary exclusions, for example, by sending children home for an afternoon, truancy rates, and the categorisation of students as having emotional and behavioural difficulties. In this respect the informal exclusion of school-age girls who become pregnant, who may be discouraged from continuing at school, continues to distort perceptions of the gender composition in the official exclusion figures.

Inclusion as about all groups vulnerable to exclusion

There is an increasing trend for exclusion in education to be viewed more broadly, in terms of overcoming discrimination and disadvantage in relation to any groups vulnerable to exclusionary pressures (e.g. Campbell, 2002; Hayton, 1999; Mittler, 2000). This is evident even in governmental and quasi-governmental usage. For instance, teachers are required by the statutory inclusion statement within the National Curriculum to be concerned with overcoming all forms of discrimination in their school (DfEE/QCA, 1999). Guidance to school inspectors requires similar vigilance (Ofsted, 2000a). Likewise, the government's early years initiative, Sure Start, has an inclusion theme, which explicitly links issues in access to services for children with special educational needs and disabilities with issues for a range of other disadvantaged groups (see http://www.surestart.gov.uk/ensuringquality/inclusion/).

This broader perspective is often associated in government documents with the terms 'social inclusion' and 'social exclusion'. Sometimes, these terms are given broad meanings, as in a series of documents produced by the Social Exclusion Unit, attached to the Cabinet Office, where social inclusion refers to interventions to reduce poverty and renew run-down neighbourhoods. (SEU, 1998, 2000a, 2000b, 2001). When used in an educational context, *social inclusion* tends to refer to issues for groups whose access to schools is under threat, such as girls who become pregnant or have babies while at school, looked-after children (i.e. those in the care of public authorities), and travellers. Yet commonly, the language of social inclusion and exclusion comes to be used more narrowly to refer to children who are (or are in danger of being) excluded from schools and classrooms because of their 'behaviour'. This is reflected in government circular 11/99, *Social Inclusion: Pupil Support*, concerned with attendance and disciplinary exclusion (DfEE, 1999b).

The broader use of the language of inclusion and exclusion is therefore somewhat fluid. It seems to hint that there may be some common processes which link the different forms of exclusion experienced by, say, children with disabilities, children who are excluded from their schools for disciplinary reasons and people living in poor communities. There seems, therefore, to be an invitation to explore the nature of these processes and their origins in social structures. However, this invitation is rarely, if ever, accepted in government texts. Instead, we commonly get a listing of vulnerable groups (see Ofsted, 2000a) or a litany of the risks to which groups are subject (DfES, 2003). As a result, 'social inclusion' and 'social exclusion' become catch-all terms which may be applied to widely differing groups with very different experiences in widely differing contexts. We find the addition of 'social' to some discussions of inclusion and exclusion but not others, unhelpful. It seems to imply that there are forms of exclusion which are not social and perhaps, therefore, natural.

Inclusion as the promotion of the school for all

A rather different strand of thinking about inclusion relates it to the development of the common school for all, or comprehensive school, and the construction of approaches to teaching and learning within it. The term 'comprehensive school' is generally used in England in the context of secondary education and was established as a reaction to a system which allocated children to different types of school on the basis of their attainment at age 11, reinforcing existing social class-based inequalities (Benn and Simon, 1972; Floud, 1961; Floud *et al.*, 1956). We argue that the idea of the comprehensive community for all children may be applied throughout the school years.

While there were moves away from such selection at secondary level to an extent in the 1970s and 1980s, some selective schools remained and selection has returned in a new form through the creation of specialist schools which can select up to 15 per cent of their pupils by so-called aptitude (see Docking, 2000; Walford, 2000). At the same time, the government's emphasis on giving parents a choice of schools based on the publication of examination results has led to an element of 'selection by estate agents', as families seek to move house in order to be in a more favourable position to gain a place in their preferred school.

Another type of school appeared in the early 2000s. Called city academies, their introduction was portrayed by government as a response to the difficulties that have been experienced in raising standards in economically poor urban contexts. These schools, which are in part privately funded, are exempt from LEA control and freed from adherence to the National Curriculum. Several such schools are funded by fundamentalist Christian sponsors and concern has been expressed about their practices of exclusion (Harris, 2005).

Interestingly, little attention has been given by those supporting inclusion to selection by religion, although one-third of schools in England remain attached to a particular religion, mainly Church of England or Catholic, but with a few Jewish and Muslim schools (Booth, 2003b). Reports of a wave of ethnic disturbances in northern cities in England in 2001 saw such religious segregation as contributing to ethnic disharmony (Home Office, 2001a, 2001b) but government support for schools attached to a particular religion remain firm and the numbers seem set to increase. Equally, the fact that approximately 7 per cent of pupils attend private schools, which segregate on the basis of wealth, is also largely omitted from the inclusion debate (see Potts (2003) for a discussion of some of the varieties of educational selection that take place within one English city).

The comprehensive school movement in England, like the Folkeskole tradition in Denmark (Hansen, 1992) and the 'common school' tradition in the USA (Franklin, 1994; Richardson, 1994), is premised on the desirability of creating a single type of 'school for all', serving a socially diverse community. However, the emphasis on one school for all can be double edged. In Norway, for example, the idea of 'the school for all' was as much about creating an independent singular Norwegian identity as it was to do with the participation of people within diverse communities. So while, in Norway, the strong emphasis on education for local communities facilitated the disbanding of segregated special institutions, it was not followed by an equally strong movement to reform the common school to embrace and value difference. As in some other countries, there was an emphasis on assimilating those perceived to be different into a homogeneous normality, rather than transformation through diversity (Haug, 2003). For us, the notion of the school for all is about a mutually sustaining relationship between schools and communities that recognises and values diversity.

Inclusion as 'Education for All'

The issue of inclusion is increasingly evident within international debates. The 'Education for All' (EFA) movement was created in the 1990s around a set of international policies, mainly coordinated by UNESCO, to do with increasing access to, and participation within education, across the world. It was given impetus by two major international conferences held in Jomtien in 1990, and Dakar in 2000 (UNESCO, 2000). While many within this movement appear to identify education with schooling, the focus on education within some of the poorest regions of the world provides an opportunity to rethink schools as one among a number of means for developing education within communities.

In response to the failure of many countries to meet the targets set a decade earlier, the organisers of the Dakar conference sought to emphasise particular areas where progress might be made, and focused attention, in particular, on the disproportionate numbers of girls around the world denied educational opportunities. Yet, while overcoming the exclusion of girls should be prioritised in many countries, in our view, setting global targets to be applied for specific groups has limited value because exclusion always occurs locally. Consequently, the priorities which need to be addressed are the barriers that need to be overcome within particular countries, regions and communities.

Disabled people and their allies, for example, were very concerned about the way they appeared to be pushed down the priority order for participation in the 'Education for All' declaration (UNESCO, 2000). This was despite the apparent progress that had been made in drawing attention to the possibilities for an education system inclusive of all children, specifically including disabled children, within the Salamanca Statement sponsored by UNESCO in 1994. Alur (1999) has documented (for India) the way disabled people are omitted when policies with apparently inclusive wording come to be implemented. We argue that the broad formulation of inclusion to which we subscribe may be used to reinvigorate the 'Education for All' movement so that it is genuinely concerned with the participation in education of all within their local communities.

Inclusion as a principled approach to education and society

The previous five ways of thinking about inclusion indicate meanings given to 'inclusion' by different people in different contexts. Sometimes, particular authors propose the general adoption of their particular definition of inclusion. We certainly differed between ourselves about the value of formulating prescriptive definitions of this sort, and this tension is evident in this and other chapters as we try to steer a path between our disparate views. On one side, it was argued that we should keep an open mind about what we meant by inclusion as we engaged in our research. On the other side, it was suggested that without a clear view of what we mean by inclusion we had no way of knowing how to support it, or of forming a judgement about when the actions of ourselves or others increased or decreased it.

We faced this tension directly as we began our work with schools. Moreover, we were entering the territory of English schools trying to develop inclusive practices in the context of a centrally driven 'standards' agenda, which had been only partially explored (for example, in our earlier study: Booth *et al.*, 1998). We wished to examine this terrain in greater depth and, in particular, to explore what inclusive practices might look like in this context and how such practices might be developed and sustained. While a detailed exploration of what inclusion might mean for a school's cultures, policies and practices had been set out in the Index for Inclusion, this did not mean that we knew in advance what actions should be taken. Barriers to learning and participation, and resources to support learning and participation, can only be uncovered and prioritised within a particular school. This implied, however, that our emphasis should be less on what inclusion might look like and more on how it might be developed with schools.

We took as our common starting point a view of inclusion which involved a broad articulation of the values to which we saw ourselves as committed and which inclusive practices, we believed, should attempt to embody. Values underlie all actions and plans of action, all practices within schools, and all policies for the shaping of practice. All actions, practices and policies may be regarded as the embodiment of moral arguments. We cannot do the right thing in education without understanding at some level the values from which our actions spring. The development of inclusion, therefore, involves us in making explicit the values that underlie actions, practices and policies, and learning how to better relate our actions to inclusive values.

Of course, we do not imply that making our values accessible is unproblematic, or that doing so is all that is necessary for us to act in accordance with them. We also require knowledge and skills, though the knowledge and skills we need to acquire are dependent on the values we wish to put into practice. Further, there has to be the opportunity for us to act, and actions are always more or less constrained by circumstances.

We articulated inclusive values as concerned with equity, participation, community, compassion, respect for diversity, sustainability and entitlement. This list is in a state of perpetual development. What of honesty, freedom, achievement, spirituality? To what extent may these further issues be derived from other concerns already on the list? For example, true participation may imply freedom to participate and perhaps not participate. However, in setting out a provisional list of concerns we invite others to think about the basis of their actions and the directions in which they would like to see the development of education.

We recognise, too, that the articulation of such principles invites two questions: What is their precise meaning and what are their implications for practice? The question about meaning is an acknowledgement that value statements such as this require considerable elucidation: they are complex, they may be disputed and they may conflict. For example, in relation to equity, it should be clear how much people differ about the acceptability of differences in income and living conditions within and between countries. There were, for example, opportunities to reflect on such issues during a meeting of our research network held at a large new football stadium. The lifestyles and salaries of footballers provide an index of accepted levels of aspiration. Once such aspirations for incredible riches and status become part of the identities of those in relative poverty, they help to police the current structured inequality on which they depend. Ideas of equality of opportunity, which do not also encourage the flattening of the pyramidal structure of opportunities, similarly act to obscure inequality.

Other 'inclusive values' similarly require elucidation. For example, participation is about being with and collaborating with others. It implies active engagement and an involvement in making decisions. It involves the recognition and valuing of a variety of identities, so that people are accepted for who they are. In valuing community the significance is acknowledged of the social role of education in creating and maintaining communities, and of the potential for communities and educational institutions to mutually sustain each other. The valuing of community may be seen to involve the development of sentiment and responsibility for groups wider than both the family and the nation state: it is about citizenship and global citizenship. Community, as a value, invites attention to the cultivating of feelings of public service. There is an irony within government policy that under the banner of school choice discourages schools from taking responsibility for their surrounding communities, yet is dependent on the public service commitment of teachers to continue to develop education in challenging circumstances.

The idea of sustainability connects inclusion to the most fundamental aim of education: to prepare children and young people for sustainable ways of life within sustainable communities and environments. At a time when global warming is arguably the most important issue affecting everyone on the planet, inclusion should be concerned with permeating within education an understanding of it and responses to it. Entitlement involves the recognition and conviction that children and young people have rights to a broad education, appropriate support and to attendance at their local school.

However, such elucidation only takes us a certain way. As we have said, we need to know not only what these values mean, but also their implications for practice and how they might be put into effect. Given our previous experiences, we could not pretend that we had no ideas about these issues. Even given the differences between us, we could agree on some of the broad features of inclusion in schools. Inclusion, we believed, referred to:

- The processes of increasing the participation of students in, and reducing their exclusion from, the curricula, cultures and communities of local schools.
- Restructuring the cultures, policies and practices in schools so that they respond to the diversity of students in their locality.
- The presence, participation and achievement of all students vulnerable to exclusionary pressures, not only those with impairments or those who are categorised as 'having special educational needs'.

Several features of these characterisations of inclusion were of particular importance to us: **inclusion is concerned with all children and young people in schools; it is focused on presence, participation *and* achievement; inclusion and exclusion are linked together such that inclusion involves the active combating of exclusion; and inclusion is seen as a never-ending process. Thus an inclusive school is one that is on the move, rather than one that has reached a perfect state**. Among the drawbacks of such a view is that it identifies education with schooling, whereas we view a school as only one of the sites of education within communities. In this sense, we see the role of schools as supporting the education of communities not to monopolise it.

We also wished to emphasise the significance of the participation of staff, parents/carers and other community members. It seems to us that we will not get very far in supporting the participation and learning of students if we reject their identities and family backgrounds, or if we choose not to encourage the participation of staff in schools in decisions about teaching and learning activities. We also wanted to connect inclusion/exclusion in education more broadly with including and excluding pressures within society.

Putting these ideas together with the approach to values means that we broadly supported a national approach to education based around comprehensive community pre-school, school and post-school education, and saw educational entitlement as worldwide. We were thus committed to the school for all and the inclusive development of Education for All. We recognised the complexity and contradictions in providing inclusive higher education but were clear that in the competitive divisive system operating within England, there was considerable scope for inclusive change.

We thus started with something specific to say about inclusion. Some may want to see this as our agreed 'definition' of inclusion. However, if so, it is tentative and open. Given our focus on values, rather than on practices and forms of provision, inclusion, we believed, could only be defined as the embodiment of those values *in particular contexts*. By the same token, of course, the broad values we were able to articulate only become fully meaningful as and when they are so embodied.

In some cases a particular set of practices are so integral to our conception of inclusion that they define themselves: for example, the reduction of bullying among children and adults in education, or the building of relationships of collaboration and respect, or the involvement in schools of parents/carers and their surrounding communities. In other respects we felt that we knew a great deal from experience about what practices and provisions were *likely* to embody inclusive values and what those values were *likely* to look like in practice.

However, what is likely to be the case may not be what is actually the case. The contexts of practice – the realities of particular teachers working with particular groups of children in particular schools where particular policy imperatives are at work – are complex and contradictory. Doing the right thing may sometimes involve choices between almost equally undesirable alternatives, and the consequences of actions may be unclear and values may conflict. Action in any particular situation requires relevant knowledge and skills, and we may be more or less knowledgeable and skilful. Yet, if the activities involved in working as a teacher, teaching assistant, school secretary or LEA officer are to promote inclusion, then they must involve knowledge about how inclusive values can be related to action, the skills that need to be acquired as a consequence, and the further knowledge that needs to be pursued.

Summary and conclusions

In this chapter we have set out some of the ways the terms 'inclusion' and 'exclusion' have been used, particularly in English policy texts. We have argued that different groups in different contexts think of inclusion differently and that there is no single, consensual definition. We have also set out our own starting position for thinking about inclusion in this study, which involves a commitment to certain broadly defined values. Inclusion in education may then be seen as a process of putting values into action; it results in the educational practices and provisions, systems and structures which embody those values. Some of these we can specify because they are integral to our conception of inclusion, others we can identify with a reasonable degree of certainty on the basis of what we have learned from experience. However, inclusion can only be fully understood as its underpinning values are played out *in particular contexts*.

The unfolding of this process of contextual embodiment provided the focus of this book. The contexts with which we are primarily concerned are those formed by the schools with which we worked. However, those schools were themselves located within a national policy environment, themselves constrained within national and international economic and social circumstances. We have already indicated some of the tensions and possibilities created by national policies. In Chapter 2, we analyse such implications for inclusive educational development in more detail.

Chapter 2

Inclusive development and the policy context

Our work with schools and LEAs began towards the end of the first term of the 'New' Labour government that was elected in 1997. This government had made no discernible attempt to revitalise the idea of 'a school for all', or to permeate its policies with inclusive values. Instead its policies were characterised by a concern with 'excellence', 'standards' and 'accountability'. In this chapter, we explore this policy context in more detail. Our aim is not to review the full range of education policy, nor to explore all of its implications. We focus only on its implications for inclusive development. In this way we provide wider contexts for the research reported in the rest of the book.

The standards agenda adopted by the Labour government involved particular approaches to the raising of achievement: that competition between schools, the setting of challenging targets for each school, regular inspections, combined with a fear of failure and the public exposure this involved would create a drive for success and ratchet up the scores of students on national tests. These approaches built on and strengthened many of the features of the preceding Conservative governments' policies which had seemed so divisive in the 1980s and early 1990s.

According to the standards agenda, whatever works (within legal limits) to push up standards is seen as good education. It therefore obscures a discussion of the values and relationships that do, and should, underlie educational change. It portrays education as a technology, and teachers as operatives within a system designed by boffins at the centre.

Labour's policies reinforced schools' accountability for 'standards' by setting national attainment targets, which were cascaded down to LEA and school level. They also reduced teachers' control over the curriculum by introducing highly prescriptive national literacy and numeracy strategies. They also sharpened competition by promoting an ever-increasing diversity of school types and infamously proclaiming, in a phrase introduced by the Prime Minister's speechwriter, the death of the 'bog-standard comprehensive school'. In this way, the comprehensive school was caricatured as a place where there was a 'tendency to uniformity' and where a doctrine had grown that 'all had the same ability' (DfEE, 1997, p. 11).

Educational debate from government itself became simplified through the uniform repetition of phrases orchestrated from within the Cabinet Office, repeated in speech after speech from a variety of different secretaries of state for education, who all wished to end the 'one-size-fits-all' secondary school (*Observer*, 23 June 2002, *Independent*, 9 July 2004). Ironically the speechwriter who coined the phrase 'bog-standard comprehensive' moved on to become a teacher at the very comprehensive school to which the Prime Minister had avoided sending his own children (BBC News, 7 February 2005).

However, it has been a remarkable feature of government policy, as we suggested in Chapter 1, that at the same time as emphasising competition and selection, it introduced an unprecedented number of policies that made explicit reference to inclusion and appeared to strongly support the idea. Government documents represented all of the strands on inclusion we have outlined in Chapter 1. They even included an implicit reference to inclusion 'as a principled approach to education', since in advocating the use of the Index for Inclusion in its statutory guidance on 'inclusive schooling' as the means for schools to 'develop their cultures policies and practices' (DfES, 2001b, p. 3), government was aligning itself, even if unknowingly, with the values which underpinned the Index and are made explicit within it.

Our view of inclusion as an approach to education informed by explicit values offers an alternative to the standards agenda approach to education in general and achievement in particular. An inclusive approach is no less concerned with achievements but with *all* the achievements of *all* children and young people, and with the meaning of achievements within communities. An inclusive approach is equally concerned with learning, but instead of focusing primarily on outcomes gives equal attention to the conditions for teaching and learning, so that the resources and relationships that support the active and sustained involvement of children, families and practitioners in education, are maintained.

Some try to recruit inclusion to the standards agenda, arguing that inclusion 'works' to push up attainment test scores and this is, therefore, its justification. Indeed, the Ofsted guidance on inclusion argues that 'effective schools are educationally inclusive schools' (Ofsted, 2000a, p. 7) and, in another Ofsted document, *Improving City Schools: Strategies to Promote Educational Inclusion*, inclusion is seen as part of the standards mix: 'At best, all the energy of the school serves the same end: raising standards' (Ofsted, 2000b, p. 7). In our view this misses the essence of inclusion. For us, the health and well-being of children, and the development of good relationships within schools and between schools and communities, are important in themselves, not as a part of the mechanism to raise educational performance.

Policy resources for inclusion

The mixed messages about inclusion within government policies have created a complex set of pushes and pulls both towards and away from the development of inclusion in education and society. These may be seen as resources for, and barriers to, the development of a broad 'transformative' view of inclusion. How school staff managed this confusing policy context formed a critical aspect of our research. Of course, it is important to remember that government policies are only one source of inclusionary and exclusionary influences on education, since these result from deep historical, cultural and structural forces, as well as local, national and global political pressures.

Resources to support inclusion within recent English national policies are summarised in Box 2.1.

Here it is important to note that some of these resources may be found *within* general education policies, despite our criticism of them. In particular, **we agree with the government view that parts of the education system have been characterised by low expectations, especially for many working-class and ethnic minority learners growing up in poor areas**. In the past few years some schools in poor areas have made radical improvements in the attainments of their children and, undoubtedly, the message about raising expectations is of considerable significance (West *et al.*, 2005).

However, other policies too may be used to support educational development based on a broad view of inclusion, as we indicated in our

BOX 2.1

Resources for inclusion in national policy

- Combating low expectations (DfEE, 1999b)
- Attending to all groups vulnerable to exclusionary pressures (Ofsted, 2000a)
- Challenging discrimination on grounds of ethnicity, religion, gender, sexual orientation and age (Ofsted, 2002a, 2002b; CRE, 2002; DfES/DOH, 2004; DRC, 2002; House of Commons, 2006)
- A concern with school responsiveness to diversity (DfEE/QCA, 1999)
- Use of inclusive language: 'barriers to learning' (DfEE, 1999c; DfES, 2001b)
- Attention to overcoming bullying between children and young people (DfEE, 2000a)
- Broadening combating exclusion to community and neighbourhood renewal (SEU, 1998, 2000a, 2000b, 2001)

discussion of the strands of inclusive thinking above. The recognition that there were other groups vulnerable to exclusionary pressures in education besides disabled children and young people, and asking schools and inspectors to grapple with the complexities of direct and institutional racism, and other forms of structural discrimination, were important steps in thinking about how barriers to learning and participation might be reduced. The consideration of the importance of overcoming the variety of discriminatory practices in education and society took the government a step nearer to the kind of comprehensive anti-discrimination legislation that Lord Lester attempted to introduce with his Equality Bill (House of Lords, 2003). This was watered down considerably with the introduction of the Equalities Act 2006, though important amendments were accepted, for example, on sexual orientation. The statutory requirements to make the National Curriculum responsive to diversity provided support for the development of 'the school for all' in as far-reaching guidance on inclusion as anywhere in the world (DfEE/QCA, 1999). There was a beginning within these documents, too, of the acceptance of the kind of inclusive language advocated within the Index for Inclusion.

The government has expressed a particular concern about bullying in schools, an issue that many children and young people continue to see as the biggest barrier to their participation in schools. The relating of inclusion within schools to inclusion within communities and society was expressed through policies to raise achievements in urban areas and support disadvantaged families, to strengthen links between schools and their communities and to a view of 'social inclusion' concerned with overcoming poverty, and to community and neighbourhood renewal.

Policy barriers to inclusion

Box 2.2 summarises what we see as potential barriers to the development of more inclusive schools within recent national policies.

As we see, possible barriers to the development of inclusion may be found within some of the same policies that also have the potential to

---

BOX 2.2

Barriers to inclusion in national policy

- Multiple and conflicting perspectives on inclusion
- Lack of coordination of overlapping inclusion strands
- Persisting special educational needs response to educational difficulties
- Initiative overload
- Attention to narrow outcomes and targets rather than good conditions for teaching and learning
- A technicist, instrumental view of educational policies that obscures the role of values in action
- Excessive accountability and the erosion of trust
- Promotion of competition between schools
- Increasing selection within and between schools
- Fragmentation of the system
- Reduction in power of LEAs to coordinate educational development
- Authoritarian views of educational development and leadership
- A rise in image management

act as resources for its development. For example, policies on 'standards' may not achieve all the effects on raising expectations that they claim. The government has argued that the raising of 'standards' is about equity; that a powerful emphasis on raising attainment does not simply benefit children who are already performing at a high level, but, implemented properly and supported by the various inclusion initiatives, the standards agenda is of even greater benefit to previously low-attaining children in poorly performing schools. It is, in words spoken by David Blunkett, former Secretary of State for Education, echoing a New Labour mantra about 'excellence for the many, not just the few' (Blunkett, 1999).

Yet while the targets set for schools, LEAs and the national system may have related to 'the many', they have certainly not related to *all* children. Only 80 per cent (rising latterly to 85 per cent) of primary schoolchildren have been expected to achieve the target level in English, for instance, and 75 per cent in mathematics. The national strategies, whatever their benefits, had at the time of our study removed the flexibility of schools to respond to the diverse characteristics of their students – and there was some evidence that children with the greatest difficulties in regular schools were receiving the least appropriate support (Hardman *et al.*, 2005). At the same time, recent research suggests that the numbers of students in the poorest areas of the country leaving school with no General Certificate of Secondary Education (GCSE) passes increased between 1999 and 2003 (Machin *et al.*, 2005).

The maintenance and strengthening of the education marketplace, and the new emphasis on school diversity, have effectively created a quasi-selective system in which the poorest children, by and large, attend the lowest-performing schools. At the same time, the lowest-performing schools fell progressively further and further behind their high-performing counterparts (Edwards and Tomlinson, 2002). In terms of its effects, through selective advantaging and dis-advantaging of schools, the standards agenda may have increased rather than decreased disparities in education between advantaged and less privileged groups (Gillborn and Youdell, 1999). Giroux and Schmidt (2004) explain how similar reforms in the United States have turned some schools into 'test-prep centres'. As a result they tend to be increasingly ruthless in their disregard of those students who pose a threat to success, as determined by measured forms of assessment.

The accountability culture, as illustrated by the inspection system in schools and other areas of the public sector, is seen to erode the confidence of people in their own professionalism. As O'Neill puts it:

> An unending stream of new legislation and regulation, memoranda and instructions, guidance and advice floods into public sector organisations. . . . Central planning may have failed in the Soviet Union but it is alive and well in Britain today. The new accountability aims at ever more perfect control of institutional and professional life.
>
> (O'Neill, 2002, Reith Lecture 3, p. 2)

The government even came up with the concept of 'earned autonomy', as specified in the 2002 Education Act, as if the natural state of teachers and schools was to operate under external directives, and freedom was a reward for good behaviour. In 2004 the government drew on this idea in its stated intention to encourage the development of a new category of schools, 'independent specialist schools'. These schools, later to be termed 'trust schools' (DfES, 2005a) were to be released from central and local control on the basis of their particular success. Such a move reveals one of the driving forces behind Labour policies in setting state education to compete with the 'independent private sector' for middle-class and more wealthy families (DfES, 2004).

The proliferation of ways in which the term 'inclusion' has been used within government policies means that they lack coherence. In fact there are so many policies, each with their own particular inclusion slant, that it is difficult for anyone to keep abreast of them all. Further, in representing inclusion in a variety of sometimes-conflicting ways, it became difficult to see how these policies could all be implemented.

A policy involves the deliberate attempt to change an area of practice in a particular direction (Fulcher, 1989). Consequently, a policy document becomes a piece of rhetoric if it is not connected to an implementation strategy. Thus in producing so many policy documents it seems that the government has sometimes manipulated perceptions of what is taking place in education rather than approaching educational change with any clarity of purpose or desire for consistent development. So, for example, the continuation of a special educational needs strand of inclusion alongside other broader conceptions has created particular policy confusion within local authorities and schools (Ainscow et al., 2000).

As LEAs contract, their continued responsibility for coordinating 'special needs education' takes up a large part of their responsibilities, and even where they wish to, it is hard to integrate the work of their departments so that a broad approach to inclusion permeates them all. Policies that limit the power of local authorities created significant barriers for our study, given the way it depended on the support and initiative of staff within the three LEAs. In theory they were restricted by the requirements of the government's Code of Practice on LEA–school relations to a monitoring and target setting role, except in those schools deemed to have serious weaknesses or placed in special measures (DfEE, 1999c), although the three LEAs interpreted these constraints in different ways. They were further restricted by the establishment of alternative coordinating structures within their borders, particularly 'education action zones' for which groups of schools and their private partners were provided with additional resources to coordinate aspects of their development. Our research enabled us to take a close look at the strengths and limitations of the LEA roles, and assess possible directions for policy revision in this area.

The government's tendency to construct policy through a series of separate initiatives, aimed at capturing a good press across the political spectrum, creates a particular form of instability in schools (see Riddell and Tett, 2001). In particular, it interrupts the possibilities for considered priority setting and development, and creates insecurity over funding. Meanwhile, the competitive climate, with its associated fear of failure, leads to an exaggerated wish within some schools and LEAs to portray themselves in a favourable light. It also tends to encourage an authoritarian approach to management, with charismatic leaders introduced into schools experiencing difficulties, to turn them round before moving on. This atmosphere puts pressure on schools to plan for the short term to meet immediate targets, rather than concentrate on longer-term improvements in the conditions for teaching and learning that sustain achievements over time.

It is interesting to relate this analysis of English education policy in terms of resources and barriers to the findings of international research. For example, some of this research highlights the discrepancy between the activities of policy makers, generating multitudes of disparate, uncoordinated initiatives, and the needs of practitioners for consistent policy implemented within a reliably funded and predictable framework (Honig and Hatch, 2004). Referring to research in the USA, Canada and the UK, Hatch talks of the 'endless cycle of initiatives that seem to sap the strength and spirit of schools and their communities' (Hatch, 2000, p. 4). In addition, Fullan has drawn attention to the critical role of policy coherence for persistent change. He suggests that in such circumstances:

> Successes [of attempts at educational development] are in the minority, they are happening despite the current system and are unlikely to be sustained because of the current system.
>
> (Fullan, 2001, p. 24)

Given that the government is advised by people who have ready access to such information, it seems relevant to ask: Why is there not a stronger critique of policy by disconnected initiatives at the heart of government? There is also a critique of the current policy climate in England, which relates it to forces that are wider than national policy. As Richard Hatcher argues:

> Education in the UK is being driven by a neo-liberal agenda, which ensures its subordination to the demand for profitable human capital for economic competitiveness in the globalised corporate economy. This indirect commodification of education is achieved through a combination of an authoritarian managerialist regime and direct forms of commodification through the marketisation and partial privatisation of provision. This education agenda is international, promoted in nationally specific forms by governments around the world and mediated by key international organisations such as the World Trade Organisation. In Europe the European Commission is supervising the gradual convergence of education policies around the neo-liberal agenda.
>
> (Hatcher, 2002, p. 1)

While the details of Richard Hatcher's analysis may be debated, what is indisputable is that a number of education systems have been strongly influenced by market economics propounded from such organisations as the World Bank and World Trade Organisation (Bonal, 2002). Any recommendations for policy change at the national level have to take account of these international influences.

Notions of school development

Whatever the source of the pressures that act on schools, teachers and other practitioners always adjust policy through their practice: in this sense they may be seen as 'street-level bureaucrats' (Weatherley and Lipsky, 1977). **Our research was concerned with assessing the degree of discretion of staff in schools within the current English policy climate, how such discretion might be increased through support and the practical adoption of inclusive values, as well as the most promising location for critical action to change current policies.**

Just as thinking about inclusive values can throw light on the nature of current educational reforms, it also highlights features of school improvement research. There is a vast amount of literature on educational innovation and development, school improvement and school effectiveness, 'good' and 'best' practice. Yet it is surprising how rarely authors mention the values that underlie their recommendations (Frost et al., 2000; Fullan, 1992, 2001; Harris, 2001; Joyce et al., 1999).

'School improvement' and 'school development' are part of the family of phrases used in education, which can appear to render unproblematic, contested views of what education should be like. They may imply that the task for academics and policy makers, as well as teachers, is simply a technical matter of identifying 'what works' to lead schools and classrooms towards 'good' or 'best practice' (Slee et al., 1998; Thrupp, 2001). It is therefore assumed that the knowledge about what works can be set out in guidance to practitioners and well-intentioned professionals, who will then set about following that guidance, particularly if they are offered appropriate technical support on classroom practices. This applies as much to avowedly inclusive approaches to school development as to those which are concerned with 'performance' and 'standards' (see e.g. Sebba and Sachdev, 1997; Thousand and Villa, 1995; Udvari-Solner and Thousand, 1995; Villa and Thousand, 1992; Villa and Thousand, 1995; Villa et al., 1992). Current educational policy in England is heavily influenced by this tradition. For example, it lies behind the award of 'leading-edge' status to some schools, to indicate that they will provide the way forward for others to follow.

There is also a body of critical literature highlighting the problems and complexities which emerge when schools attempt to develop towards greater inclusion (see Booth and Ainscow, 1998). Some of this literature is concerned with the way in which even those national policies and prescriptions which appear to support the development of inclusion become progressively more ambiguous and compromised as they are formed and re-formed at various levels of the education system (Fulcher, 1989; Slee, 1996). Other researchers have focused on the ways in which non-inclusive aspects of the policy environment generate compromises and tensions even in schools with a strong explicit commitment to develop themselves in inclusive directions (Dyson et al., 2003). Others again have emphasised the complex dynamics of schools as organisations and the capacity of exclusive practices and assumptions to resurface, despite the best efforts of 'hero-innovator' headteachers (Dyson and Millward, 2000). These literatures point to the internal complexities of schools as organisations, and the constraints and contradictions that are generated by the policy environments in which they exist. As such, they usefully problematise the assumptions underlying the more mechanistic approaches to improvement, but stop short of saying how inclusion might actually be developed.

A more promising family of approaches to development start from the assumption that increasing inclusion is less a set of fixed practices or policies, than a continuous process of deconstruction and reconstruction (Thomas and Loxley, 2001); what Corbett and Slee (2000) have called the 'cultural vigilantism' of exposing exclusion in all its changing forms and seeking instead to 'foster an inclusive educational culture'. Where writers have addressed these questions, they tend to give particular attention to the characteristics of schools as organisations which stimulate and support this process of interrogation. The American scholar Tom Skrtic, for instance, argues that schools with what he calls 'adhocratic' configurations are most likely to respond to student diversity in positive and creative ways (Skrtic, 1991a, 1991b, 1991c, 1995). Such schools emphasise the pooling of different professional expertise in collaborative processes. Students who cannot be educated easily within the school's established routines are not seen as 'having' problems, but as challenging the schools to re-examine its practices and make them more responsive and flexible. Similarly, Mel Ainscow's work talks about 'organisational conditions' – distributed leadership, high levels of staff and student involvement, joint planning, a commitment to enquiry and so on – that promote collaboration and problem solving among staff, and which therefore produce more inclusive responses to diversity (Ainscow, 1994, 1995, 1999, 2000; Ainscow *et al.*, 1994). Such conditions, he argues:

> create a culture within mainstream schools that will enable them to be more flexible in responding to all children in the community. Such a culture would encourage teachers to see pupils experiencing difficulties not as a problem, but as a source of understanding as to how their practice could be developed.
>
> (Ainscow, 1994, p. 26)

These themes reflect some of the recent international literature, as summarised in a review carried out by members of our team that examined the effectiveness of school actions in promoting inclusion (Dyson *et al.*, 2002, 2004). The review concluded that **there is a limited, but by no means negligible, body of empirical evidence about the relationship between school action and the participation of all students in the cultures, curricula and communities of schools.** In summary, it suggested the following:

- Some schools are characterised by an 'inclusive culture'. Within such schools, there is some degree of consensus among adults around values of respect for difference and a commitment to offering all students access to learning opportunities. This consensus may not be total and may not necessarily remove all tensions or contradictions in practice. On the other hand, there is likely to be a high level of staff collaboration and joint problem solving, and similar values and commitments may extend into the student body and into parent and other community stakeholders in the school.
- The extent to which such 'inclusive cultures' lead directly and unproblematically to enhanced student participation is not clear. Some aspects of these cultures, however, may be seen as participatory by definition. For instance, respect for diversity from teachers may itself be understood as a form of participation by students in the school community. Moreover, schools characterised by such cultures are also likely to be characterised by forms of organisation (such as specialist provision being made in the ordinary classroom rather than by withdrawal) and practice (such as constructivist approaches to teaching and learning) which could be regarded as participatory by definition.
- Schools with 'inclusive cultures' are also likely to be characterised by the presence of leaders who are committed to inclusive values and to a leadership style which encourages a range of individuals to participate in leadership functions. Such schools are also likely to have good links with parents and with their communities.
- The local and national policy environment can act to support or to undermine the realisation of schools' inclusive values.

On the basis of this review of international evidence, the review team make a number of recommendations for policy and practice. They suggest that attempts to develop inclusive schools should pay attention to the development of 'inclusive' cultures and, particularly, to the building of some degree of consensus around inclusive values within school communities. This leads them to argue that headteachers and other school leaders should be selected and trained in the light of their commitment to inclusive values and their capacity to lead in a participatory manner. Finally, they conclude that the external policy environment should be compatible with inclusive developments if it is to support rather than undermine schools' efforts.

According to the review, there are general principles of school organisation and classroom practice which should be followed: notably, the removal of structural barriers between different groups of students and staff, the dismantling of separate programmes, services and specialisms, and the development of pedagogical approaches (such as constructivist approaches) which enable students to learn together rather than separately. It is also argued that schools should build close relations with parents and communities based on developing a shared commitment to inclusive values.

The implications for practice of such an orientation are illustrated in the Index for Inclusion (Booth and Ainscow, 2002). The Index, mentioned earlier, is a set of review materials that enable schools to draw on the knowledge and views of staff, students, parents/carers and governors about barriers to learning and participation that exist within the existing 'cultures, policies and practices' of schools in order to identify priorities for change. In connecting inclusion with the detail of policy and practice, the Index encourages those who use it, to build up their own view of inclusion, related to their experience and values, as they work out what policies and practices they wish to promote or discourage. The Index can support staff in schools in refining their planning processes, so that these involve wider collaboration and participation and introduce coherence to development (see Rustemier and Booth, 2005).

Such approaches are congruent with our view that inclusion is essentially about attempts to embody particular values in particular contexts. Unlike mechanistic views of school improvement, they acknowledge that decisions about how to improve schools always involve moral and political reasoning as well as technical considerations. Moreover, they offer specific processes through which inclusive developments might be promoted. Discussions of inclusion and exclusion can help, therefore, to make explicit the values which underlie what, how and why changes should be made in schools. Inclusive cultures, underpinned by particular organisational conditions, may make those discussions more likely to occur and more productive when they do occur.

However, the knowledge to be gained from such approaches remains partial. We know a great deal about what sorts of conditions, cultures and processes *should* be in place for inclusive development to occur, and we have examples of the positive outcomes when this is indeed the case. However, our review of the inclusion literature (Dyson *et al.*, 2002, 2004) highlighted the extent to which what we know rests on rather superficial studies and, moreover, on studies of somewhat *exceptional* schools. We know what happens when charismatic headteachers, working with supportive staff, set out in a determined way to enact the values of inclusion. We know much less, however, about the prospects for inclusion when these conditions do not obtain, when school cultures are not supportive of inclusion, or when teachers find themselves working in a hostile policy environment.

It may well be unlikely that inclusive provisions and practices can emerge in the face of determined opposition or a resolute refusal to question the status quo. However, what happens in those schools – the vast majority, we suggest – where heads and teachers are neither determinedly opposed nor unflinchingly committed to inclusive developments? What happens in those schools where well-intentioned staff, broadly committed to the well-being of their students, encounter the daily challenges of responding to classroom diversity in the context of demands for ever-higher standards of performance from their heads, their LEAs and central government? Can inclusive values be realised in such ambiguous contexts? If so, how?

Summary and conclusions

In this chapter we have described the tensions between the 'standards' and 'inclusion' agendas within the English education policy context. At the point where our work with the twenty-five schools began (spring 2000), it is arguable that the standards agenda was at its fiercest. Primary schools were in the early stages of implementing national strategies on the teaching of literacy and numeracy, and secondary schools, already under pressure to raise attainments and reduce exclusions, were awaiting the implementation of their own national 'Key Stage 3 strategy'. Effectively, government policy meant that the schools had three overriding priorities: (1) they had to comply with national definitions of 'good practice', particularly as enshrined in the national strategies on teaching and learning; (2) they had to meet increasingly challenging attainment targets; and (3) they had to maintain a sufficiently positive presence in the education 'marketplace' so that they could attract enough students to remain viable.

By the end of the study, three years later, there was evidence that some of the pressures from government were easing, as indicated in a speech by the chief inspector of schools. Although he stressed that targets still had an important part to play in educational development, he argued:

> An excessive or myopic focus on targets can actually narrow and reduce achievement by crowding out some of the essentials of effective and broadly-based learning. . . . [There are] teachers, heads and local authorities for whom targets are now operating more as a threat than a motivator. . . . The harder the targets become, the more tempting it is to treat them with cynicism or defeatism. . . . It is only by focusing on fundamental questions of teaching quality that we will meet challenging targets. This requires schools to engage in intelligent long-term planning . . . so that they are maximising progress for all pupils. My advice to teachers is be bold and take the initiative, doing what you think is right in your school.
>
> (David Bell, 28 February 2003)

However, as the New Labour government entered its third term of office in 2005 it seemed intent on pushing through an increase in selective, specially resourced schools. So as we shall see in later chapters, government policies provided staff in schools with real dilemmas. Should they, for instance, focus their energies equally on all children, on those with greatest difficulties, or disproportionately on those whose attainments were at the borderline of national targets? Should they maintain children who they categorised as having 'learning' or 'behavioural difficulties' in regular classes, even if they thought this might slow the progress towards target levels made by other children? Should they seek to serve all children from their local communities, or should they market themselves aggressively to higher attaining 'middle-class' children from more affluent areas? In answering these questions, moreover, schools had to bear in mind that the standards imperative was clear, operationalised through detailed prescription and so strongly enforced that it was, to all intents and purposes, unavoidable. The inclusion agenda, on the other hand, as espoused within government 'policies', was ambiguous, tentative and contradictory.

In order to exercise a degree of control over their own development, schools had to resist simply reacting to new pressures as they emerged, or place unmodified into their development plans the requirements of government. They had to recapture or initiate a degree of rational planning, in which they could attempt to interpret the requirements placed on them in the light of their values, and initiate principled change for themselves. We wanted to see how schools juggled rational, short, medium and longer term planning with the improvisation that responds to opportunities as they presented themselves, and the more passive reactions to external pressures. In particular, we wanted to explore the opportunities for inclusive development that might be created through collaborative research with schools. We aimed to generate the kinds of dialogues and challenges that could help teachers and others take a degree of control of their development, and where they wished, change their policies, practices and, most importantly, cultures, in the direction of greater inclusion. Our approaches to establishing these opportunities are described in Chapter 3.

Establishing the research network

In this chapter we describe the development of the research network 'Understanding and Developing Inclusive Practices in Schools', explaining how partnerships were created between researchers and practitioners in schools and LEAs. These partnerships explored the nature of barriers to learning and participation in the schools, and attempted to reduce them through a process of collaborative action research. In this way, we set out to explore how inclusive school development can be encouraged. In this process, the members of the network negotiated their way through the tensions within English educational policies between inclusion, standards and accountability, discussed in Chapter 2, in order to generate understandings that would be of interest to wider academic and practitioner communities.

While the terms of the Teaching and Learning Research Programme (TLRP) grant required us to set up 'a network', they did not specify what such a network would look like, except that it required collaboration between a number of higher education institutions. We decided to take the idea further, establishing learning partnerships not only between ourselves, but also within and between the schools in each of the three LEAs, and between the three LEAs and their groups of schools.

From our previous work we recognised that providing opportunities for those working within schools and LEAs to learn from their own experience and the experience of others, and increasing the capacity of people to make use of such opportunities, were keys to development. We also believed that contrary to a widespread view, particularly promoted by government, the fact that activities in a particular school or LEA were designated as 'good' practice made very little impact on the practice of others unless they shared the basic values or educational principles which underlay them. Equally we took the view that practice which some people might not regard as 'good', could be fertile for supporting ideas about development, if it connected with the current concerns and stimulated the thinking of those observing it. Thus we favoured the designation of examples of practice as being 'instructive', rather than seeing them as being 'good' or 'best'.

The network involved the creation of opportunities for people to learn how to learn from differences in experience and context. With this in mind, we set up a variety of meetings between schools, and a series of local and inter-LEA conferences. At the heart of these meetings were structured opportunities to observe and discuss ways of intervening in teaching and learning in order to promote more inclusive cultures, policies and practices.

The research agenda

The university groups adopted a broad definition of inclusion, as discussed in the previous chapters, and encouraged schools to work in a similar way, supported by the 'Index for Inclusion' (Booth and Ainscow, 2002), and, to a lesser extent, by Ofsted's guidance document, *Evaluating Educational Inclusion* (Ofsted, 2000a). These documents had been made available by central government to all schools to support the inclusion aspects of national education policy.

Work with the Index had been taken up widely both within schools in England and in many other countries, and it had also had an impact on the wording of government policy documents. However, not everyone involved in the university groups saw as equally useful the setting down of the implications of inclusive thinking in this detailed way. Indeed, there was a debate between members of the research team about the extent to which the Index liberated or constrained thinking about inclusion in schools. So, while there was some work with the Index in all three LEAs, it was not used systematically to assess changes in the development of inclusion, or as the approach to the research throughout the network.

We set out with a common set of questions to explore inclusion in the schools:

- What are the barriers to participation and learning experienced by students?

- What practices can help to overcome these barriers?
- To what extent do such practices facilitate improved learning outcomes?
- How can such practices be encouraged and sustained within LEAs and schools?

The third of these questions was perhaps the most problematic for us. It was there, in the main, as a requirement of the research programme, yet we knew how difficult it was to tease out from the complexity of influences on schools the particular effect of one initiative. This was perhaps most obviously exacerbated in those cases where there were multiple projects going on within the same school. Yet all schools were subject to a multiplicity of influences affecting the extent of their including and excluding practices.

The emphasis of our work gradually underwent a subtle change from 'understanding and developing inclusive practices' to 'understanding the development of inclusive practices'. **We saw the schools and projects within them as grounding, and providing opportunities to test, our emerging understanding of how inclusion could be developed.** Nevertheless, at an early meeting between the university teams from the four networks set up as the first phase of the TLRP and the directors of the overall programme, it was suggested that we had to attempt to show 'an unequivocal connection between the performance of children in the schools and [our] interventions'. Given the conceptual and practical problems in carrying out such a request we understood it as part of the context affecting our research: it was, we felt, an ideological feature of the 'standards agenda' and 'accountability culture', which affected those working in higher education as much as those in schools and LEAs.

Within a largely qualitative research study there is an inevitable refinement of the research questions as information is gathered from the field and analysed. In the case of our research this involved a process of progressive focusing, leading eventually to the two questions presented at the beginning of Chapter 1. These are:

- When and how does improvement in schools become inclusive development?
- How can inclusive school development be best supported?

Furthermore, while the title of the research and the original questions were directed at schools, we came to see 'the case' as being wider in scope. In particular, we became increasingly interested in exploring the way researchers from institutions of higher education could work on the development of inclusion with schools and LEAs within the cultures and policy contexts which shaped them.

Selecting the LEAs

In setting up the network, each of the three research groups agreed to work with one LEA. In each case these agreements built on previous relationships between the researchers and the particular LEA. As we will explain in later chapters, factors within these local districts proved to be significant in the way schools interpreted their involvement in the network. At the same time, this was also affected by the particular people who supported the work of the network from within the LEAs and the positions they occupied.

Since we approached the research with a broad perspective on inclusion, we wished to avoid the narrowing of view that might result if we linked our work solely with the special educational needs teams in the LEAs. We were particularly interested in the involvement of teams variously called 'school improvement officers' or 'school development advisers'. However, we were inevitably constrained by the structures of LEAs that did not themselves fully integrate the work of their different sections.

Many within the LEAs continued to see inclusion as an aspect of education rather than as an overall approach. For example, the difficulty of the task of encouraging people to see inclusion in broad terms was revealed well by the ethnic composition of conferences within the network. Participants at these events were predominantly white and did not reflect the ethnic composition of the staff in the participating LEAs. It seemed that, despite our discussions, there remained a split between issues of 'ethnicity' taken up within LEAs following the Stephen Lawrence Enquiry (Macpherson, 1999), in which ethnic minority staff were relatively well represented, and the issue of 'inclusion' seen as primarily about issues of 'special educational needs' and the concern of primarily white professionals. We even noticed evidence of the use of the term 'diversity' to mean non-white, rather than all groups.

In what follows we provide brief introductions to the three LEA contexts, drawing attention to certain factors we see as being important to the reader's understanding of the accounts we present in subsequent chapters.

Southminster LEA

The Canterbury team worked with Southminster LEA. Created in 1990 on the demise of the Greater London Council and Inner London Education Authority, this is a relatively small authority but it has one of the highest population growth rates in the country. The area has long been a first place of arrival for immigrants from other parts of the world. In one street, for example, there is a mosque that was formally a synagogue and before that a church.

The Borough has one of the largest communities originating from Bangladesh, in Europe, making up some 33 per cent of its population. Altogether, 48 per cent of the total population (compared to 9 per cent in England as a whole) and 76 per cent of the school-age population are from minority ethnic communities. The Borough comes at, or close to, the top of most indices of deprivation, but contains striking contrasts. Wealth is represented by luxury apartments and multi-storey office blocks which exist alongside extremely poor housing, with the highest level of overcrowding in England, particularly affecting families with a Bangladeshi background.

At the time of the research, schools in Southminster contended with many pressures, not least staff shortages and recruitment difficulties exacerbated by very high house prices. In January 2001, one year into our research, the teacher vacancy rate was 8.6 per cent, compared with 3.5 per cent generally for Inner London boroughs and 1.3 per cent nationally. In 1998, Ofsted gave the LEA an unfavourable report, arguing that it had been mismanaged, that standards of achievement had risen insufficiently, and that it had to reduce the money held centrally for support services. The effects of this report were made more compelling by the spectres of nearby authorities, which had been seen as failing and had been privatised in whole or part. The new Director of Education, who had arrived in 1997, was not implicated in the perceived failure and was to be given time, though relatively brief, to turn things around. In the event, improvements in measured performance on tests in primary and secondary schools were dramatic. When it was re-inspected in 2000, the LEA was given a glowing report, and by 2002 it was said to be the fastest improving authority in the country.

Inclusion was defined in the LEA's Inclusion Strategy as 'the process of increasing the participation of children in the curriculum, culture and community of their school, thereby raising education standards for all', and it is evident that this definition relies heavily on previous collaboration with the research team (Booth, 1996a). An Inclusion

Policy Steering Committee was set up to develop inclusion policy in the LEA, and this group saw its task in part as shifting conceptions of inclusion away from a concentration on special needs education towards developing schools that remove barriers to the learning and participation of all children and young people within a neighbourhood. An Inclusion Action Plan was produced, structured around the dimensions of the Index for Inclusion: creating inclusive cultures, producing inclusive policies and evolving inclusive practices. In 2001, the new 'Service Head: Access and Inclusion' described the Index as the 'lead document' for inclusion within the authority and circulated a copy of the revised version to every school.

Northfields LEA

The Newcastle team worked with Northfields, a unitary authority established in the mid-1990s. The area is relatively large and mixed geographically, extending from an industrialised riverside in the north of the Borough, through increasingly affluent residential suburbs, to a mixed area of farmland, small industrial villages and a market town in the south. Industry, both along the riverside and in the villages, had experienced severe decline in recent years, with consequent problems of unemployment and poverty. The area as a whole was experiencing depopulation.

Members of the Newcastle team had previously worked with Northfields' schools on a series of developmental projects that typified the LEA's approach to school improvement. It subscribed to the national standards agenda and, at the time the network began, shared in the current national concerns about standards of writing and boys' under-achievement. However, unlike some LEAs which had reduced their contact with schools and concentrated on setting schools challenging achievement targets and monitoring progress on them, Northfields officers tended to work closely with schools. They supported and encouraged grass-roots development, rather than engaging in wholesale change processes or making sweeping policy statements. By and large, this approach was seen to be successful, at least to the extent that the LEA had never had a school in special measures. An Ofsted inspection of the LEA during the course of the life of the network was able to report 'a picture of at least reasonable standards and consistent, sometimes rapid, improvement'.

Castleside LEA

Finally, the Manchester team worked with schools in Castleside LEA, which was the twenty-sixth most deprived authority in England. It was a relatively new unitary authority, which, at its inception several years earlier, was described by Ofsted as having 'a formidable legacy of under-performance'.

Prior to the establishment of the network, a team from the University of Manchester had spent three years evaluating the LEA's strategies for school improvement and found evidence that, in terms of raising standards as measured by test scores, its strategy was having a positive impact (Ainscow and Howes, 2001; Ainscow *et al.*, 2006). Test and examination results had risen across all phases of the service, with improvement rates in the Key Stage 2 tests among the highest nationally. Over the same period there were fifteen schools in the LEA which were seen as requiring special measures or having serious weaknesses, but by early 2001 there were just two 'with serious weaknesses'. Despite these successes, officers of the LEA recognised that they were vulnerable to criticism about the development of inclusion policy and practice. Indeed, they understood that some of their success in schools had been achieved through the use of exclusionary tactics, and there was a desire to develop in a more inclusive direction.

On being invited to consider involvement with a network about inclusion, those officers recognised an opportunity to work publicly and collaboratively on this issue. By this time, considerable trust had developed between the Manchester research team and several senior LEA staff regarding ways of working with schools, and a decision was made to become involved.

Selecting the schools

The involvement of the schools was negotiated through officers of the LEAs, taking account of what they saw as the local priorities. Whereas in the past it might have been possible for an LEA to be more directive, strongly encouraging the involvement of those schools that officers and advisers thought would benefit most from an inclusion project, their reduced powers meant that they were much more dependent on schools volunteering their involvement. While this was mainly a positive basis for engagement, in some cases these were schools that volunteered for involvement in many external initiatives and so had limited time to give to any one of them.

This created a tension for us. We did not want schools to see us as bringing an additional project or initiative to the schools. Rather, **we saw ourselves as offering a way of approaching the development of their schools more generally, which would help them to integrate the mass of government initiatives and local projects within a single inclusive framework.** But within an initiative culture, it was inevitable that we would often be seen as one among many projects with which particular schools engaged, and that this would limit the possibilities of their according the network the central role that we envisaged.

In general, as we have argued, schools did not join the network because they were believed to have made exceptional progress in relation to inclusive development, although a few might be seen in that light. In general, they were schools with a broad commitment to 'doing the best' for all of their students, and a sense, on the part of themselves and their LEAs, that they might have something to learn from looking more closely at how particular students, or groups of students, were faring within their current practices. These were 'typical' schools, struggling with the practical challenges of educating diverse populations and with the imperatives of a particularly demanding external policy environment. They included some schools that had been placed in special measures or defined as having serious weaknesses as a result of external inspections by Ofsted. The typicality of our twenty-five schools strengthened the possibility for learning about how inclusion might be increased more generally.

The research process

The network set out to explore ways of identifying and overcoming barriers to participation and learning experienced by students in English schools. **We started from the assumption that schools were capable of developing more inclusive practices and that such development could be facilitated by intervention from within and outside the schools, amounting to a process of 'critical collaborative action research'** (Macpherson et al., 1998). We gave considerable attention, therefore, to the development of social processes that could facilitate group engagement with evidence about these issues. We had developed a loose conception of the kinds of changes that might arise within schools as they increasingly permeated inclusive values through their organisation, relationships, teaching, learning and play activities. We worked with schools on a critical analysis and development of their practice in the light of broad inclusive principles. This led us to examine how that practice related to national policy requirements and where they could find room for manoeuvre within those imperatives.

The development of an effective method for supporting and analysing the inclusive development of schools represented a major challenge (see Appendix). We wanted to refine and record ways to encourage the development of inclusive cultures, policies and practices within schools and LEAs that could also be taken up within other practitioner and research communities.

Our previous research had led to a commitment to collaborative research with practitioners as a means of understanding the development of inclusive practices. It had led us to believe that greater understanding of the development of schools and LEAs could be helped considerably when 'outsiders', such as ourselves, work alongside teachers, students, parents and local authority staff, as they attempt to explore ways of overcoming barriers to participation and learning in schools.

Such an orientation is intended to overcome the traditional gap between research and practice. It has been assumed, by some, that this gap has resulted from inadequate dissemination strategies: that educational research would be seen to address the concerns of practitioners 'if only the right people would listen' (Robinson, 1998). However, we argue that research findings will continue to be ignored, regardless of how well they are communicated, if they bypass the ways in which practitioners themselves formulate the problems they face and the constraints within which they have to work (Poplin and Weeres, 1992).

However, this does not mean that academics should give up their critical scrutiny of practice and merely follow the way priorities are formulated by teachers and others. For the formulation of approaches to problems by practitioners may be constrained by their professional histories and the pressures acting on them, such that they cannot productively address areas of concern, or may work against the interests of others, such as students and their families. It would be foolish to place the views of any group involved in collaborative research, whether drawn from academic or school communities, as above critique. Further, if values play a fundamental role in deciding on educational actions, then there can always be fundamental disagreements between participants. Nevertheless, the potential benefits of collaborative enquiries, through which an open dialogue may develop, are enormous.

The participation of university staff in the schools' action research was intended to strengthen these activities by providing research training and support, while at the same time helping to overcome some of the reported limitations of action research; these include the failure to provide adequate explanations as to how new insights come to be generated through the research process (Adelman, 1989). A central strategy in this respect was the use of 'group interpretive processes' as a means of analysing and interpreting evidence. These involved an engagement with the different perspectives of practitioners, students and academics in ways that were intended to encourage critical reflection, collaborative learning and mutual critique (Wasser and Bresler, 1996). The use of statistical evidence regarding student participation and achievement, and feedback from students regarding their experiences of current practice, were seen as being essential elements in providing challenges to practitioners about their existing approaches (Ainscow et al., 1999). The varied theoretical perspectives of members of the research team also provided a valuable means of questioning taken-for-granted assumptions and helping teachers to reconsider neglected possibilities for moving practice forward.

The overall strategy of the network may be seen to comprise two interlinked cycles of action research. The first of these cycles was driven by the agendas of the partner LEAs and schools, and sought to use existing knowledge within these contexts, supplemented by further research evidence, as the means of fostering developments in the field. The second cycle attempted to scrutinise these developments in order to address the overall agenda of the network, using existing theory and previous research, including our own work, as a basis for pursuing deeper understandings. As we will explain, however, the complex connections between the two cycles were both important and, indeed, potentially powerful in relation to the generalisability of the knowledge obtained.

The research in practice

Schools were asked to establish a small project coordination group. This generally included the headteacher, who was assumed to be a dominant figure in determining the scope of the work in the schools. However, while we recognised that heads are essential in coordinating or, indeed, in sometimes undermining change, we wanted to ensure that other voices were heard, not least because this would broaden our understanding of barriers to learning and participation and how they might be addressed in schools.

Workshops were held in each LEA where these groups were encouraged to collect and analyse evidence in order to reflect on and develop aspects of their practice, with the support of the university teams. Each school then made their participation in the network a part of their development plans. Emphasis was placed on schools having control over the selection of areas of focus. These took the form of an aspect of current practice and provision that those in the school wished to review and develop in order to become more inclusive. In some schools more than others, deciding on a focus that would be fertile in encouraging change towards, and debate about, more inclusive ways of working was the result of careful negotiation between coordinating groups and the university research teams.

What schools chose or negotiated as their focus of concern has to be seen in relation to the specific situation within the English education system during the three-year period in which the network existed, as described in Chapter 2. Thus, in many schools there was a focus of activities that they believed would directly affect the results on national tests and examinations.

In a similar way, the research process itself varied from site to site in response to local priorities and possibilities. We also created an arrangement between the research teams that allowed flexibility but retained elements of a common approach so that evidence accumulated in the different LEAs could be combined.

The evidence gathered during the study was, then, substantial, ranging across twenty-five schools, three LEAs and nearly a hundred teachers and LEA personnel groups, covering a period of just over three years. It comprised interview data from professionals, parents and students, notes from informal discussions and meetings, school-generated evaluation data, attainment and attendance profiles, observation notes and videos, discussion documents prepared by school and university teams, and the recorded outcomes from local and national conferences.

Cameo accounts of each partner school and LEA were written according to shared guidelines, which focused on salient features of each institution and its context, and set out, in particular, the initial context of the action research that schools undertook. In the final year of the study, the research teams developed detailed summative accounts, describing and analysing developments in each of the three LEAs and the twenty-five schools. These accounts were prepared in relation to an agreed framework that specifically addressed school and LEA cultures, policies and practices; and national policies.

The research process was extended by the meetings of schools within each LEA and in the conferences across the network. These became a focus for coordinating the involvement of LEA and university staff in the schools' projects. The meetings were also used as opportunities to share, record and celebrate progress; and to ensure continued enthusiasm in the face of competing commitments. Those within the schools were then assisted in monitoring the impact of their interventions on student participation and attainment. In these ways the aim was to increase their capacities for using data for strategic purposes.

Learning from difference

Our critical engagement with the schools over an extended period meant that we were able to avoid the trap of describing apparently inclusive surface changes, or 'window dressing', beneath which lurked distinctly less inclusive values and processes. This was complicated by the tensions that existed in some schools between the need for immediate action to satisfy the demands of inspection, and a wish for deeper sustained development as a result of the careful analysis of current circumstances and the values which should underlie proposed change. Thus, some schools engaged in relatively small-scale, discrete initiatives, while others reviewed their practice more fundamentally. We also had to avoid a belief that collaboration with a small coordinating group meant that we were working with all staff, students, parents and governors, or indeed that all these voices were represented.

As we worked with schools we tried to maintain a consistent challenge to existing practices. We were aware of the social pressures towards collusion that could arise within any group, such that unwelcome ideas or evidence might be overlooked. So, during meetings of the coordinating groups from the schools we tried to facilitate techniques that invited challenge and might later be used more widely in the schools. During one such meeting, for example, groups of three were formed, made up of members of staff from different schools. These groups were given detailed suggestions as to how to act as critical friends to one another in relation to their school's action plans: each member of the group was given time to 'think aloud' about their ideas. While this was going on, the other two group members were asked only to interrupt if they needed to seek clarification. In this way each group member was supported and, to some degree, provoked to think more clearly about their current plans. Towards the end of the meeting colleagues re-formed themselves into school groups in order to compare notes on their varied experiences and, where necessary, to reformulate or refine their school's strategy. School staff reported that they learned much from an environment in which it felt safe to share difficulties as well as accomplishments.

In working in the schools we were conscious that what we did was at least as important as what we said. Our school colleagues observed our styles of working and decided for themselves whether or not our suggestions had credibility. We found that this became particularly important when participating in staff meetings or professional development days. For example, at one such day two of us collaborated with two teachers in planning and leading a day for the whole staff, including non-teaching staff. We adapted group discussion techniques, such as circle time, that the school had been using to foster greater participation from children during lessons. Members of the staff team felt that the day had been successful in supporting them to share ideas and develop a more focused plan for their research, while, at the same time, enabling them to experience the potential contributions and drawbacks of the approach they were taking to activities with children.

Significant efforts were made to foster collaboration between the academic research teams within the network. Regular meetings of the group of ten academic staff were held, including five residential events and also regular video conferencing. These processes were frequently supplemented by the exchange of discussion papers and memos about emerging issues. A strong sub-network was established between the three research associates, one from each research team, who were in regular contact through meetings and also by telephone and e-mail. The growing database about what was happening within the partner LEAs and schools could be accessed by all members of the university teams through a 'closed' website. In addition, an 'open' website was established that encouraged wider involvement in the activities of the network.

The learning that was necessary for academics to take advantage of their differences of view and experience was at least as complex and fraught with difficulties as such learning within schools. Over the three-year period we gradually learned to take advantage of differences in our experiences, beliefs and methodological assumptions. The academic teams within the network were therefore both instruments of research, gathering and reporting evidence about developments in LEAs and schools, but also the focus of research, as their own thinking and practices were subject to scrutiny. As we engaged with data about the work of practitioners in a different context, we too were constantly challenged to think through our own practice as researchers.

The approach to research in the network was, then, essentially a process of learning how to learn from difference. Practitioners and researchers had to find ways of bringing together their different understandings in a way that was of direct benefit to the children, young people and staff in the schools. As we show in later chapters, at its best, this provided many opportunities for developing new understandings. However, we also found that such possibilities can only be utilised if potential social, cultural, linguistic and micro-political barriers are overcome.

We found too that many of the schools interpreted 'inclusion', in the context of standards and target setting, to mean enabling low-attaining students to meet national targets in key areas. In this way, the target-setting agenda was seen to colonise the notion of 'inclusion'.

It became clear that carrying out collaborative research of this kind is particularly difficult within the current educational context in England. The government's reform agenda is demanding of time among LEA and school staff, and there was a danger that in some schools this initiative would get lost among a host of competing priorities. In addition, of course, particular events, such as school or LEA inspections, were always likely to distract attention. On the other hand, there is no doubt that since the network was addressing the key dilemma arising from the tensions between 'standards' and 'inclusion', it was seen within the three LEAs as an important development.

As the research deepened it revealed different levels of collaboration within the network. In practice, many interconnected and overlapping learning networks were being created. These included the learning networks within each of the schools; those between schools; those between school and LEA practitioners; those within and between the three teams of researchers; and, of course, those between practitioners and researchers. Reflecting on the research process has helped us to understand how collaborative action research can contribute to sustainable development within education systems. We found that we learned much about how to make use of different perspectives to stimulate critical reflection and creativity. In this way, we developed a much better understanding about what we meant by a 'collaborative action research network'.

As we learned more about how to do collaborative action research, we noted the complexity of what this involves. We were reminded here of the work of Fulcher (1989), which illustrates how education policies are created through struggles that occur within and across a series of interconnected levels in education systems. So, for example, as we engaged with teachers in relation to the dilemmas they experienced within their classrooms, we were conscious of the influence of tensions and contradictions within school, LEA and national policies. Indeed, these engagements helped us to develop a better understanding of the nature of these policy contradictions and how they affected school and classroom encounters. And, of course, it is within this complex process that barriers to learning and participation are created for some students.

Summary and conclusions

This chapter has described the setting up of the research network. This was a collaborative process involving practitioners and university researchers. Indeed, we believe that the strength of the research reported in this book is the deliberate way in which so many varied experiences and perspectives were brought together in order to carry out the investigations, critique findings and generate understandings that are of relevance to both practitioners and academics. At the same time, the research has thrown considerable light on the nature of the tensions between national policies for raising standards and reducing marginalisation and exclusion within the English education service.

In the following three chapters we present and compare the experiences and findings of the three research teams in working with their partners in the LEAs and schools. Chapter 4 mainly focuses on developments in Southminster LEA in order examine the role of communities and LEAs, as schools attempt to move in a more inclusive direction; Chapter 5 focuses more specifically on the way teachers in the Northfields schools interpreted the idea of inclusion in relation to the pressures they faced in their work; and Chapter 6 moves closer to the action by analysing the detailed exchanges that occurred in Castleside schools in order to determine factors that can help to generate inclusive practices. Then, in Chapter 7, we further compare and contrast the developments in the three LEAs in order to make recommendations for the development of practice in the field. Finally, in Chapter 8, we consider the implications of our research for future policy development.

Part II

What does the research tell us?

Chapter 4

Manoeuvring space for inclusion

In this chapter we begin to describe and analyse the attempts by staff in the network schools to overcome barriers to learning and participation for their students. We focus in particular on the effect on schools of external pressures from central and local government policies on inclusion, the standards agenda and accountability culture. The chapter is illustrated by developments in Southminster LEA. We provide accounts of some of the inclusion activities that occurred within the eight schools which participated in the network. This leads us to reflect on the possibilities for staff in the schools for integrating their work on inclusion into long-term development strategies. Finally we draw together ideas about the space that can be created in schools for the development of inclusion within a particular policy climate.

As we described in Chapter 3, Southminster had substantial areas of economic deprivation but was characterised by dramatic contrasts in wealth. Yet, in some other ways, it provided a favourable context for the work of the network in promoting the development of inclusive practices in schools. There was a wonderful and vibrant mix of ethnicities, heritages and languages. There was, as we indicated, a strong commitment to a broad notion of inclusion from some sections of the LEA. The Director of Education had worked previously with a member of the Canterbury team on the inclusive development of her school, when she had been a headteacher in another authority, and several schools, including some which had signed up to join the network, had a reputation for their work on inclusion.

Nevertheless, **developing inclusion in the LEA and its schools proved to be complicated in a multitude of ways, not least because of the huge pressure to increase scores on national tests.** While we saw evidence that this pressure distorted the activities of schools at times, the Director of Education had herself become something of a convert to several of the government approaches to improving such results. She explained:

> When I came to the Borough I was absolutely opposed to all I'd read about the literacy and numeracy strategies. We were trialling them here. I'd been here about three months when I had to change. I've since become an absolutely passionate advocate of them, used in a customised way, because when I went into schools I saw teachers committed to what they were doing, I saw kids really enjoying what they were doing. So whatever is said about the dire side of it, the 'you will do this' side, I saw teachers and children really enjoying what they were doing and children making much more progress. That gave us the very good base for the GCSEs which really jumped forward last year. Anybody looking at the results ten years ago or five years ago they would never believe what was possible in [Southminster] which is why I have more of a commitment to targets really. Not the number sometimes suggested, but a minimal number of targets as just signposts, about how you're moving forward.
>
> (Director of Education, May 2003)

The school development advisory service had been commended in the successful re-inspection of the Authority for its role in 'negotiating' targets with the schools. The advisers had adopted a way of working, which in comparison with the other two authorities in the network, conformed more closely to the letter of the Code of Practice on LEA–School Relations (DfEE, 1999c). This focused in particular on working in schools with serious weaknesses and those in special measures to raise their performance on the tests, and in setting challenging targets for, and monitoring the progress of, others. This left very little room for our research team to work with them to encourage the inclusive development of schools and, while we saw our work was essentially about school development, our collaboration within the LEA was primarily with others involved in developing inclusion policy and equality issues.

There was a history of racism in the area, with the first British National Party candidate to win a local election elected within a ward containing some of the network schools. However, it appeared not to have the same level of inter-ethnic tensions as in areas of the North of England near to Castleside LEA, which were subject to disturbances in 2001 (Home Office, 2001a, 2001b). While there was a continuing problem between 'gangs' of youths, these usually involved different groups of young English-Bangladeshi men. In surveys the great majority of residents saw the Borough as a place where people from different ethnic backgrounds get along well. Yet the potential for conflict was well illustrated from notes made following a discussion with the headteacher of one of the schools:

> Shortly after the events of the eleventh of September 2001, groups of young people gathered outside the school. They were divided by skin colour, English-White to one side, English-Bangladeshi to the other. As one group chanted 'Bush, Bush, Bush', the other responded: 'Bin Laden, Bin Laden, Bin Laden'.

The authority had made considerable strides in appointing teachers from ethnic minorities, their proportion rising from 14 per cent to 22 per cent in three years. Ethnic minorities made up almost 40 per cent of support staff. On the council, ethnic minority councillors exceeded their proportion in the general population. Nevertheless, some teachers and LEA staff felt that progress was slow and were concerned at the continuing under-representation of staff from ethnic minorities in conferences and discussions about inclusion, partly caused by the continuing separation of strands of the inclusion agenda promoted by central government that were reflected within LEA structures.

There were other features of the policy environment which were significant in the development of inclusion. For example, the numbers of teaching assistants had trebled in the five-year period 1997 to 2002, and encouraging them to work in ways that carried forward inclusion was a major task of the schools in this as in other areas (see Balshaw, 1999; DfEE, 2000b). We should also mention a particular feature of the English education scene at this time, which, because of the penalties of being seen to fail, LEAs and schools were concerned with conveying an image of success. This might have been exaggerated, further, for an authority under the London spotlight.

A critical account of practice inevitably reveals more of the messiness of ordinary life than easily fits the clean-cut image of an authority striding forward in its achievements. At one meeting of the coordinating group for the research, one of the headteachers remarked: 'I hope you are not going to do a Martin Bashir on us.' She was referring to an interview with Michael Jackson where the interviewer had gained the singer's trust before portraying him in an unfavourable light.

Views of inclusion in the schools

In some of the schools, then, there was evidence of a widespread and long-standing commitment to a broad view of inclusion that pre-dated their involvement in the network. Thus, for example, it was noticeable how one of the primary schools had integrated inclusive values into the detail of its practices, and was able to articulate and spread its approach within and beyond the school. Another striking example of this was provided by one of the secondary schools, where there was a shared view among staff that the development of inclusion had to be built on a common culture which they should develop among themselves, and with students and their carers.

The headteacher of this particular school related her ideas on inclusion to 'equal opportunities' and 'the comprehensive ideal', and this inclusive message seemed to pervade the whole environment. The school has to meld students from a range of primary schools, each with their own cultures: all of this in an area with a strong history of racism. Posters were prominently displayed which made clear the school's commitments to combating bullying, racism, sexism, disablism and homophobia. Photographs of students in the entrance spaces reflected the diversity of the school population under the heading 'All Different, All Equal'. Such values seemed to be well understood by students. For example:

> Someone can't say just because someone's getting more help that he's a favourite person. Everyone's all different and we get all equal. But not at the same time.

> Yea, there's nobody higher than me, nobody lower than me.

It was noticeable that students accepted that they were expected to look beyond the friends with whom they associated when they joined the school, and that this was a justification for a strict classroom seating policy which required them to mix:

> Yeah, you get mixed up to get to know all different lots of people, instead of just sitting with your mates and looking at 'em. You make new friends and all that.

In talking with visitors to the school, teachers, teaching assistants, learning mentors and supervisors were quick to mention the school's inclusive culture and their concern with welcoming and celebrating student diversity. It was also clear that there was no separate policy on inclusion. Rather, it was seen as being integrated into the fabric of the school.

In another primary school, the headteacher claimed that the school's 'vision' of inclusion owed a great deal to the use of the Index for Inclusion. Indeed, on a number of occasions she expressed a wish that her staff should 'have the same vision of inclusion as the Index':

> We believe in inclusion. This means that we are all the time striving to build a community which creates inclusive cultures, policies and practices. We want to break down the barriers that we have created, either inside the community between each other, or between our community and others. We particularly want to break down the barriers that stop all children achieving their best. We do this by constantly evaluating our practice in the light of our philosophy.

The explicit commitment to inclusion in these three schools was striking in the context of Southminster. However, as we will show in subsequent chapters, it was even more so when contrasted with the traditions that existed within the schools in Northfields and Castleside. Yet inclusion continued to be problematic in the schools in the area. Apart from concessions to the standards agenda and accountability culture, and the contradiction of actions arising from these with inclusive principles, some schools differed in the extent to which they drew together the variety of strands of the inclusion agenda. For example, the research notes of one of the team revealed how categorisation could shape expectations about the way particular children were viewed in the school:

> Kim has been described to me as having 'severe language delay'. I join the class during the whole class activity of a numeracy lesson. Kim has a teaching assistant near her on the carpet who encourages her to respond. The class is broken up into groups and Kim is on a table with those thought to be attaining least and given the simplest task. This group is supported by a teaching assistant and I join the group and sit next to Kim and work with her. She greets me and then introduces the children next to her: 'Hello Tony, this is Peter and this is Ahmed'. She has been given ten counters. I am to cover

some and she has to tell me how many I have covered. She accomplishes the task without difficulty. At the end of this activity I ask the teaching assistant how she feels the activity went. She replies: 'It went pretty well but Kim wouldn't have been able to do it'. I try to understand what is going on here. Why is Kim's apparent linguistic and numeracy progress not noticed?

During other observations it was clear that many staff in this school rejected the specialist model of educational difficulties. For example, when a speech therapist who occasionally saw Kim recommended that she be transferred to the speech and language provision at another school, her teachers were adamant that she should remain where she was.

Teachers in this school were concerned, too, about grouping policies, and felt that since the introduction of the national literacy and numeracy strategies they often grouped by attainment within classes, against their better judgement. The observation of Kim's lessons seemed to provide support for these concerns. In a school and classroom where commitment to inclusion was very evident, a group of lower attaining students was created for some activities. This reduced the opportunities for peer support from students with relatively high attainment and also led to the group being given assistance, for some of the time, by a member of staff without teaching qualifications.

In most respects, however, this particular school was adept and assertive in bringing together policy strands reflecting different and perhaps conflicting agendas. Thus, for example, the school had volunteered to be in a pilot scheme for 'gifted and talented' children. The headteacher told a story about a neighbouring school, where the co-ordinator had asked during an assembly for 'the gifted and talented pupils to stay behind after the assembly', as an example of how not to incorporate this initiative into the school. The coordinator for this work attended the training and found it to be naive. He felt that the children would be better served by courses on inclusion involving teachers in making classrooms responsive to learner diversity, so that no child was impeded in the development of their learning. They were using the 'gifted and talented' money to increase the opportunities for all children to widen their cultural experience, through theatre and other visits. Nevertheless, children were identified as 'gifted and talented' and knew they were, and this could put additional pressure on them as well as send messages to other children about their absence of gifts and talents. In one classroom several poems were placed on the wall, the most stilted of which, in the eyes of one of us, was by the student labelled as 'gifted and talented'.

In one secondary school where there was evidence of a well-articulated commitment to inclusion, there were also examples of what seemed to be contradictions between principles and actions. So, for example, the headteacher was happy to argue that her response to what she called 'EBD' (emotional and behavioural difficulty) was to use disciplinary exclusions. This was the school where one of the deputy headteachers described the difference between her and the learning support coordinator's roles as: 'She's inclusion – special educational needs, and I'm social inclusion – naughty boys.'

Although this school had not permanently excluded any students in three years, there were 192 fixed-term exclusions involving 122 different students in the school year 2000 to 2001. This was a significantly higher figure than elsewhere in the LEA. The deputy head was planning to introduce an exclusion room, to replace external disciplinary inclusion with internal exclusion, and to bring this figure down. She and the head saw such a move as an improvement in avoiding the consequences of students being out on the streets during the day.

Like the exclusion room, an alternative curriculum provided for some 14- to 16-year-olds, applied disproportionately to white working-class boys. The Director of Education and others within the Borough were aware of the importance of addressing the issue of class, and an understanding and valuing of class identities in particular. Exhibitions were established to reflect the working and cultural history of these children and their families. But there was some distance between this recognition and the development of school cultures that would prompt the avoidance of practices which devalued or especially valued children on the basis of their class.

In another secondary school, the research team assumed that a broad view of inclusion had been developed because of its involvement in the network. They also assumed that this went beyond (and incorporated) support for students categorised as having special educational needs. However, it became evident that this was only true to a certain extent and at certain times. For example, when a photographer visited the school to document aspects of its work in the network, he was directed to classrooms containing named students who were seen to experience difficulties.

Making changes in the schools: developing inclusion?

The work of the network had to fit into an unusually flourishing project culture in Southminster. This meant that the schools were simultaneously juggling several different initiatives emanating from central government or the LEA that were attached to different sets of funds. One school had a list of twenty such initiatives in which it had been involved over a one-year period. Several of the schools became particularly adept at integrating the funds for these apparently separate activities to support the priorities they had already identified. The way this project culture impinged on the work of the network was perhaps best highlighted by the operation in several of the schools of a parallel inclusion project entitled 'Reaching Out to All Learners'. This project began shortly before the network and started by getting school teams to identify priorities for development using questionnaires from the Index for Inclusion, an activity that overlapped precisely with what the research team intended to do with the schools.

Nevertheless, throughout the three years of the network, all the schools developed activities concerned with increasing the participation of their students, families and communities. This was not always a continuous process, since energy to engage in such work might be interrupted by an impending inspection, emerging from an unfavourable report, or by a dip in Standard Attainment Test (SAT) scores. In what follows, we illustrate the range of these activities.

Developing inclusive values

It was noticeable that one of the primary schools in the network was regarded by some as a think-tank for inclusion in the Borough. Staff in that school argued that inclusive values should underpin everything that they do, and staff meetings and conferences were used to extend the implications of these values for the school. This gradually led to such values permeating the fine details of practice. For example, the names of all the members of a class were on the classroom door, conveying a message about the shared ownership of the space beyond it. Within lessons, the routine of orchestrating a classroom with a variety of group activities, with language support and support for those whose learning is prompting concern, was described by one teacher as 'bog-standard differentiation'. This was an allusion to the decrying of the 'bog-standard comprehensive school' mentioned in Chapter 2.

The atmosphere in the school was noticeably calm. Teachers and teaching assistants were called by their first names and relationships were usually respectful. This calm seemed to be the result of a careful strategy of routine intervention in classrooms, halls, corridors and playgrounds at the first signs of potential conflict. Thus, play-fighting in the playground was seen to be a potential precursor of aggression and a stimulus to the aggression of others. During circle-time discussions, students learned to avoid disparaging remarks ('That's stupid') or laughter at the contribution of others, whether meant playfully or not. Children were expected to understand that some children needed more help than others to settle.

In one class the temporary absence from the classroom of a child, who had been aggressive to others in the class, was used to appreciate how understanding the rest of the class had been:

> We don't want him to think we don't like him. You are handling what's happening so well. We want him to feel good, we all have our off days.

The perennial conflict between children over friendships and the potential for friendship power to turn into bullying power was given particular attention. Children were supported to avoid competing to be best friends and to widen their social circles.

The use of interventions for one child for the benefit of others was well illustrated by Lee, who learned Makaton (a British Sign Language basic vocabulary) because he found it difficult to articulate his speech. The class teacher used signs alongside speech when teaching the whole class. Other children and staff learned some signs and sign-supported songs were sung in assemblies. The picture signs and visual timetable that had been developed for Lee were also used with other children who needed prompts for reading English. This approach was extended into a more visual curriculum, using drawings, photographs and objects to stimulate the contribution of those who have more visual learning styles. His classroom teacher noticed that Lee had begun to develop real friends, as sign supported the communication between them. His teachers also noticed a marked increase in Lee's concentration after he exercised real choices about what he was learning, and this had obvious implications for the learning of others.

The school developed a variety of other schemes to promote participation. For example, transparent weekend play bags were produced, drawing on suggestions from parents/carers and children, containing dressing-up clothes, videos, books and puppets. Children could choose from one of the transparent bags on a Friday. The school also prepared learning kits to support the education of children when they had gone on extended leave to Bangladesh.

Encouraging student participation

Another primary school set up a school council comprising two elected members from each class, which met twice a term. An early task was to help to frame the school aims, which was built from the children's statements into an acronym, PRAISE – Pride, Responsibility, Achievement, Inclusion, Success and Entitlement.

Members of the school council expressed concern about the amount of fighting and aggressive behaviour in the playground and suggested that more organised playground activities would help to reduce these. In response, the school developed a playground buddies scheme and adopted a zero tolerance view of fighting, which dramatically reduced the number of incidents. It also provided a variety of games for children to use, managed by Year 6 children, and, as a result, teachers reported that playground accidents had decreased. Staff members responsible for the playground also involved the children in fundraising activities for new equipment.

Inside the classroom, the staff felt they were increasingly successful in engaging children in their own learning, through sharing with them the setting of learning intentions at the start, and the evaluation of what they had learned towards the ends of sessions.

Conflict resolution was a theme running through many of the activities that schools used to involve students. At one of the secondary schools students could apply to become 'conflict resolution trainers' at the end of Year 9. The chosen ones were generally a mixture of high-attaining students and others with general 'street credibility'. After intensive training, the mentors were each allocated to a Year 7 tutor group and their photographs were put on the tutor room wall. They attended registration and helped to deal with issues of conflict between students, and between students and their teachers as well as checking homework diaries. They made a record of serious incidents and were expected to report them to teaching staff.

A similar scheme was developed within one of the other primary schools, following a survey of views using the Index for Inclusion. One student priority stood out from the survey: there was a concern that bullying needed to be reduced. The response of the school was to develop a wide-ranging behaviour policy in which anti-bullying was not the direct focus. This may have made strategic sense, but also owed something to the protection of the school's image, as the head explained:

> What is bullying? I don't think it helps when the word is used by the media to beat educational professionals over the head, we have to be careful about overusing the term and it being seen as a problem here.

Further perceptions of bullying, and of good and bad relationships more generally, were obtained through interviews and discussions with teachers and teaching assistants, and, indirectly, through a week of activities on the theme of 'getting along together'. This included class assemblies, circle time, role-play, discussing videos and responding to books on bullying. A wide-ranging behaviour policy was developed through a series of meetings, including a two-day residential conference, involving governors and all staff. This focused on issues of culture, including detailed attempts to develop collaboration across the school and attention to visual displays.

The new policy was introduced to students during another week of activities, including a special assembly attended by parents and carers. They were also given copies of the policy document. This emphasised ways of reducing bullying, agreed rules of behaviour and the links between good relationships and approaches to teaching and learning which held student interest and encouraged cooperation. A group of Year 6 conflict resolution mentors was established to work with younger students. However, the school staff regarded the core of the policy as good-quality, well-focused teaching.

Involving parents and community

All the schools were concerned about the involvement of parents and local communities. This was also a priority for the LEA, which had worked with a consultant to develop a set of materials to encourage parental involvement in children's learning (Bastiani, 2003). Significantly, this work built on the approach used in the Index for Inclusion, but was created as an entirely separate initiative with its own meetings and attempts at implementation. It highlighted the presence of an initiative imperative that existed within the LEA as well as to an extent within central government, and indeed ourselves, whereby engagement in an activity inevitably required a new document to add to the pile. This does not mean that such documents were not immensely valuable, just that few had the capacity to get around to them all, or to integrate them into their work.

For two schools, parental involvement was a particularly fraught issue due to the perceived racism of some white parents. One of these schools focused on this issue from the start of the research. The school had been through a period of difficulties, and staff referred to a previous era when they had 'a thriving parent–teacher association' and 'many mothers worked in classrooms'. The communities surrounding the school had changed and now originated principally from Bangladesh. The school itself remained mainly white, with a minority of African-Caribbean children but with no Bangladeshi background students at the start of this work. One member of staff described the school as 'like a white village transported to Bangladesh'. It was felt that some parental aggression arose due to parental fear of school. The headteacher instituted controlled change because of the danger, she felt, that she might otherwise be 'setting myself up for a slanging match'. She hoped that 'the word may filter through'.

A monthly parental forum was established where 'representatives' of the parents were consulted on issues and where they could raise concerns. Gradually, relationships with parents become less formal and parents once again began helping in classrooms. As one parent commented:

> It's much more relaxed, the children sense that too. Before it was always teachers on this higher level; now it's like, do you want to make an appointment to see Margaret? Much as I loved Miss___, even if I'd known her first name I would never have associated it with her.

Including categorised students

Southminster has a policy of progressively moving children from special into mainstream schools and basing them within resourced schools, rather than in their local schools. One primary school had incorporated a group of students with physical impairments and another group categorised as having severe learning difficulties.

At the start of the research, another primary school became the local authority resource for students categorised as having speech and language difficulties. This school already had a reputation for taking children seen to be difficult within other schools and there was concern about some staff, as one commented:

> They're so exhausting, the stress levels are enormous. It's also a question of balance. If you reach a critical mass the whole thing goes.

Taking a group of students categorised as having 'speech and language difficulties' was seen, in part at least, as a way of controlling the intake in a school with spare capacity. Nevertheless, the headteacher voiced a deep commitment to inclusion. He regarded it as a 'state of mind', which recognised 'the right to belong as a basic human right'. He explained that his job was to 'deal with the practicalities of what that mindset looks like in everyday life'.

After two years, the number of categorised students in the school had risen to twenty, most of whom had settled in well and made friends. This belied the fears of some staff that the school would become 'a special school in all but name'. According to the head:

> The progress those children have made, from assessments done in the summer, the general feedback from their parents at the reviews, there's been a very positive start. Unfortunately there aren't many in this school who step back and look at the big picture.

Deploying support staff

All of the Southminster schools were integrating an increasing number of support staff, such as teaching assistants and learning mentors, into their work. These colleagues worked in a variety of ways and often become sensitive to assisting all students within a group or class.

A particularly innovative use of assistants to support students *outside* classrooms was developed at one of the secondary schools. These 'supervisors' were at the school from early in the morning, when they were involved in the breakfast club, through to the end of the school day, when they saw students safely away from the immediate area of the school. Team members circulated throughout the school, patrolling the corridors, grounds and lavatories, during lesson times as well as break times. They maintained radio contact with each other and wore bright red polo shirts.

We observed how the supervisors significantly reduced the spaces and opportunities for conflict and disaffection. They were trained to defuse conflict situations and to detect signs of bullying in an isolated student, a reduced lunch or a student burdened with carrying several bags. They were also responsible for following up lateness and truancy. Each day they spent a period sharing problems with each other, deciding whether they needed to refer on any issues to senior teaching staff.

Students who were described as most in danger of disciplinary exclusion spoke positively about the supervisors and the contribution they made to the order and safety at the school. For example:

> We listen to them like we listen to the teachers. At lunchtime, like, we know that they're there and we can't get up to any troubles. So it's safe for all of us then.

> I know all of 'em 'cos my mum knows all of 'em. They only live round here. [_____] lives bang next to us.

The supervisors also showed prospective parents around the school, and acted as a powerful bridge between the school and its communities.

School-to-school collaboration

Despite the competitive assumptions of the standards agenda, participation in the network seemed to encourage schools to share ideas and resources. For example, one school offered considerable support to a neighbouring school in special measures, both before and during an inspection. Other schools were part of an Education Action Zone (EAZ), which viewed the development of inclusion as a main assumption. It specifically encouraged the sharing of ideas on how to reduce racism and racist incidents.

A particularly strong working relationship developed between the new heads of a Roman Catholic primary school, with its predominantly white population, and a nearby junior school, comprising almost entirely students from a Bangladeshi background. The heads of the two schools wanted to address the divisions between their communities barely a hundred metres apart. It had been reported that children from the junior school might cross the street rather than walk too close to the church, and a group of parents at the Catholic school had expressed open hostility towards people from Bangladesh. Apparently, a Muslim student on teaching practice in that school had experienced racist remarks from parents and students, and a Bangladeshi visitor to the school had been harassed in the playground. The junior school head was also concerned about the limited monocultural experience of her students and that they could be influenced by any racism within their families.

Collaboration started with an invitation to a nativity play at the church. Despite opposition from some Catholic parents, who 'sent a posse in to complain', and initial objections from some parents at the junior school, the event went ahead. Several parents attended from the Catholic school but none from the junior school. The visiting children were said by the head of the Catholic school to have performed 'a beautiful spellbinding dance' as their contribution to the occasion, although the other headteacher found irony in the choice of a Hindu dance by her teachers:

> It always amuses me, this school: Muslim children doing a dance for Diwali. Do they understand what they are doing? A dance for Diwali and all of that in the church.

In return, the junior school created its own version of the nativity to which staff and students from the Catholic school were invited. The head from the Catholic school remarked: 'We found out how many kilometres it was to Bethlehem, which a Catholic would have absolutely no interest in.'

A theatre-in-education project built on what the students at the junior school had learned about prejudices within and between the communities. A play was performed for the students at their partner school. Joint staff development days followed and then a more ambitious theatre-in-education project, which involved all the 8-year-olds from both schools. This had the theme of making new friendships. The children reflected on the lessons they had learned. For example:

> I didn't know them much before – they used to be bad to me, I used to be bad to them – but we're friends now, that's my favourite part.

> When you have friends you shouldn't just let them go away or throw away your friends.

Parents from the two schools travelled together in one coach to a performance of the new play. A difference in 'assertiveness' was noted (parents from the Catholic school commandeered the best seats) but, despite the fears of the headteachers that prejudices might be voiced, the journey went peacefully. The play was a great triumph and many tears were shed. The head of the Catholic school recalled that she had deferred to the head from the Junior school: 'I was feeling too emotional, so you had to speak first.'

Since the collaboration began, the Catholic school has admitted ten Bangladeshi background children, and its staff has become more ethnically diverse. Both schools have developed race-equality policies that build on their work together, supported by an anti-racism consultant funded by the LEA. The head of the junior school argued that inclusion 'is a mirror you hold up to your practice'. She saw her relationship with the headteacher of her partner school as the foundation of a model of collaboration: 'Staff and children seeing us working together well.' However, these efforts were to some extent overtaken by events when a sudden and unanticipated drop in the SAT scores in the junior school narrowed the attention of the head and her staff. We discuss this in a little more detail below.

Pressures on school development planning

During their three years of involvement in Southminster, the Canterbury team attempted to understand how the variety of inclusive activities in which schools engaged might be connected together through an inclusive approach to school development planning. This was informed by their view that sustainable development required a balance between rational, improvised and reactive planning. Improvisation is important in planning, as practitioners see new ways to connect values to a course of action, or recognise the need to seize opportunities that emerge. The importance of a degree of improvisation in planning was well made by one headteacher:

> School development plans are all very well . . . but you can't legislate for seeing something out there you didn't know about before and thinking that would really do well in my school . . . I make no apologies for that, I'm not going to say 'well it's not in my school development plan'.

Our view is that inclusive values provide a framework for such improvisation in planning, as in moment-to-moment interactions within the classroom, though, if change is to be coherently related to principles and sustained, it must also involve medium- and long-term rational planning. Furthermore, there is a considerable difference between improvising change within a coherent framework and being forced to react to disparate and contradictory initiatives.

Yet, some teachers spoke about the impossibility of making considered plans while trying to patch up the consequences of teacher shortages and the consequent instability provided by temporary inexperienced teachers; or while preparing for impending inspections, or responding to their aftermath. One headteacher argued that the constant flow of initiatives and policy changes from central government made a long-term improvement plan virtually unworkable. She argued: 'Talk of a plan in our present culture is meaningless.' In a similar vein, and for the same reasons, another head considered that she did not have 'a realistic plan for the next three years'.

Pressures from the standards agenda

It was particularly evident that the approach to planning and development in these schools was affected considerably by the prospects and verdicts of an Ofsted inspection. Despite the rapid increase in overall performance on SATs and GCSE examinations, there was still a higher proportion of Southminster schools said to have serious weaknesses, or to be in special measures, than the national average. This was, of course, unsurprising given the degree of disadvantage within the Borough.

The stress associated with inspections and the protectiveness of heads towards their staff also interrupted the schools' involvement in the network. It was noticeable, for example, that in the lead-up to an inspection, headteachers were reluctant for anything to distract their staff's attention. In one case a head cancelled a planned day of observations and interviews, and all other contact with the research team, for the 'foreseeable future' in the light of her receipt of a letter from Ofsted informing her that the school was going to be inspected in two months' time.

The response to inspections is well illustrated by what happened in one of the primary schools. This was a school operating in challenging circumstances by any definition. Sixty-one per cent of its students were in receipt of free school meals, it had the most transient student population in the Borough, and 58 per cent of students were at the 'beginning stage' of acquiring English at the time of the initial inspection. In addition, along with many other schools in Southminster, it had suffered from teacher shortages and high turnover. When a member of the Canterbury team first visited the school he was greeted with a large wall display in the foyer, with a headline banner: 'CELEBRATIONS'. It had been put up to mark the fact that the school had recently been taken out of 'special measures'. It included an invitation to parents and others to join an afternoon of festivities, including 'food from around the world'. There were also a number of mock newspaper reports by students describing the efforts by them and their teachers to 'work harder', as well as cards sent to the school by well-wishers. A Year 2 student explained that everyone was now working a lot harder so that the inspectors would say, 'well done'.

When the school was eventually taken out of special measures, the inspectors praised the high quality, strength and decisiveness of the new leadership, brought in to 'turn things around' and raise standards of attainment. This seemed to have been achieved by putting the whole school staff on a kind of war footing. The headteacher described her deployment of teaching assistants in pursuit of this aim with a mixture of medical and military analogies when she said:

> We target groups of students and then we use them [teaching assistants] like, I don't know, to blast cancer out of a cell. In they go, then we bring them back, evaluate their impact, push them somewhere else.

She further described the development of 'an assessment culture' whereby all students were assessed 'in every subject every half-term', and placed in sets for maths and literacy:

> Let me tell you now . . . there's nothing more exciting than teachers assessing children and walking down the corridor smiling and the children get that buzz as well.

However, there was a drastic narrowing of the curriculum accompanying this focus on standards in the core subjects, which was cited by the Ofsted report taking them out of special measures. However, the headteacher reacted to such criticism by asking her critics to put themselves in her situation:

> At one point I had all the Ofsted Inspectors with me in this room and they said, 'You don't have a broad and balanced curriculum', and I said, 'I know, but what would you do? I mean, I'm only a headteacher, tell me what you would do in your school?' And they said, 'We would do exactly the same.'

Another primary school had a good reputation for meeting the needs of a wide range of students, many of whom arrived there after experiencing difficulties in their previous schools, but it had failed to meet what the headteacher described as 'fairly challenging targets' set by the LEA's school development advisers. The school then changed its priorities to a new focus on improving results in SATs, as the deputy headteacher explained:

> Because we didn't have that kind of agenda we took our eye off the ball in terms of ensuring *what you need to do to get children to be able to pass those tests* and that's what we're addressing right now [emphasis added].

For most schools, 'what you need to do to get children to pass those tests' had become an important element of their day-to-day thinking and working. They often felt it necessary to put students into attainment groups, direct resources to getting them to cross the borderlines from SATs level 3 to a valued 4 by the end of primary school or from a D to C grade in secondary school GCSEs, drastically narrow the curriculum, hold revision sessions before and after school and at lunchtimes, and to single-mindedly 'teach to the test'.

Most of the headteachers resented the inflexibilities in the way that ever-rising targets were set by the LEA, with no allowance being made for cohort characteristics. They were aware of the danger that some schools may 'in the past' have simply 'coasted along' and had not set sufficiently challenging targets. However, the current system was often regarded as being irrational and unfair.

One head, who felt that she was working long hours to raise attainment at her school, had a particularly strong reaction to a visit from her school development adviser following negotiation over fresh targets. She felt that the adviser was not only ignoring the characteristics of the student cohort but also of the staff:

> Well, I had a mauling from my inspector. He asked very tough questions and that's his job, but he won't accept the cohort argument and he will not accept that I have to work with what I've got staff-wise. My maths coordinator, she's super, but the feedback I've had this morning, if she got that she'd go back to the leafy suburb from whence she came.

> I thought they're bloody lucky to have me. He asked: 'how can I help you?' I nearly said: 'Just stay away and don't come back. I know how to raise standards – sack all the LEA people and get them back into class.' I'm sick of cobbling together a teaching staff.

Some teachers argued that it was part of their professional competence to monitor and evaluate teaching and learning at their schools by taking account of 'cohort characteristics'. They felt that they were in the best position to respond to national curriculum requirements 'to set suitable and appropriate learning challenges' for students and 'respond to their diverse learning needs' (DfEE/QCA, 1999). Such an approach seemed to be in contrast with the LEA's determination to reach 'political targets'. One head admitted that she had used the very small amount of leeway she believed heads possessed in their negotiations with the LEA to underestimate what her students might achieve in order to give herself some 'breathing space'.

Simplistic explanations that might be given to a fall, or indeed, a rise in results on SATs sometimes caused particular difficulties. There was an assumption among LEA school development advisers, in particular, that all changes in SATs results were due to good or bad teaching. Yet cohorts could vary, not least because of movement in and out during a school year, and that this was a particular problem for smaller schools, where a couple of new children could affect the percentages sufficiently to be noticed.

There was also evidence that Year 6 teachers adopted different approaches to the way they supervised the tests and the degree to which they encouraged and relaxed the students. Some teachers saw the SATs tests as more important than other teachers, and might vary in the keenness they felt to enhance the image of their school. After two 'successful' years, the head at one school felt under considerable pressure as a result of the drop in SATs scores. Some in the LEA interpreted difficulties at the school as her fault, and it was even suggested that she should 'have the sense to leave'. It was argued by others that the drop in results might have less to do with the failure of this head to bring about sustained improvement at the school and more to do with the fact that her Year 6 teachers were moving on to a different school to rejoin the person who had been acting head at the school before she was appointed, by governors keen to see greater ethnic minority representation at the school. With the support of other heads and her family, she decided to 'weather the typhoon'.

Grappling with teacher shortages

Perhaps the most significant single external pressure affecting school development in Southminster during the period of our research, however, was that of teacher shortages. Some schools had to replace more than half of their teaching staff at the beginning of a new year. At the start of one year, three new staff failed to appear at one of the primary schools. Meanwhile, most of the schools were only able to stay open with the support of temporary agency teachers. One school put a half-page advertisement in *The Times Education Supplement* inviting prospective staff to an open day, with a buffet lunch, and offering to arrange overnight accommodation for those from outside London. The headteacher of another school travelled to Australia in order to recruit teachers for the Borough generally, and at the same time she found two maths teachers for her school.

It was reported that some teachers from other countries arrived without knowledge of the English education system, or a readiness to understand the particular cultural circumstances of a complex social environment like Southminster. Thus a teacher in one school, recruited from Australia, referred to the large numbers of 'immigrants' in the school, most of whom, unlike him, were born within the locality. There was also a feeling, expressed during a meeting of the Bangladeshi Teachers' Association, that white teachers recruited from other countries found it easier to find teaching posts and then to get promotion than local English-Bangladeshi graduates. Meanwhile, staff turnover was increasing and the average age of teachers within the schools was dropping.

Students in one of the secondary schools expressed particular resentment at the high staff turnover. They felt unsettled when they were 'left in the lurch' by teachers who moved on and were difficult to replace. They preferred teachers who were qualified in the subject that they were teaching, had been in the school for some time and who therefore knew them well. New teachers and supply teachers were seen as liable to misjudge their capabilities and to give them 'the wrong work'.

In a primary school, the headteacher described how, in the face of shortages and the need to employ agency supply teachers, the small number of strategically placed permanent members of staff held the school together:

> It's like a peg going through the school. I've got Diana holding together 5 and 6. I've got Vic in 3 and 4, Alice in 1 and 2 and Jean in reception, and then I've got one NQT (Newly Qualified Teacher) who isn't too strong and one NQT who is very strong.

In another school in special measures, progress had to be made while coping with a high turnover of mainly overseas agency staff. Several staff simply felt unable to stand the pressure of the constant scrutiny associated with being in special measures. During the school term of the re-inspection, two-thirds of the teachers were agency staff. By the end of the research period the school had a full complement of permanent staff for the first time in three years and felt that this liberated them to engage in longer term planning.

Views of leadership

An understanding of inclusion as developing participation among adults as well as students would lead to a view of leadership as distributed through the staff of a school. However, observations of the work of the Southminster schools suggested that current approaches to school improvement may, sometimes, reduce the inclination of headteachers to seek a participative approach.

Nationally, there is an image of the 'super-head', wheeled into a school in difficulty, turning it around and then passing it on to another sort of leader once it has been pressed into shape (Morley, 2006). This image adds to the pressure on heads to make improvements in the short term. Thus, one head felt she had to demonstrate that she could achieve change quickly:

> Experience has taught me that in this school you can get quick results, because I have done. Investors in People after a year, amazing isn't it! And the Ofsted, I know it can be done, I provided the vision and leadership, and motivated a huge amount of people.

Given the constant pressure to boost test results, there was an inevitable tendency to marginalise developments less likely to provide short-term evidence of impact on pupil performance. Although work to decrease bullying, or to encourage greater engagement with parents, might contribute to a long-term strategy for raising the attainments of pupils, such concerns might be seen as peripheral in the short term. As one head commented:

> My priority is quite simply to raise attainment however it is done. We're having booster classes . . . rearranging timetables . . . we're gonna do it!

Who participates in planning?

So, if leadership tends to be concentrated in one or a few people within a school, how can the staff, students, parents/carers and other communities connected to the school feel ownership of planned developments? An approach to school development that rests so heavily on success or failure of the headteacher, besides emphasising short-term rather than long-term planning, is likely to be in direct conflict with wide and sustained staff participation.

In a primary school taken out of special measures, the inspectors praised the high quality, 'strength and decisiveness' of the new leadership. Indeed, the 'strength and decisiveness' of the headteacher was evident from the first engagement of the Canterbury team with the school. An atmosphere of a 'new broom sweeping clean' pervaded the school, and casual staff room conversations were peppered with comments about the changes the head had brought about, contrasting these with 'the way we used to do things'. One member of staff described her as 'a woman in a hurry, she wants results yesterday'. The head saw herself as having to change both parental and staff attitudes to achievement, behaviour and attendance. She felt she needed to 'get her message across' to both groups, 'so that they may come to buy into my vision'. Both groups were seen as needing to be worked 'on', rather than 'with'.

All the schools described the process of development planning as participative to some extent, involving staff, governors, and, in some cases, parents and students. However, all reported, too, that their procedures were less inclusive than they would have liked. In one school that had had a stable staff and management team, and a long-standing commitment to building a culture they defined as 'inclusive', there was a strong element of rational planning and an approach to initiatives that mitigated their disruptive effects.

Yet where, as in Southminster, there is a reliance on consultants to support development, an emphasis on maintaining existing staff, and inducting a stream of temporary agency staff, wide participation may seem an irrational luxury. A number of heads described their position as 'fire-fighting', or engaging in 'knee-jerk' reactions to external events. Indeed, one head argued that it was these pressures that prevented a more participative approach:

> It's just something I had to get stuck in with, which hasn't given us the luxury of spending a lot of time on this sort of thing.

Staff at another school set out 'to develop strategies to increase the involvement of the local community in the school'. This was an aim from the action plan, written in consultation with the Ofsted inspectorate and Local Education Authority advisers, to bring the school out of special measures. It was made clear to the research team, however, that this was impractical and that it was counter-productive to consult too widely. In the event, a number of meetings were held, to which parents and governors as well as staff were invited. However, when attendance of parents and governors was low, this was accepted without analysis, or a strategy for increasing their involvement. The lack of involvement of the governors was justified in terms of the many calls upon their time that had been made over the past few years, and the 'sterling work' that many of them had done in assisting the school to get out of special measures. For the headteacher, that had been a more important role for them. Similarly with the parents, the attitude was: 'Oh well, we have tried.'

Whose priorities?

It seems, then, that while the development of relationships with the community might be an inclusive aim for a school, when it is part of the means for a school to rid itself of the stigma of 'special measures' or 'serious weaknesses', it can become another externally imposed target to be seen to be reached as quickly as possible. Some informants were also quite explicit about the way plans were designed more to impress others than to provide a practical way forward for the school. One school produced a development plan, ninety-seven pages long. It contained an enormous amount of detail, amounting to a collation of each individual member of staff's action plan. As seen by the headteacher:

> It was an attempt to chart every moment of change and development, and to demonstrate everything we were doing. To say: 'this is what we're going to do next and boy aren't we doing an awful lot?'

Eventually this long plan was replaced by a twelve-page version, with five priorities derived from a new Ofsted report. Three of these related to the raising of standards of attainment. The plan produced by a second school was described by the headteacher as 'huge . . . because there were so many elements that had to be put into place'. Again, staff had been involved in the production of a much 'simpler' and more strategically oriented plan, with three key headings. The years when the school was in special measures were seen as extremely stressful for staff at the school. The headteacher spoke of staff feeling that she (or Ofsted) were 'doing things to them . . . rather than their having ownership of their actions'. She described a 'shell-shocked atmosphere', whereby the school had been under so much scrutiny that they preferred to employ their own teacher-consultants rather than use LEA services. Although often very helpful, there was a feeling that all such advice and support was linked to the LEA agenda, and that such advisers were unable to switch off from a monitoring role.

Where schools employed consultants provided by the LEA to work on particular areas, these became, almost by default, priorities in their planning. The use of consultants, either from the LEA or independently contacted by the schools, to help them with the implementation of priorities in their improvement plans, was a way in which hard-pressed schools could see that progress was being made. But it could also limit the understanding and ownership by staff of their own development, as well as the opportunities for them to learn skills in supporting each other through observing and analysing each other's practice.

Some primary school heads described, too, how their planning was skewed by the requirements of government programmes and initiatives, and the support for these through the LEA and their advisers. The most frequently mentioned were the national literacy and numeracy strategies. For example, there were comments on the way the LEA reinforced messages about grouping by attainment for the literacy hour. One school wanted to redress this practice in line with their principles and the practice prior to the introduction of the literacy hour. Staff at the school commented on the difficulties created by the setting up of groups of children experiencing the most difficulties in literacy or numeracy. The staff involved felt that through such arrangements, pupils would receive little peer support with their work, and, in practice, were often supervised by a teaching assistant with limited knowledge and experience of overcoming such barriers to learning. However, when it was proposed that such an issue might be the topic for a workshop at a network conference, a local authority officer was concerned that it would contradict local orthodoxy.

Drawing together the analysis

In reflecting on our observations of what happened in Southminster, we characterise staff in schools as being constrained within a series of policy tensions (see Box 4.1). These will be taken up in more detail in the final chapters of the book.

In particular, we saw how schools had to contend with multiple and contradictory policy strands, reproduced within the LEA and passed on to schools through lines of funding and accountability. In such a context, it becomes difficult for schools to bring together the separate support resources associated with difficulties in learning, disabilities, English as an additional language, behaviour and discipline, and students categorised as 'gifted and talented'. Such separate support streams make it even more difficult to develop a truly inclusive notion of support, to do with increasing the capacity of schools to respond to the diversity of students within their communities. The structural separation of inclusion, equalities and school development also make it difficult for LEA staff to promote a common agenda and provides conflicting messages to the schools.

At the same time, schools are constrained to adopt an approach to achievement within the standards agenda that can pressurise them

---

BOX 4.1

Policy tensions in schools and LEAs

- Integrated vs. separated strands of inclusion
- An inclusive vs. 'standards agenda' approach to achievement
- Teaching and supporting diversity vs. special needs education
- Emphasising reality vs. attention to image
- Long-term and sustainable change vs. short-term meeting of targets
- Attending to conditions for teaching and learning vs. attending to outcomes
- Rational vs. reactive planning
- Commitment to inclusive values vs. compliance to directives
- Shared vs. charismatic leadership
- Coordination of schools vs. LEAs 'pared to the bone'
- A new framework for education vs. responding to initiatives

to narrow the curriculum and deflect them from a broader understanding of achievement. This can lead them to adopt selective grouping strategies against their better judgement, and the development of exclusive values that see some students as more important to the school than others. In being pushed to attend to a narrow set of outcomes of education, schools can reduce the attention they give to providing the conditions which develop children and young people as active, interested, whole learners. As we have seen, it can also lead central government to ignore the need for a long-term strategy for proper teacher supply and replace this with short-term recruitment strategies which export teacher shortages to other countries, or de-professionalise teachers by replacing some of their duties with the work of teaching assistants.

The persistence of the categorisation of large numbers of students as 'having special educational needs', and the ideas of special education to which it is connected, also continue to exert considerable barriers to inclusion. In several of the Southminster schools, a specialist and selective response to difficulties in learning had not been replaced by practices which support teaching for, and learning from, diversity. Much of the work of teaching assistants provides a default position to which practice appears to return, despite training on a broader role. Frequently, assistants remained attached to individual students, rather than aiming to help students to become independent from adult support, and encourage their working and social relationships with other students. As we have explained, special education as a response to educational difficulty also fosters a professional and administrative response to categorised students, leading to the grouping of large numbers of categorised students within particular 'resourced' schools, even when they leave special schools, rather than entering their local schools.

An overall emphasis on competition, failure and its consequences within an education system can encourage schools and LEAs to be over-concerned with image, rather than building from a keen awareness of the reality of what is happening in classrooms and schools. In this way, opportunities for development may be overlooked. We encountered a striking degree of openness in some contexts, but also times when information from within the school or LEA that might take practice forward was resisted.

Despite all of this, **some schools were incredibly adept at consuming a succession of external demands and initiatives, and fitting them into a framework of their own concerns and values.** But most were pushed, at times, towards a short-term reactive approach, particularly in relation to the achievement of targets, and away from medium- and long-term rational planning. Meanwhile, an approach to school leadership that places undue emphasis on the responsibility of headteachers for 'success' or 'failure' can work against the development of shared leadership and participatory development that is assumed to be a necessary element of strategies for developing inclusive practices.

As we have analysed the material collected from the network schools, we find ourselves repeating a common story. Schools are under pressure from 'the standards agenda' and 'accountability culture', the way these are interpreted within the LEA, and from local circumstances. These pressures frame their approach to school development, and therefore limit the attention they can give to the development of inclusion and how they formulate it.

Nevertheless, there is considerable commitment within LEAs and schools to put inclusive values into action and to develop inclusive 'cultures, policies and practices'. Such developments meet a relatively rigid structure moulded by the standards agenda and accountability culture, which for some staff in schools are also integrated into their professional identities. It can seem that inclusion can only flow into the spaces that are left. In some cases, where inclusive developments have continuous support and/or little conflict with other activities, remarkably persistent changes have been made, but in general the development of inclusion encounters conflicting activities and structures, and remains relatively incoherent and fragile.

Schools have limited discretion to develop themselves according to their own values. However, the process of making values explicit, attempting to put them into action and resolving contradictions between them extends this discretion. It helps to clarify the frame within which new initiatives are absorbed and around which day-to-day practice is improvised. While inevitably some planning itself is reactive, we argue that coherence over values helps to reinstate an emphasis on rational planning and the building of long-term sustainable inclusive development.

Summary and conclusions

The accounts in this chapter illustrate how national policy tensions impact on the efforts of those within an LEA and its schools who are apparently committed to notions of inclusion. In so doing, they highlight how policy factors can act as barriers to progress while, at the same time, revealing resources that could be mobilised to move practice forward. As we have seen, the achievements of the eight Southminster schools are particularly encouraging in this respect. They draw our attention to the fact that progress *is* possible even within the context of these policy tensions and contradictions. In Chapter 5 we look more closely at how teachers in some other schools within the network interpreted and dealt with these tensions and contradictions.

Chapter 5

Winding up to inclusion

In this chapter we look more closely at the processes that took place within network schools as they struggled to make sense of policy tensions and were prompted to think about the inclusive development of their schools. We draw on the experience of the Newcastle team, working with schools in Northfields LEA. We explain how the schools decided on their areas of focus and how they saw these in relation to notions of inclusion and, indeed, the wider context of government reforms. We then describe the variety of activities taken up within the schools and points to the factors that influenced these developments. These differed from the developments discussed in Southminster in being focused more directly on activities to support student learning.

In the previous chapter we looked at the experiences of schools working in an LEA that had a strong, explicit commitment to the development of inclusion. However, it became apparent that the complexity of LEA organisation meant that not everyone had a similar understanding of the meaning of inclusion, nor equal commitment to the values underlying it. Further, contradictions of policy nationally as well as locally, and the multiple strands of inclusive thinking, required schools to constantly manoeuvre their way around policy tensions. The schools also clearly demonstrated the huge resource for the development of inclusion represented by their staff, who returned to the task of putting their inclusive values into action when pressures on them from other sources eased. This task of reflecting on inclusive values itself played a significant role in allowing staff to mediate the pressures of the standards agenda, and make space for themselves to think their own thoughts about how to develop education in what they saw as the interests of children and their communities. Such values took them beyond the vision of education within government policy documents. Indeed, in a very important sense, it added considerable value to them.

The LEA view of inclusion

The Newcastle team brought with them to this work their realisation of the complex interplay of inclusionary and exclusionary processes within even those schools which had an explicit commitment to developing inclusion, or indeed felt that they had reached an 'inclusive' position. They were interested to find out whether a study of the development of schools not pre-selected because they felt themselves to be, or were seen by others to be, particularly successful at developing inclusion, would yield different results.

Northfields is not as polarised as Southminster in its economic and social conditions. While it contains pockets of severe deprivation, these are less concentrated and there is less of a contrast with extreme wealth. It also has a much smaller minority ethnic population and only one of the schools in this branch of the network had a significant number of minority ethnic students. Northfields teachers also tended to be less likely to express their view of education in explicitly political terms than those in Southminster. Thus, while they were probably as committed to principles of social justice as were their colleagues from the London Authority, they did not tend to express this commitment in terms of an explicit discussion of the relationship between inclusive principles and policies and practices in schools.

However, Northfields LEA did see itself as actively encouraging more inclusive practices in schools. Indeed, in terms of a strand of inclusion connected to special needs education, its predecessor LEA had been one of the early pioneers of 'integration'. It had set up a series of resource bases for students categorised as 'having special educational needs' in several of its schools, including some of those that took part in the network. There was a sense, however, that this pattern of provision was beginning to look dated, though it was typical of the LEA's style that it was not engaging in wholesale changes and had not yet formulated either an explicit definition of inclusion, or an inclusion policy. This may be seen as an example of what the government referred to as a 'pragmatic, not dogmatic' approach to inclusion (DfEE, 1997). Those critical of government policy interpreted this stricture to mean adopting a position of sitting on a fence in the centre while appealing to potential voters on both sides of it. Such a characterisation would be entirely unfair of those working with the team from Northfield LEA, where staff adhered strongly to a concern with social justice and traditional motives of public service. In their own way they shared many of the inclusive values set out in Chapter 1.

Looking across developments in the eight schools, then, it is interesting to examine what they did and why, and how they related their initiatives, begun for a variety of reasons, as fitting under the aegis of 'inclusion'. Whereas in Southminster the research team negotiated activities as foci for the research that related to inclusion as understood by the research team, in Northfields, school groups formulated their own understandings and set their own priorities. What, then, were the factors at work in this process?

Inclusion and the standards agenda

The foci of the work in the schools were clearly affected by the so-called 'standards agenda'. Although early results from the national literacy strategy had been encouraging, there were particular concerns that it was failing to make much impact on the teaching of writing and that the attainments of boys lagged behind those of girls (Ofsted, 2000c). It was scarcely surprising, therefore, that the LEA should view the improvement of attainments in writing as a priority in its development plan.

The prominence of the standards agenda and its influence on LEA planning goes a long way towards explaining why the primary schools chose to focus heavily on issues to do with the attainments of their students and particularly, in most cases, on the standard of children's writing. Thus, for example, even a school that decided to focus on staff culture was actually seeking to address similar concerns:

> It is important that we're up there. You're judged on your success, and the only way that we're going to get more pupils into the school, and I know falling numbers with the birth rate and everything are an issue, so the best will survive. I know this school – I went to this school, and I think it's rather nice that my children have gone to this school, but I want them not to have average [sic]. So I think there's a big expectation for me that I want these SATs results up.
>
> (Chair of Governors)

Those within the schools, like national policy-makers, seemed to operate with a notion of 'underachievement' that stemmed from a belief that there were significant numbers of students who could attain more highly, if only the school could find more effective ways of teaching them. This tended to be seen as not encompassing students who were identified as having special educational needs, on the grounds that the schools were already doing all they could for such students – and, in any case, there might be little room for improvement. As one headteacher explained: 'We have tended to pour resources into the weakest at the expense of the majority.'

Since achievement was measured through national assessments, any attempt to address underachievement would necessarily have the effect of raising student – and hence the school – performance on these assessments. Another primary head noted: 'I hope the strategies have an effect on the SATs. We're under huge pressure.'

In some cases, this meant that work within the network was equated quite instrumentally with the raising of national assessment scores. In one primary school, for instance, the focus on non-fiction writing was a more or less straightforward attempt (at least initially) to maximise the proportion of students achieving target levels in the writing SATs. Indeed, the emphasis here was less on whether children would become better writers, in some sense, than on whether they would choose the non-fiction option in SATs, which seemed to be rather easier. The headteacher reflected:

> Now also, in past years, when it's come to SATs – I know everything shouldn't hinge on SATs but – when we look at past SAT papers, very few of our children have chosen the non-fiction option . . . but interestingly enough, those children who have chosen it, when we've analysed their pieces of work, they've got level 4s and yet we wouldn't have thought if they'd been doing pieces of story writing they'd have got level 4, they'd have got level 3. So there's something about non-fiction that encourages children to attain higher.

Even where schools were less overtly instrumental, however, the inclusion agenda, understood as being about addressing underachievement, was seen as broadly compatible with the standards agenda; that is, it was understood as being about raising school and student performance on a narrow range of measures. Another head made the link in the following way:

> What all [these] strategies do really, is tend to pick up those
> children who for one reason or another – either maturity or
> absence, or inability to make connections between different stages
> of learning, or principally they just don't have the intellect to be
> able to cope with that more focused teaching, and they need a
> small steps approach. They haven't arrived at that level, and what
> you're trying to do essentially is before they meet the hurdle, you
> give them the boost and that will get them to that level. . . . It's a
> policy of inclusion basically, which recognises the varying abilities.

However, a different head expressed succinctly the difference between
an inclusive view of the meaning of achievement for personal and
community development and the narrow view of achievement in the
standards agenda, when he commented, 'It's all about level 4s really,
isn't it?'

The two secondary schools, untouched at that time by the influence
of the national literacy and numeracy strategies, and accountable for
performance across a wider range of curriculum areas, had concerns
that were somewhat different. In both cases, they focused on those
students who were, or were at risk of becoming, disengaged from the
process of schooling. However, they too were responding to local and,
especially, national concerns about 'pupils who are at risk of disaffection
and exclusion'. In this context, one of the schools established a student
support service which was, in fact, simply paralleling and complying
with the establishment of learning support units (LSUs) in Excellence
in Cities areas (DfEE, 1999a). Meanwhile, the other secondary school
was part of such an area and was already in the process of establishing
its LSU. The initiative it chose to explore as part of its 'developing
inclusive practices' project, although couched in the liberal language
of pupil empowerment, was in fact clearly focused on the issue of
attendance and truancy. The project coordinator explained:

> We want to look at inclusion positively and identify what we do that
> is inclusive. The school is doing something right on attendance –
> but we really don't know what it is. The project is another way of
> monitoring what happens, but asking more groups what they feel.
> . . . The management team has a perspective, policy is to improve
> attendance. But to improve attendance, what helps?

Children who 'don't fit'

Given this equation of inclusion with raising achievement, schools were not in any simple sense opposed to the general direction of national education policy. On the contrary, some teachers (particularly in the primary schools) spoke very positively about how their own teaching practices had been improved and the learning of their students had been enhanced by recent developments at the national level. For example:

> There's a mass of stuff come out with the literacy, and ideas for teaching in a different way, using different methods – there's the spelling book and the grammar book and it's got a wealth of new things, so many that you can sift through them, try them and think, well that doesn't work. And the same with the numeracy strategy, and I'm a great fan of it because it's so well set out, and the INSET stuff was so good. But there's loads of ideas for presenting things in a different way to get children interested.
>
> (A primary schoolteacher)

However, other teachers were dissatisfied with what they saw as the inflexibilities of the current system, including the distorting effects of a too-narrow concentration on performance in national assessments:

> The rest of the curriculum, I don't think we've actually sorted that yet. I think we need to be looking again, but it's all about getting SATs results again, and this is where I'm thinking that . . . if you concentrate on your SATs results, OK you're getting what the government wants to hear, but we're not doing what we're paid to do, which is the all-round education. So it's a bit of a cleft stick really. At the moment I think we're concentrating on the SATs results more than we are on the other things.
>
> (A primary schoolteacher)

Running throughout all of this, however, was a recurrent theme that there were groups of students who did not do well under teaching and learning arrangements seen to be inappropriate and ineffective. In some schools this was the view of a relatively small number of overtly disaffected students. In others, the opinion was that most, if not all, of the school's students suffered from this 'lack of fit' to some extent, either because they brought significant difficulties with them into school, or because the school's responses to them did not engage their interests, or build on their attainments and experience. Other schools placed themselves somewhere between these two extremes.

Intake and social class

The schools began with the view that some students had characteristics, derived in turn from facets of their families and communities, which led to a mismatch with the educational opportunities on offer to them. The clarity of the analysis varied considerably between schools and teachers and the emphasis in primary schools was slightly different from that in secondary schools but the same set of factors emerged from all of them. It was felt that some children came to school from families where education was not valued, where experiences were limited, and (particularly in primary schools) where language skills were poorly developed:

> Well, the children we take in, particularly have problems with language. Because I think their first-hand experience is quite little. And from the nursery, talking to the nursery, we do have a lot of children with speech impediments. And I think their lack of experience with language, perhaps at home, already has created a problem when they come into school.
>
> (A primary schoolteacher)

This was attributable to the unwillingness or inability of children's parents to engage with them fully in activities which promoted development, for example, by providing them with stimulating experiences to expand their vocabulary or by acting as positive role models:

> But there is a good proportion I would say, where nobody reads. Where they don't see their parents reading. Maybe they might see somebody reading a newspaper, but I'm willing to bet that quite a large proportion have never seen mum or dad read a book, for pleasure, as we would.
>
> (A primary schoolteacher)

In time, this produced underachievement which might be manifest in poor literacy skills. As another primary teacher said:

> When we were thinking in terms of making education more inclusive for everyone, even for our more able children, they don't often

have the skills – the language and the thinking skills, that they need to maximise their potential, I suppose.

Underachievement was seen as resulting in increasingly difficult behaviour, low expectations and ambitions, and progressive disengagement from schooling. At the same time, parents were perceived as failing to develop the sustained and meaningful involvement with the schools which would enable them to support their children's education. One teacher explained:

> We send a reading diary home with the children. And I sent it out at the beginning of this year, and I wrote a little note saying, 'If you read with your child, would you like to write comments, record the book that they've read, any work that you've been doing at home would be lovely.' And there is a very small proportion of parents who write in that book in my class. And I think it's the same for classes across the school.
>
> (A primary schoolteacher)

Implicit in this analysis was a distinction between children and families who understood and supported the norms of schooling – the families who behaved 'like we would' – and those who did not. By and large, the children and families who were not supportive of the teachers' view of what they should be doing, or not effectively so, were seen to come from lower socioeconomic groups. Some schools could discern a clear divide in their populations between the two groups:

> we're quite interesting because we have . . . we really are in the middle of two sides here, socially. And it is apparent where our children are not achieving, as much as perhaps we feel they could be, which side of the school they emerge from. And linked to that of course is the parent response.
>
> (A primary schoolteacher)

This situation was exacerbated for schools by what they believed to be a change – indeed, a 'downward' shift – in their intakes. For example, a learning support assistant in another primary school commented:

> What does tend to happen is we lose the brighter children. . . . They move on and up. And the children that tend to come in, I think it's

all to do with catchment isn't it? People get better off, don't they, and they move to a better area. So then we're increasingly taking children from nearer the centre of town.

It was evident in many cases that the systems and practices which schools had in place for their 'historic' intakes were breaking down in the face of these changes. In some cases, this breakdown was little more than a minor irritant. For instance, staff in one primary school explained how its hitherto stable and largely skilled working- or middle-class village was beginning to receive a small number of significantly poorer families who were being rehoused from one of the Borough's most deprived areas. This was seen to be difficult for the school, though not overwhelming; indeed, the teachers could name the handful of individuals who had entered the school as a result of this process. Elsewhere, however, the effect was felt to be 'overwhelming', not least in one of the secondary schools, where an entire intake year was seen as posing significant and unprecedented difficulties.

There was evidence that these changes were neither imagined nor the result of a 'moral panic'. Socioeconomic indicators suggested a small but noticeable change in all but two of the schools. Significantly, one of these was the only school where the staff did not complain of an increasingly problematic intake, or feel the need to take action in respect of one or other problematic group in its population. The other was a primary school which continued to serve a historically highly disadvantaged area.

The ambiguities of inclusion

One reading of the responses which schools made to the invitation to 'develop' inclusive practices is to see them as seeking quite radical possibilities for injecting inclusive values into dominant agendas that were patently failing some students – not least those who already experienced the greatest social and economic disadvantages. One primary school, for instance, claimed to be developing a radically alternative pedagogy, leading to outcomes much broader than those envisaged in the national strategies:

> Well, we're going down the route of looking at our teaching strategies, and how children learn, and the skills they need to learn, as learners – not the curriculum bit, but the actual learning techniques

and strategies they have, because that tends to be very limited with our children. And we actually want to broaden their range of learning strategies, their thinking skills. We want to create more opportunities of first-hand experience, the discussion, practising these thinking skills.

(Headteacher)

However, it was equally if less dramatically true of one of the secondary schools, where the establishment of the student support service was presented by the head as a radical alternative to exclusion, giving real opportunities to students who might otherwise be lost to education. The Chair of governors supported this view:

> [If a 14-year-old] is given the right help and support, at 16 you've got a nice, tolerable human being, which you never thought possible eighteen months previously. All right there are some kids who have problems all the way through, and there are some, but I think very few, who at the end of the day need to be somewhere other than here, but those who have minor problems or temporary ones who could get the help [from the Service] and be easily reintegrated back into the normal mainstream of things, you know I think that's a great way to do it.

However, the view that schools as a whole were interested in radically shifting the values they brought to education, or the practices that flowed from them, could not be sustained. As we have seen in this and in previous research, apparently radical challenges to dominant agendas often turn out, on closer inspection, to be somewhat less ambitious – and in some cases narrowly instrumental – attempts to deliver those agendas by alternative means. Moreover, the analysis of the difficulties faced by some students remained firmly rooted in a deficit model in which educational difficulties were seen to be caused by problems within students, rather than in teaching and learning arrangements. Such deficits were also frequently generalised to their families, communities and social classes.

Under these circumstances, the approaches set in train by these schools tended to be marked by deep ambiguities. Insofar as they located the source of children's difficulties in the characteristics of the dominant agendas from government, or of schools' interpretation of those agendas, they opened up the possibility for radical critique and radically alternative practice. At one primary school, for example, the head saw problems as located within staff cultures rather than in student characteristics. Likewise, at another primary school, the hide-bound practices of long-stay staff were seen as significant contributory factors to children's underachievement, and involvement in the network was understood as a way of problematising teachers' assumptions: 'What I'm really interested in is teachers realising the effect they have on children through their attitudes and practices' (Headteacher).

However, insofar as the schools' approaches continued to conform to the standards agenda and to locate the source of difficulties inside the children themselves, their families and their communities, they reinforced the correctness of the government's diagnosis of, and remedies for, the problems faced by schools. As a consequence, the government's agendas were themselves seen to be marked by deep ambiguities – at one and the same time both liberating and constraining, opening up new possibilities and shepherding children back into well-trodden and problematic paths. Thus, a secondary school's student support service was both a form of inclusion – maintaining disaffected students in the school – and a form of exclusion – removing them from lessons in some cases, but, more commonly, policing their behaviours until they conformed with school norms and expectations. Likewise, at a primary school, the powerful – and powerfully enacted – rhetoric of finding alternatives and opening up new opportunities for disadvantaged children, brought them back to the need to write and, ultimately, the need to reach the magical Level 4 at Key Stage 2.

Developing inclusion

So far, in focusing on the way schools interpreted the task of inclusion, we have outlined the contexts, dilemmas and views that the schools tended to have in common. However, it was clear that they responded to the complexities of their situations in various ways. In particular, there were differences in the scope of their initial actions and in the way those actions developed over time. In this section, we try to understand more clearly the course of that development.

The initiatives taken by schools, then, followed distinct trajectories. Thus, for example, one of the primary schools adopted a very narrow focus on performance in the writing SAT. Another took the potentially larger issue of student grouping, but dealt with it in a narrow manner, through the actions of a small and semi-secret project group undertaking small-scale experiments in two classes and within a small segment of the literacy hour. Another primary school focused likewise on a specific curriculum area and on a specific group of students, while a secondary school had a relatively small initiative to address concerns about behaviour which had already been planned and made minimal impact on practices and systems across the school as a whole.

Other schools, however, took a much broader view of what they should do. One looked, as we have said, at an all-pervasive issue of school culture; another set in motion a free-wheeling review process, which could, in principle, look at any aspect of the school; while two of the primary schools tackled fundamental issues of pedagogy.

In some cases, schools remained with the initial focus for the duration of our involvement with them, and their project was little more than a process of implementation. For instance, the secondary school retained its narrow focus on the evaluation of its student support service and resolutely refused to accept any invitations to explore wider issues. Elsewhere, although initial plans were certainly implemented, that process led to new insights, a deepening of teachers' understanding of their situation, and, at times, a broadening of the scope of their action. In some cases, this broadening and deepening was quite dramatic, as in the example of one school, whose original focus broadened into a wholesale review of teaching and learning, which encompassed a rethink of the school's unit for children categorised as having moderate learning difficulties and how these children might be more fully included in classroom activities.

In the case of a secondary school, however, the process was very different again. Its original broad conception remained broad, but the Newcastle team found it difficult to pin the school down in terms of how the project was progressing, what was planned to happen next, or how an evident flurry of action in the school related to the original focus.

The role of leadership

This last example points us towards the nature of leadership, particularly from the headteacher, as a significant factor in determining the focus and direction of work in the schools. In that particular school there was a view that the head might not be sufficiently in touch with what was happening and therefore not in control. One teacher explained:

> I think, well . . . there's a real strength in the management team in how to get the best from people and how to approach people to get

the best from them, and accessibility anyway . . . I think that side's very good. There's always gripes with staff about senior management, because senior management don't teach, and they feel that they don't know what it's like at the chalk face. I don't know that they've forgotten; they're not under the same pressures that – you know, the things that come down, not fully aware of things that are going on.

By contrast, at the other secondary school, the head seemed very much in control, but equally reluctant to widen the project's focus. On a number of occasions the research team and members of the LEA team raised questions about the apparently high level of student disaffection, and the relationship between this and the culture and established practices of the school. While the headteacher recognised this as a legitimate issue, it was never followed up: 'The sense of unfairness. I accept the view, but it's a very hard one to tackle.'

In other schools, it was a combination of qualities in the head that seemed to be crucial to the development of the school's work, including an openness to examine problematic issues. A teacher in one of the primary schools commented:

> I think a headteacher willing to take part in a project like this, and have the school evaluated from top to bottom straight away, is a big plus in favour of the school.

Headteachers also needed to be able to coordinate and motivate a group of key staff to drive a process of development:

> It's about communication. Sometimes a staff of sixteen/seventeen teachers is too big, and actually a small working party like this one can take a lead in curriculum innovation. I mean it's a fairly powerful group when you consider it's got the Head, the Deputy, the SENCo [special educational needs coordinator] and the foundation stage leader, plus a reasonably young teacher.
>
> (Primary headteacher)

Such leadership was not seen to be about outstanding skills, charisma, or filled with visionary zeal. Rather, the heads of most of these schools were careful managers, aware of the realities of budget control, target setting and staff development. As one head said:

> It's not enough just to say, 'well we are an inclusive school'. It's looking at how it impacts on the finances of the school, how it

impacts upon the professional development and training plan, how it affects the support assistants and the teachers in school. How it's perceived by members of the community. How parents feel. How would the children feel? So it's not enough just to skim the surface and say, 'well we're developing a culture and we're making everybody feel involved'. It's beginning to look at it on a much deeper level and say, 'OK we are, but how are we going to do it, and how is that going to affect the management of the school within the confines of the school budget as well?' And it's actually looking at other practices that are going on, and learning from best practice, and seeing how we can apply that practice in our school.

This head, and other teachers, demonstrated a powerful sense of liberal values to do with equity (though variously understood), which informed their work and guided them in plotting a more or less steady course through the complexities and contradictory imperatives which they faced on a daily basis. However, what was important for them was not the powerful articulation of rhetorical positions, but actions which, at one and the same time, realised some broad values and 'worked', especially in terms of classroom practice:

> And it's also about teaching strategies. . . . It's about saying 'these are the strategies and these strategies will work'. Whether they will or not, we'll wait and see! But that's the aim.
>
> (Primary headteacher)

This propensity paralleled that of the LEA, which also preferred to see inclusion as a broad informing principle, to be worked out in action, rather than requiring a more developed position set out in policy documents, as in Southminster. As a teacher commented in a discussion at the end of one the national seminars held in Southminster LEA: 'Southminster has an ethos of inclusivity. In Northfields it's bottom up!'

The importance of staff culture

While the actions and attitudes of headteachers were important factors in what happened in the schools, these could not be understood separately from those of other staff. This was most obvious in schools where some staff were hostile to the inclusive developments which the heads and school project teams were trying to initiate. In two schools the actual or anticipated resistance of a sizeable proportion of the staff limited what the head was prepared to attempt. In one of these schools, this led to the covert approach to experimentation on the part of the staff team until a number of the long-stay teachers left the school. At the other, although the head maintained a resolute approach to changing staff attitudes, this was a constant source of stress for her. In both of these schools, there were distinct signs of change by the end of the project towards a more open and collaborative approach.

In some of the other schools, however, there was evidence of such an approach from the outset. For example, one head said:

> If there are any initiatives, they're always collaborative. Nobody does anything on their own in this school. I mean that's how we spread good practice basically.

What seemed to be key in these cases was a shared identification and definition of problems, joint problem-solving and sharing of ideas, and mutual support and mentoring. By and large, these processes were not managed through separate structures and events, but had become part of the culture of the school: 'the way we do things round here', as one of the heads put it. In such a context, the network was simply one more opportunity (albeit a particularly highly structured one) to work on problems together and to share experiences.

The way in which such collaborative cultures could support head-teachers is clear. If the head could enlist the support of the staff for an initiative – or, as was more usually the case, if the head was part of the whole-staff problem-solving group – there was every prospect that the staff would see the initiative through to fruition. Where universal support was not immediately forthcoming, however, the head could use more committed staff to work with more sceptical colleagues to bring them on board. However, a reliance on collaborative and supportive structures sometimes prevented heads from taking risks which they were convinced would bring about improvements in the school. Indeed in a number of cases, heads preferred to wait for staff to leave rather than force their compliance:

> there are some little pockets, not of resistance – it's not that people are being difficult at all – but it's hard to let go when you know

there are pressures at the end. In some places, and in some cases, I don't know how much shift we will see. You know, it's a fact, there are some cases . . . we've got some long-established staff here, we've got some staff due to retire. I'll be sorry to see them go as well, because they'll be taking some wonderful skills with them and great experience . . . but the fact that this is a long-term project and there will be staffing changes, people will be expected to sort of come in and come on board at our level.

(Headteacher)

Headteachers did not always make a great fuss about the changes they wanted to see happen, both because they did not wish to alienate staff and also because they wished as many staff as possible to take ownership of developments for themselves.

This analysis did not apply equally well to the two secondary schools. The scale of these institutions meant that whole-staff collaboration was less viable. It also made the research team more cautious in claims about the views and practices of the large number of staff who were not directly involved in the project initiatives. Certainly, there was little evidence of widespread collaborative approaches in one of these schools, as evidenced by the rather detached nature of its student support service initiative. In the other secondary school, there was a great deal of what Hargreaves (1991) calls 'contrived collegiality', and the project there was intended to be managed by a relatively large cross-school group of staff brought together for the purpose. However, the failure of this group to sustain itself and its fragmentation into a series of disconnected initiatives confirmed an impression that a collaborative approach was not firmly embedded within the culture of the school.

Using evidence

Much of the collaborative problem-solving activity that took place involved teachers in drawing on their professional experience and knowledge to identify problems and find solutions. However, they were also able to use a variety of other forms of evidence in forming a view about their work. To some extent this pre-dated and was independent of the network. Thus, for example, the schools were very familiar with the performance data on which they expected to be judged, which was supplied to them annually by the DfES or their LEA. As we have seen, in some cases, a desire to make immediate improvement in performance indicators was one of the main factors in determining the initiative the school would take.

However, involvement in the network encouraged schools to collect and analyse other forms of evidence to help them monitor and evaluate their initiatives. Moreover, the research team collected additional data themselves, both in accordance with their own agendas and in response to requests made by schools. This meant that the schools could make use of such additional information as reports of stakeholder interviews, lesson observation data, questionnaire analyses, detailed assessments of students' work, examples of teachers' planning records and teachers' logs.

All of the schools in Northfields engaged with this additional information and performance data, albeit in different ways and to different extents. One approach was to seek quantitative data that, they anticipated, would demonstrate conclusively that their initiatives were having the effects for which they hoped. One school set up an experimental group and a control group, which the school team hoped initially would yield results proving conclusively that mixed-attainment grouping produced better outcomes than attainment grouping. The team in the school that set up the student support service was likewise happy to provide attendance and exclusions data to prove that it was having a positive impact and were reluctant to respond to suggestions which might indicate the complexity of interpreting such evidence.

An alternative approach, promoted by the Newcastle team, set performance and other quantitative data alongside other, more qualitative forms of evidence. This involved asking questions about the nature and effects of current practices and the impact of any initiatives taken to develop those practices. It was hoped that this approach would lead to a cycle of action research in which school teams interrogated data and used them to interrogate their practices on a recurrent basis, as it did, for example, in one of the schools, where the focus was on the use of questions:

> If we go back to the first year when we started to look at teacher questioning and we collected evidence from that and you sent back [analyses of teachers' questions], the first time you observed me I think I asked one evaluative question, and a couple in the higher order. Most were in the lower order. By the next time you came back, because that had been analysed and we'd rethought it . . . it was nowhere near that.
>
> (A primary schoolteacher)

In general, there was a move during the lifetime of the network, from attempts to 'prove something' towards a more exploratory, reflective approach. The two schools that had placed most emphasis on an experimental approach, for instance, found that they could not use data to 'prove' the superiority of one practice over another and became amenable to a more dialogic approach. However, it would be a mistake to assume that there was a simple process of development here. The use of data at one of these schools remained as opportunistic and, at the other, as tightly constrained as most other aspects of the school's project work. Another school collected 'portfolios' of evidence about the occurrence of particular activities, which involved little in-depth enquiry into the quality or impacts of the school's initiatives.

What emerges, therefore, is a somewhat mixed picture. Where schools were relatively open about their work and had (or developed) a view of the way the use of evidence could challenge their previous thinking, the data collection and analysis process played a part in helping to guide developments in the school. However, where schools (or powerful members of the school team) were less open, or where there was a narrow conceptualisation of data, its analysis and collection tended to be used to demonstrate the worthiness of their actions for any potential external audience, rather than for a developmental process which they owned themselves.

Making use of alternative perspectives

An important element in the development process for all schools was the availability of a range of external perspectives on the work that they were doing. The most obvious of these was the critical friendship provided by the university research team through a series of formal feedback sessions and informal discussions. The responses to these interventions varied.

In one of the schools, the Newcastle team felt they could identify ways in which their feedback had prompted a clear change of direction by the school. They had drawn attention to the segregation of students with 'moderate learning difficulties' in the school's 'unit'. At first, this brought no response, but some months after raising this issue, the school decided to increase the amount of time these students spent in ordinary classes and reported the positive outcomes with some satisfaction.

Elsewhere, the interactions were less dramatic. One school, for instance, used a regular flow of feedback to make corresponding adjustments to its work. In other schools, the commentaries of the team appeared to be strongly welcomed but then were followed by little response. Not surprisingly, this was the case in the secondary school, where the project remained tightly controlled and delimited. However, it was also the case in the other secondary school, where the project seemed more far-reaching and, in the view of the school team, more risky. As in this school's use of data, the approach here was to repeat the justification for what had been done rather than to further explore its consequences.

There were two other sources of external perspectives. Through their half-termly meetings as an LEA project group and through the national seminars, the Northfields' schools had contact with each other and with schools elsewhere. Some of these contacts had a significant impact, particularly when teachers were able to undertake short visits to schools in the other two LEAs. These visits had been initiated by the team in Southminster, and we were able to reflect on the experience and refine them during subsequent conferences in Castleside and Northfields.

Responses from the Northfields teachers to some of the schools in Southminster had been rather polarised, particularly in respect of the explicit and powerfully articulated commitment to inclusion in that LEA. This was in marked contrast with the more low-key approach adopted in Northfields and its schools. Some teachers (and LEA officers) were quite negative about claims about the progress towards inclusion in Southminster LEA, seeing it as rhetoric disguising a less impressive reality. For example:

> I picked up the projects in Castleside, but not Southminster. Southminster seem to be already very inclusive. But I haven't picked up specific things to tackle barriers to learning. What data are they collecting – how will it feed into our data and Castleside's? I've lost the plot.
>
> (Headteacher)

For others, however, the Southminster approach was something of a revelation and gave them a very different standpoint from which to view their own work:

> I think certainly the visit to Southminster, to [named] school, was quite significant, because we came away enthusiastic about changes that we could introduce here. And some we have introduced.
>
> (A secondary schoolteacher)

Even one of the initial cynics later found some cause for reflection in his experience in Southminster:

> I wonder now whether we started at the 'wrong end'. I feel we focused very much on improving learning. Maybe we should have taken a broader view like Southminster. Maybe you [Newcastle researchers] influenced our decision to take the route that we did.
>
> (Headteacher)

Teachers from one secondary school in Northfields made a strong link with a secondary school in Southminster to gain support in developing their own conflict resolution work.

When the Northfields teachers visited schools in Castleside they found the approach closer to that in their own context. By and large, they saw the visit less as being transformatory and polarising, but none the less highly illuminating because they were invited to interview children in order to provide feedback to the host schools about their work.

As a direct result of these experiences in other LEAs, the Northfields schools set up a programme of equivalent visits to one another, realising that they now knew more about schools in other LEAs than in their own area. Again, they tended to see these as a powerful stimulus to their development. Thus, for example, one school invited visitors to observe one of the lessons in which teachers were employing new questioning techniques as part of its development of thinking skills with children and to discuss their observations afterwards. One of the host teachers commented: 'The talking through the lesson afterwards with visitors has helped us to develop a more complex way of analysing the questions used.'

For her part, the visitor to the lesson noted: 'Because we have begun working on thinking skills, the visit was really, really useful, particularly analysing the questions.'

It is worth adding that schools that were unable or unwilling to make use of other forms of information about their development besides simple quantitative measures saw less value in such opportunities. One of the secondary schools, for example, did not participate in the programme of visits and felt there was little to learn from visiting other schools.

The other important external perspective available to schools was that of advisers and advisory teachers. All the schools, as a matter of course, received regular visits from an adviser attached to the School Effectiveness Service, and for six of the schools, these advisers were members of the steering group for the network in Northfields. What seems to have been valued by schools was less the critical perspective they could offer than their positive support for schools' actions, even where these actions might be viewed as 'risky'.

Two advisory teachers played a different role. One of these was a literacy consultant, whose impact was restricted by the large number of schools with which he attempted to work and because he focused on technical issues to do with writing. None the less, the feedback from schools about his contribution was positive. More dramatic was the impact of a second advisory teacher working on an LEA-designed 'Quality in the Classroom' project. She was a former secondary school learning support coordinator who was concerned to extend the repertoire of teachers' classroom strategies. She was particularly interested in using activity-based learning and group work to develop thinking skills and provide children with strategies for problem-solving. She had developed a number of ways of recording information that did not rely on extended writing, such as the use of mind maps and spider diagrams. This particular adviser was a charismatic teacher who related well to both teachers and children, and was universally popular. Crucially, her approach involved her working inside the classroom, taking over the class from the teacher, modelling a range of approaches, and supporting class teachers when they used these approaches themselves. For some teachers her involvement had been, in their view, transformatory. For example, one teacher explained:

> She's already done three sessions with us – I would say more than a year ago. So we all loved her ideas. It was revolutionary in school! Every teacher was doing it.

Teachers could see new techniques being used with their own classes, producing responses which they would not have believed possible:

> I also think that all the alternative things, all the things that she's given me, are – any teacher could execute, *but* – I think they need to see you do it. You see it's all right her giving us the book of alternative forms of recording, but like a lot of teachers, if she'd just given me it and I hadn't had knowledge of what she meant, I might have thought 'oh yes very good', and pushed it in a drawer

and never picked it up again. I think you actually need to see her doing it with the children.

(A primary schoolteacher)

In this respect the way teachers learned from this advisory teacher overlapped with what they gained from visiting other schools; teachers saw with their own eyes practices that they did not commonly use themselves and, indeed, that they might have considered impractical. It seems to have been the opportunity to see a respected colleague doing something that helped them to recognise that they could learn how to do it themselves.

Impact on students

It is, of course, important to consider both the actions which schools might take in the hope of becoming more inclusive, however defined, and the impact of these actions on students' experiences and learning outcomes. As with the schools in the other two LEAs in the network, there was good evidence from, for example, teachers' plans, accounts and observations, that identifiable changes in practice and provision occurred, to some extent at least, in all of the schools in Northfields. Importantly, schools were also able to provide evidence for impacts on student outcomes.

In some cases this was apparent in standard forms of performance data. At one primary school there were rapid improvements in the attainments of a targeted group of children who were involved in a 'better writing partnership'; another primary school achieved rapid improvements in its overall performance, since it developed as a learning community and introduced a learning support service; and one of the secondary schools permanently excluded fewer students and improved levels of attendance significantly.

However, staff within the schools were also enthused by, and sometimes taken by surprise, by the effects their actions seemed to have on other less readily measurable outcomes, such as the motivation, confidence and self-esteem of students. A teacher at one school provided an illustration of this:

I'm concerned about the outcomes that couldn't be measured which [the headteacher] mentioned quite frequently. The confidence that our children have got in verbalising their thoughts, and just thinking, often comes through in our discussion now. We can't measure that but we know that it's a change that's happened and a significant change, and I'm not sure that's come through [in the feedback report]. That has been one of the most powerful things.

During the course of the three years, in their schools and at network meetings, the teachers articulated a view of the outcomes important for students that are much broader than their attainments on national tests. While teachers remained committed to raising achievement through their initiatives, they progressively asserted the importance of outcomes which mediated learning, both because these were crucial to sustaining achievement and because they were important in their own right. Such a view was often echoed by those of their students. For example, children at one of the primary schools spoke keenly of the way new approaches had helped them 'to have ideas', and, at another school, they talked of new approaches that had taught them 'other ways of doing things, not like the usual boring ways'. This seemed to be a way of asserting the presumption we brought to the project that inclusion emphasises the conditions for learning and teaching as much as it celebrates achievements of all children, and indeed staff, in schools.

An unpredicted result in a number of schools was how more general initiatives seemed to have a specific impact on students seen as experiencing particular difficulties. Unexpectedly, for example, a number of children targeted for a programme called 'Write Away Together' in one school made significant progress in their spelling, and this included some students who were identified as having problems in this area. Teachers at another school talked about dramatic strides made by children who had been placed on 'the special educational needs register' because of their low attainments. They attributed this to their focus on the development of children's thinking skills:

> Their thinking skills have improved, developed at least as much, if not more, than the brighter children, and they have become much more articulate, in expressing their thoughts or their questions.

The case of another primary school was slightly different. In the second year of the project the school chose to explore the potential of new ways of organising learning within the classroom for increasing the participation in mainstream classes of children who had 'statements of special educational need'. However, these children were not targeted as a discrete group but with the rest of their peers as part of the school's investigation. Children in the school talked of the impression made upon them by the progress of these students. One boy described his realisation of this as being 'like a bomb dropping on me':

> She has brought [boy with a statement] on to be – like if he's stuck, he'll have a try. His behaviour is much better. Some abilities are just unreal. Since [the 'Quality in the Classroom' coordinator] has come in his ability has risen above other people.

In spite of all these positive findings, however, there remained an essential ambiguity in relation to the outcomes of schools' actions, as there was in relation to their interpretations of inclusion. The way schools identified priorities for action in relation to the standards agenda had inevitably influenced the kinds of outcomes that it had been possible to achieve in the network project. In one school, for instance, the programme 'Write Away Together' undoubtedly had a significant impact on students who were in turn part of a different intervention in the network targeted for the intervention. However, in selecting students for the intervention the school could clearly be seen to be operating the kind of 'rationing' that has been identified as a feature of the schools trying to maximise their successes on national tests (Gillborn and Youdell, 1999). Using the criterion of a two key stage sub-level difference between students' writing and reading attainments, the school used an apparently 'objective' way of selecting children to take part. However, in prioritising children for the intervention, it chose 'mid- to lower ability' children, rather than 'higher ability' children, even where there was an identical discrepancy in their reading and writing attainments. The justification for this was that the 'more able' would do well anyway and that therefore the other children were more in need of the intervention. An alternative interpretation may be that the children who were targeted could make the most difference to the schools' performance on national tests.

Sometimes, too, the maintenance of a rigid view of the purpose of their initiatives, and the reluctance to consider alternative aims, prevented schools from making a difference to particular areas of students' experiences and learning. Thus, for example, students who were directly involved in the support service set up in the secondary school were very positive about it. One said, 'If it wasn't for the Service, people like us wouldn't be in school.' On the other hand, many of the same students were also equally forthcoming about their continuing dissatisfaction with school in general. They continued to feel that some, even many, teachers did not treat them fairly. Some students talked about being 'scapegoated' because of their reputations: 'Because I've been on report an' that, some teachers try and make my life hell – keep me back from lessons and that.'

One student even felt that teachers' attitudes could be described as discriminatory:

> The school gives out a message that it doesn't discriminate, but it does. Trendies can keep make-up on ['Trendies' are 'nice' girls' who look like 'Steps singers' – a bland pop group] but me and my mates can't.

Changes in schools, then, were not simply at the level of rhetoric. They commonly made real differences to students in the areas where they sought to make a difference. This, however, is the key. Although wider changes towards more inclusive cultures, policies and practices did sometimes occur as a by-product of the interventions that schools engaged in for the project, the main effects, naturally enough, were on the particular groups and the issues that had been singled out. There were therefore aspects of schooling where a difference needed to be made urgently but which were, in the main, simply overlooked by these schools.

Putting it all together

Where, then, do these accounts of developments in Northfields leave us? Are we seeing here the progress of committed schools towards an unequivocally more inclusive future? Or are we simply seeing the reproduction of existing patterns of exclusion? We would find it hard to argue that we are seeing the former. As we have explained, some, though not all, of the schools identified barriers to learning and participation and took definite steps to overcome them. However, for the most part they did so in limited and unspectacular ways, and their efforts were characterised by the sorts of ambiguities which the earlier research by members of the Newcastle team had led them to expect. Indeed, if anything, **the advent of the 'standards agenda' appeared to have reinforced exclusive tendencies in schools' work and reduced their freedom to develop more inclusive responses to student diversity.** Above all, there is little evidence here of the radical transformations sometimes reported in the inclusion literature brought about through charismatic leadership, or the emergence of collaborative staff cultures or organisational reconfiguration.

There is therefore much here that could drive us into a more pessimistic position: the willingness of schools to submit to the more exclusive aspects of national policy; the analyses based on deficit models of children, families and communities; and the attempts to manage students who do not 'fit' with established practices. However, this is not quite the whole story and the notion of children who do not 'fit' seems to lead to other possible explanations of what was happening.

Certainly, schools had different types of responses to children who did not 'fit' with existing practice, and one such response was simply to try harder to fit the child to the practice. However, there were other responses which were much more concerned with a critical interrogation of practice to understand why it was inappropriate for these students. In these latter schools, the interrogation of practice did lead to its reconstruction. Moreover, this reconstruction was not simply a technical matter of finding more effective means to reach the same ends. Rather, it led to new practices based on different understandings of how children learn, how their teachers should relate to them and the broader purposes of education.

It is important not to romanticise this point. We have seen how even the most apparently radical reconstructions of practice ultimately served the 'standards' agenda. However, through their involvement in the network, some teachers came to view this agenda in a different light. They acknowledged that their work was, indeed, aimed at the measurable outcomes which were the focus of the standards agenda. However, they questioned whether a frontal assault on these outcomes, as advocated within the national numeracy and literacy strategies, and embedded in much of the schools' established practices, was the best way to achieve them. They argued that they could only achieve year-on-year improvements in attainments for their children, and particularly for children who experienced difficulties in schooling, by working more holistically to develop self-esteem and engagement in learning. These latter outcomes might not be so easily measurable, but they felt confident that they had evidence of their significance as a result of their network activities.

Thus, **teachers in these schools felt that the best way to increase the achievements of children was by making the school more 'individually responsive'; that is, able to take into account the human and personal characteristics of all of its students.** This, it seems, is an important characterisation of what 'inclusion' had come to mean for these teachers. It was not a set of fixed practices or forms of provision, but an understanding of how to respond to student diversity in ethically defensible ways.

In this sense, these accounts seem to differ from those presented from Southminster. As we saw in the previous chapter, there was a tendency for schools in that authority to see their approaches for developing inclusive practices as being mainly *outside* of and alongside the standards agenda. By and large, this was not the case in Northfields, where raising the achievement of those below the target levels in maths, English and science, or unlikely to achieve five A–C grades at GCSE, tended to be seen as a form of inclusion. This was deeply ambiguous in itself, but it did mean that these schools saw a way through standards towards inclusion, rather than seeing themselves as facing insuperable and externally imposed barriers to developing inclusion.

It is also true that the emphasis placed on 'children who don't fit' in Northfields was full of teachers' deficit explanations of educational difficulties. This suggests that the lack of a well-articulated ethnic dimension made it more difficult for these explanations to be exposed and challenged. By the same token, it made it possible to see driving up the achievements of these pupils as an inclusive move in a way that would have been far more difficult in the context of Southminster.

Summary and conclusions

The accounts presented in this chapter illustrate how some schools, or more accurately, some teachers in these schools, were able to interrogate critically the assumptions behind certain aspects of their practice. Such interrogation was not always widespread or sustained, and, in some instances, led to reconstructions of practice which were limited and deeply ambiguous. None the less, schools were engaged in processes which were not simply reproductive of the status quo. Even within the context created by powerful external imperatives, these schools were able to create limited spaces within which alternative approaches, understandings and values could be developed.

In terms of prospects for the development of inclusive practices, therefore, there are causes for cautious optimism here. The first, as we have seen, is that the essential dynamic in this process is not exceptional but endemic in schools. The reality of diversity means that approaches to education which fail to recognise it inevitably turn some students into misfits. The second, perhaps even more surprising finding, is that the powerful external imperatives which appear to threaten inclusion may actually catalyse the very process which is most likely to bring it about. Whatever else the 'standards' agenda did in these schools, it caused them to question their own practices and, if not yet to reject explanations for low attainment in terms of children's innate characteristics, then at least to develop responses which were focused on what they, the schools, could do about this situation. If this does not quite hold out the prospect of an 'inclusion revolution', it at least makes it possible to consider how current agendas could be modified and school processes strengthened, so inclusive practices are more rather than less likely to emerge.

In the next chapter we look more closely at the types of processes that seem to make space for such developments and that encourage productive interrogation of thinking and practice in schools. In this way, we point to ways of making and taking opportunities for the development of inclusive practices.

Chapter 6

Creating principled interruptions

In this chapter we step closer to the action in order to look at the processes that encouraged productive interrogation of thinking and practice in the network schools. We draw on accounts of the experience of the members of the Manchester team in working with schools in Castleside LEA. These accounts of collaborative action research point to promising approaches for developing inclusive practices in schools. As we will show, these approaches have the potential to interrupt existing thinking about teaching and learning, and, in so doing, open up possibilities for exploring new ways of working. At the same time, we show that the use of these approaches is far from straightforward, not least due to organisational factors within schools that can provide yet further barriers to progress. This analysis leads us to consider the implications for the way researchers and practitioners can collaborate in addressing these barriers. We also explore the potential of school-to-school cooperation as a means of providing support for such developments.

In the previous two chapters we illustrated how involvement in the network led schools to make changes that could be related, by and large, to inclusive values. Whether or not they managed to do this was complicated by a need to separate an inclusive view of student achievements from the narrow view of the standards agenda. Some of the activities in which schools engaged within the network involved relatively straightforward actions designed to increase the attainments of particular groups of students within a framework prescribed by government. In other cases, the activities involved a much deeper process of questioning the assumptions that guided practice and could be seen as parallel to and, to some extent, in tension with the requirements of the standards agenda.

The Castleside context

Castleside was different from both Southminster and Northfields as a context for the network's efforts to explore the development of inclusive practices. While as an authority it had not articulated a set of inclusive principles, as in Southminster, its short history had led it to a point where inclusion was seen as a policy priority. One issue in this respect was the worrying evidence of ethnic segregation within the local community, so that the issue of cultural diversity was perhaps more evident within educational debate than in Northfields.

The idea of the network was introduced at an LEA conference, when schools were invited to express interest in a project on 'teaching and learning for all'. At the same time, some headteachers were approached directly and encouraged to participate. Indeed, it was discovered later that for one head, at least, participation in the network was offered as a consolation for not being selected for another LEA project on 'accelerated learning'.

Initially, some secondary headteachers seemed unpersuaded of the value of being involved in the network, not least because it offered very little additional funding. One secondary school withdrew after several months of negotiation, and it was only later that a secondary special school was invited to join. As it turned out, the presence of this school eventually opened up possibilities for the involvement of other secondary schools in the work of the network.

By June 2000, then, the Castleside network consisted of a medium-sized secondary school, a special school for students categorised as having moderate learning difficulties, and seven primary schools ranging in size from 110 to 330 pupils on roll. The social and economic context of these schools was quite varied, with six schools serving relatively deprived areas, with high family mobility. Free school meal eligibility ranged from 10 per cent to 60 per cent. In an LEA where over one-third of schools are church schools, four of the nine were aided by the Church of England, while the others had no religious affiliation. Schools were less representative of the LEA with regard to the ethnicity of the intake. Nearly 30 per cent of school-age pupils in the LEA were from ethnic minority backgrounds, but only two schools had a substantial proportion of such youngsters.

Prior to their involvement in the network, some of the schools had experienced periods of recent turbulence. Four had been labelled by Ofsted as having 'serious weaknesses' and one had been subject to special measures within the preceding three years. Only three of the headteachers had been in their schools for more than three years, while four had been in post a year or less. There were two further changes of headship during the period of the network.

Working closely with coordinating groups in each of these nine schools as they attempted to move practice forward, the Manchester team became active partners, to various degrees, in their attempts to develop more inclusive practices. This led the team to conclude that the development of such practices was not, in the main, about adopting new technologies of the sort described in much of the existing literature (e.g. Stainback and Stainback, 1990; Thousand and Villa, 1991; Wang, 1991; Sebba with Sachdev, 1997; Florian et al., 1998). Rather, they found that it involved social learning processes within a given workplace which influenced people's actions and, indeed, the thinking that informed their actions (Ainscow, Farrell and Frankham, 2003). This led the team to seek a deeper understanding of what these processes involved. As we will show, these involved the use of various forms of evidence generated within schools that created a sense of interruption to existing ways of thinking and working.

The role of challenge

The approaches described in this chapter link to the currently fashionable idea of evidence-based practice (Hargreaves, 1991). However, there is a significant difference about the strategies that emerged from the work of the schools in the network. This relates to the ways in which the actions of staff involved were guided by meanings constructed in the context of *particular* schools. This being the case, **we see these approaches as involving what we prefer to call 'evidence-stimulated reflection'. Our observation was that such a process can sometimes lead to a reframing of perceived problems that, in turn, draws the teacher's attention to overlooked possibilities for addressing barriers to participation and learning.**

Here our analysis is informed by the work of Robinson (1998), who argues that practices are 'activities that solve problems in particular situations'. This means that to explain a practice is to reveal the problem for which it serves as a solution. So, in working closely with practitioners, members of the Manchester team found that they could make inferences about how school staff had formulated a problem and the assumptions that were involved in the decisions they made. They also saw how initial formulations were sometimes rethought as a result of their engagement with various forms of evidence. The examples that follow illustrate the different types of activity involved and how in each case evidence provided the *challenge* that was needed in order to move thinking and practice forward.

Challenging thinking

A group of staff in one of the primary schools decided to analyse barriers to participation and learning experienced by children with hearing impairments. In supporting this initiative, members of the research team interviewed some of these pupils and also some of their hearing peers. This generated evidence about the effects of grouping arrangements and about the pupils' experiences of what they saw mainly as a supportive school culture. Some observations were also carried out, focusing on issues such as the way younger children with hearing impairments appeared to be socially isolated. For example, when asked why they were not being friendly with one boy who was sitting nearby during one lunchtime, two of his classmates said it was 'because he is wearing hearing aids and he speaks funny'.

For some staff, evidence such as this seemed to act as an interruption, providing them with a reason to stop and think. For example, an e-mail from the headteacher to a member of the research team read:

> I found this transcript fascinating! Teachers do not have these sorts of conversations with children and they are very revealing. I felt pleased that the children understand a lot of the social and moral education, which creates the climate of the school. I was proud that the children in the interview wanted to put everything in a positive light; they obviously care about the image of the school. The questions and comments from the observations made us think. Some of the comments felt uncomfortable and were based on incorrect or incomplete assumptions but this is bound to be the case. However, please keep asking questions and making comments because it makes us delve into reasoning which might otherwise not be explored, [which is] the whole idea of doing this research.

The response of this headteacher seemed to embody what Lambert and her colleagues talk about as creating 'an inquiring stance' (Lambert *et al.*, 1995). At the same time, the data generated in this particular school discomfited some staff initially, particularly those with a specialist background in teaching children with hearing impairments, seeming to threaten their deeply held interpretations of what was possible and desirable with pupils for whom they assumed responsibility. Nevertheless, members of the research team found that it was possible to maintain and develop a dialogue from this starting point.

Similar processes of rethinking, stimulated by a social engagement with evidence, were observed in the other Castleside schools at various stages during the three years. At a secondary school, for instance, members of the research team worked with a voluntary group of teachers set up to improve teaching and learning. Initial discussions in the group provided some indications of the beliefs that informed teaching and learning in the school, not least the negative views some teachers had of certain groups of students. Indeed, some of these discussions provided indications of attitudinal factors that were likely to create barriers for these learners.

In order to challenge some of their preconceptions, the team agreed with the teachers that video recordings would be made of lessons taught by members of the group. At the same time, some staff conducted interviews with students about their experiences of learning in school. Watching the videos seemed to encourage reflection on thinking and practice, and the sharing of ideas about how colleagues could help one another to make their lessons more inclusive. For example, the recording of a modern language lesson focused the group's attention on issues of pace and support for participation, while discussion of the strengths of a science lesson indicated the value of students generating their own questions to deepen their understanding of subject content. In each case, discussions created moments of uncertainty for some members of the group, as they were confronted with examples of practice that challenged their assumptions about what was possible with particular classes. At times this was potentially threatening, not least because the school was getting ready for an external inspection. Nevertheless, the group did manage to nurture a somewhat fragile hope for improvement by providing mutual encouragement and sharing practical ideas. After one meeting, the coordinator of the group explained:

> We had a good meeting tonight. We looked at positive starts to lessons and identified things that inhibit a positive start. We then broke these down into things that we have no control over, things

we can control and things that we could minimise the effects of. There was a good discussion.

Exploring and interpreting evidence in a social context was an important step in both of these schools, and there was no doubt that this provoked a process of reflection and some degree of rethinking. Other schools provided further examples of similar processes, showing how an engagement with evidence provides interruptions that can lead people to reframe the problems they face in new and more productive ways.

In another primary school such a process led to a radical reformulation of notions of ability by members of staff. Here the 'core group' decided initially to focus on the progress of their 'most able' pupils, and interviews were conducted with groups of pupils about this topic. It was striking that most of the children spoke in rather restricted ways about their abilities, and that older children, in particular, spoke only of their abilities outside of school. The teachers were particularly shocked when some pupils even reported 'not being good at anything' as far as school was concerned.

The interview data were discussed during a series of staff meetings, where they generated considerable debate about what was meant by 'ability'. This led some teachers to hold discussions about the same theme with their classes. As a result, the focus of the action research gradually shifted to the way members of the school community think about children's abilities, and to how the school could give the message that many kinds of ability were valued.

Challenging established agendas

In another relatively large primary school there were difficulties in involving staff in the action research initiatives that were planned. Consequently, the coordinating group decided to hold a staff development day in order to clarify the goals of these activities and to encourage greater involvement of staff members. The explicit aim of the day was to agree the priority themes of the action research project, and to develop a plan for the rest of the year that would involve all staff.

The day involved a series of small group activities that focused on what staff had learned through circle time and interviews with pupils about their experience of school. Having read evidence from pupil interviews, groups developed stories of surprising things they had seen and heard at school that were connected with children and lessons. Each of the groups then challenged the rest of their colleagues to predict the outcomes of the story in a way that revealed some deeply held beliefs about particular children. Staff also interviewed one another to find out what each had learned about children's similarities and differences. Then, during the afternoon session, a 'mind map' was constructed in order to try to bring together the changes that had been taking place in school in terms of action and learning. As a result of this activity, members of staff agreed a title for the strategy that they felt the school should adopt: 'Supporting Achievement for All.'

During the following months, many staff became much more involved in thinking about changing practice in relation to their agreed theme. As a result, various new ways of working were introduced and evaluated, although there were still some difficulties in maintaining involvement in the action research activities that were planned. Here, the mind map proved to be a useful tool for maintaining and communicating strategic direction. For example, a governors' meeting focused on one neglected branch of the mind map, 'the school in the community', after which visits by governors to the school were significantly increased. All of this provided an example of how a shared experience can influence processes of adult learning within a school. It also pointed to the use of visual imagery as a means of recording the learning that has taken place and, as a result, encouraging greater involvement in development activities.

Challenging expectations

In another primary school, evidence from tests showed that a significant proportion of children in the school were struggling with writing, as compared to their scores in mathematics. As with some of the schools in Northfields, the original emphasis had been informed by national debates on boys' underachievement, and certainly it was a group of boys who struggled most with their writing. Nevertheless, a focus on boys alone was clearly unjustified, given that boys were also some of the highest performers and that many girls were barely out-performing the lowest performing boys. This was one of a number of occasions on which test results were used to positive effect by schools in the network.

In this particular case, further evidence was generated by interviewing a small number of children while they were writing, some of which pointed to their feelings of fear of failure. Members of the school coordinating group were fascinated by the insights gained and wondered how widespread were these feelings about writing. With this in mind they decided to devise a questionnaire, which was completed by all children in years 5 and 6, with teaching assistants scribing for some children. Once again, coordinating group members were surprised and intrigued by the factors that children identified as barriers to good writing and began to consider how their own practices might be changed to alleviate some of these issues.

It was decided that this was a moment to engage other staff in the school. So, the coordinating group decided to use the data from interviews and the questionnaires, alongside examples from the tests, to inform the planning of a teacher development day. The emphasis throughout was on interpreting the data from 'their' children and how they might respond in terms of their own practice. The meeting generated a lot of debate, with many teachers giving examples of how they intended to try out new ideas in relation to the insights gained. Teaching assistants were involved in these discussions, providing valuable and specific insights from their one-to-one work with pupils. The elements of 'fun' during the day – for instance, trying out a drama activity linked to writing a story – also helped to remind staff of the continuing good relationships within the school and encouraged discussion about their priorities in the face of many challenges. Even so, follow-up interviews with some teachers revealed how they struggled to see ways of changing their practice within the constraints of the national literacy strategy. Indeed, only later, after Ofsted had judged the quality of teaching in the school to be 'very good', did teachers start to trust their own judgement again in determining how they might develop their practice.

Significantly, two years later a number of staff were still using data from the questionnaire to inform continuing developments. 'Trials' of different approaches to encouraging writing also continued to take place, with a continuing emphasis on checking things out with the children concerned.

The focus of the action research in a small primary school was on the impact of a 'nurture group' created during the first year of the network (Howes et al., 2002). Most of the staff saw its purpose as being to help children struggling to settle into the school, due to their disruptive or withdrawn behaviour. However, the headteacher hoped that the introduction of the group would in some way lead to the use of more appropriate teaching and learning strategies by all staff. The evidence collected by observations and interviews, and through an analysis of pupil records, suggested that the behaviour of children in the group improved rapidly. Perhaps the most significant outcomes, however, were the possibilities it encouraged for creating new relationships between parents and teachers. It was noticeable, for example, that some of the parents involved became more confidently engaged in their children's learning, using reading diaries and talking freely about their children's difficulties. Insights from interviews with some of these parents helped teachers to understand how much most parents wanted to support their children and to 'get on' with teachers. As a result, parental interpretations and concerns about teachers' behaviour in the past helped staff to see how they needed to be more sensitive in the way they talked to parents in the future. All of this assisted in breaking a continuing cycle of mutual suspicion.

Challenging roles

Sometimes, interruptions to thinking were associated with changing roles. For example, the coordinating group in a primary school, which included some of the support staff, focused originally on the effect of break and lunchtime play on pupils' attitude to and participation in learning in the classrooms. They made extensive systematic observations and used questionnaires with pupils to find out about their experience of playtimes. However, the school struggled to make a useful response to the findings until a school council was established. One of the first things the pupils on the council proposed was that they should act as playtime helpers. Consequently, they received training on how to approach this and learnt how to deal with issues that might arise, such as how to calm down both sides in an argument. As playground behaviour improved significantly, it was noticeable that relations changed between adults and children, with some staff beginning to see pupils as active partners. For example, the headteacher explained how she had involved three boys in a system of care for another boy who was often marginalised and sometimes bullied.

The written case study accounts drafted by the research team challenged organisational arrangements in some schools. One of these focused on developments in the special school, where a group of staff developed a variety of inclusion-related activities with mainstream secondary schools. Some of these involved individual special school pupils attending particular lessons in the mainstream, while other pupils would be there for most of the week. In addition, some of the special school classes went into mainstream schools to use facilities unavailable at the special school. In a similar way, the excellent facilities for computer-based learning in the special school were used by groups of pupils from mainstream high schools.

Members of the research team produced a written account describing the experiences of the special school pupils involved in these exchange activities. This explained how some were found to be initially resistant to visiting the mainstream school. Here the issue was often one of self-confidence, and teachers used evidence to question the assumptions of these young people about their feelings of inferiority. As one teacher put it: 'They said, "Oh I don't want to go, they're all clever." Whereas in actual fact, one of our children got the highest mark in maths last week.' The account also described the potential for much more collaborative work with mainstream schools. During a conversation about these ideas, the head of the special school reflected:

> The secondary heads want to work with us. . . . We have got a good reputation, which really does help. It could be the next phase with our inclusion. [Here he paused, then continued] I suppose I have got to be brave . . . I have got to be brave, haven't I?

This statement marked the beginning of a new phase of the action research that went on to involve teachers in three local high schools working together with special school staff on issues related to differentiation within lessons and the use of learning support.

Surprises and interruptions

Examples such as these, then, illustrate how involvement in the network sometimes challenged aspects of thinking and practice, and, in so doing, proved productive for the development of more inclusive practices in Castleside schools. They indicate that **when headteachers and other staff within a school adopt an enquiring stance, their engagement with evidence can provide surprises and produce moments of shared uncertainty, leading to a rethinking of assumptions and the development of new ways of addressing barriers to participation and learning.** However, it can also create feelings of uncertainty or disequilibrium that can cause further entrenchment of views – a rush for steady ground rather than a desire to explore the 'choppy' waters of new thinking.

All of this suggests that an engagement with evidence can, under certain conditions, help staff in schools to develop more inclusive ways of working. As we have seen, this involves interruptions to the usual ways of thinking that exist within a school that can create space and encouragement for reflection and mutual challenge. However, this is not in itself a straightforward mechanism for the development of more inclusive practices. To have a chance to move practice in the direction of greater inclusion, interruptions must be welcomed and they must follow an invitation to engage in dialogue. They must also be principled, introducing values as a motive for action, or allowing connections to such motives that have previously been hidden.

Of course, any space that is created may be filled according to conflicting agendas. **Deeply held beliefs within a school may prevent the experimentation that is necessary in order to foster the development of more inclusive ways of working.** So, for example, at the end of a lesson in a secondary school during which there was a very low level of participation among the class, the teacher explained what had happened with reference to the fact that most of the class were listed on the school's 'special educational needs register'. Such explanations make us acutely aware that it is easy for educational difficulties to be pathologised as difficulties inherent *within* students, even when those same difficulties are used productively, at other times, to interrogate some aspects of school practice. This is true not only of students with disabilities and those defined as 'having special educational needs', but also of those whose socioeconomic status, race, language and gender renders them problematic to particular teachers in particular schools. Consequently, the research teams found it necessary to explore ways of developing the capacity of those within schools to reveal and challenge deeply entrenched deficit views of 'difference', which define certain types of students as 'lacking something' (Trent et al., 1998).

This involved being vigilant in scrutinising how deficit assumptions were influencing perceptions of certain students. As Bartolome (1994) explains, teaching methods are neither devised nor implemented in a vacuum. Design, selection and use of particular teaching approaches and strategies arise from perceptions about learning and learners. In this respect even the most pedagogically advanced methods are likely to be ineffective in the hands of those who implicitly or explicitly subscribe to a belief system that regards some students, at best, as disadvantaged and in need of fixing, or, worse, as deficient, and therefore beyond fixing.

Communities of practice

In examining how such beliefs influence practice and how they might be challenged, it is helpful to use the ideas of Etienne Wenger (1998), focusing specifically on the way he sees learning as 'a characteristic of practice'. He explains that practice consists of those things that individuals in a workplace do, drawing on available resources, to further a set of shared goals. In schools, this goes beyond the activities practitioners set up to complete the demands of the curriculum and includes, for example, how they make it through the day, commiserating about the pressures and constraints within which they have to operate.

Wenger provides a framework that may be used to analyse learning in social contexts. At the centre of this framework is the concept of a 'community of practice', a social group engaged in the sustained pursuit of a shared enterprise. Practices are ways of negotiating meaning through social action. In Wenger's view, meaning arises from two complementary processes: 'participation' and 'reification'. He notes:

> Practices evolve as shared histories of learning. History in this sense is neither merely a personal or collective experience, nor just a set of enduring artefacts and institutions, but a combination of participation and reification over time.
>
> (Wenger, 1998, p. 87)

In this formulation, *participation* is seen as the shared experiences and negotiations that result from social interaction within a purposive community. Participation is thus inherently local, since shared experiences and negotiation processes will differ from one setting to the next, regardless of their interconnections. So, for example, within schools in the network we saw how hours of meetings, shared experiences and informal discussions over hurriedly taken lunches also involved the development of particular meanings of frequently used phrases such as 'raising standards' and 'inclusion'. These shared meanings helped to define a teacher's experience of being a teacher. In the same way we may assume that groups of colleagues doing similar work in another school would have their own shared histories which give meaning to being a teacher in that particular context.

According to Wenger, *reification* is the process by which communities of practice produce concrete representations of their practices, such as tools, symbols, rules and documents (and even concepts and theories). So, for example, documents such as policy documents, or the posters that were displayed in some of the Southminster schools and the mind map used in the Castleside primary school, may be seen as reifications of the practice of teachers. They include representations of the activities in which teachers engage, and some illustrations of the conditions and problems a teacher might encounter in practice. At the same time, it is important to remember that such documents often provide overly rationalised portrayals of ideal practice in which the challenges and uncertainties of unfolding action are smoothed over in the telling (Brown and Duguid, 1991).

Wenger argues that learning within a given community can often be best explained within the intertwining of reification and participation. He suggests that these are complementary processes in that each has the capacity to repair the ambiguity of meaning the other can engender. So, for example, a particular strategy may be developed as part of a school's planning activities and summarised in guidance for action, providing a codified reification of intended practice. However, the meaning and practical implications of the strategy only become clear as it is tried and discussed by colleagues. In this way, participation results in social learning that could not be produced solely by reification. At the same time, the reified products, such as policy documents, serve as a kind of memory of practice, cementing in place the new learning.

Wenger offers some guidelines for judging whether a particular social collectivity should be considered a community of practice. Since such a community involves mutual engagement, a negotiated enterprise, and a repertoire of resources and practices, he says that we should expect members to:

- Interact more intensively with, and know more about, others in the community than those outside of the community;
- Hold their actions accountable (and be willing for others in the community to hold them accountable) more to the community's joint enterprise than to some other enterprise;
- Be more able to evaluate the actions of other members of the community than the actions of those outside the community;
- Draw on locally produced resources and artefacts to negotiate meaning more so than resources and artefacts that are imported from outside of the group.

This is a useful formulation, though it may itself be seen as a form of reification which overemphasises the importance of single corporate-style allegiances to institutional colleagues over those based on a more diffuse community of common interest, or emotional and spiritual ties with others. Perhaps in this respect it may be seen as a masculinised view of relationships. Nevertheless, we find the idea of communities of practice, and the cultures that are developed within and by them, as useful for thinking through the conditions for principled development. According to the above criteria, the staff teams in the network schools may be seen as communities of practice. They may have shared common aims with colleagues engaged in related work in other schools within the LEA and with those who had similar roles in other LEAs. However, Wenger's conceptualisation is a reminder that much of the learning which led to their particular practices was grounded in their shared experiences.

The notion of communities of practice is particularly powerful in explaining the networking and linking processes that occurred between schools. Through a set of strategies and sometimes more accidental processes, the research teams facilitated processes of participation and reification, and, through these, the growth of communities of practitioners from more than one school. Meetings within the LEAs, and also those involving staff from other LEAs, proved to be powerful shared experiences on which to base learning. Newsletters, conference reports and contact lists constituted artefacts that supported the development of an identity as part of the network.

Wenger himself notes the particular value of interconnected communities of practice. He uses the term 'constellation' to describe a grouping of discrete communities of practice that are related by some form of common meaning – whether purpose, membership, identity, artefacts, history or environment – across these communities. Our collaborative research encouraged the growth of some continuities that were intended to give a strong sense of identity among those within the network, such that, in Wenger's terms, it may be correct to view it as a 'constellation of communities of practice'. At the same time, we came to recognise that common meanings between those in different schools were more partial, more temporary and not as fully shared as those within a more discrete community. This also led us to explore how this very partiality and lack of commonality could be provocative, providing opportunities to learn from difference through processes of school-to-school collaboration.

Such an analysis provides a way of describing the social processes that were observed taking place in the schools. These processes were, we argue, the means by which practices developed, and through our research we have thrown light on what this involved. This social learning argument also provided further justification for the way the three research teams positioned themselves in relation to the developments that took place. While their engagement varied considerably in character and detail from school to school, and from person to person within the teams, they too participated in social learning in schools, albeit in more or less peripheral roles.

At this stage in the argument it is important to stress that we are not suggesting that the strengthening of communities of practice is in itself a simple route to the development of inclusive practices. Rather, the concept helps us to attend to, and make sense of, the significance of the social processes of learning as powerful mediators of meaning. Wenger (1998, p. 85) notes:

> Communities of practice are not intrinsically beneficial or harmful. . . . Yet they are a force to be reckoned with, for better or for worse. As a locus of engagement in action, interpersonal relationships, shared knowledge, and negotiation of enterprises, such communities hold the key to real transformation – the kind that has real effect on people's lives. . . . The influence of other forces (e.g. the control of an institution or the authority of an individual) are no less important, but . . . they are mediated by the communities in which their meanings are negotiated in practice.

This suggests that **a methodology for developing inclusive practices must take account of the social processes of learning that go on within particular contexts**. From our experience, this requires a group of stakeholders within a particular context to look for a common agenda to guide their discussions of practice and, at the same time, a series of struggles to establish ways of working that enable them to collect and find meaning in different types of information. The notion of the community of practice is a significant reminder of how this meaning is made.

Cultures and structures

As members of the research team became more closely involved in such processes of change, it became evident that some elements of school organisation were themselves barriers to the development of more inclusive practices. Carvita and Hallden (1994) argue that learning from one another requires contexts where there are 'shared goals, recognized distributed expertise, credibility to be gained, need of the others' support, different legitimate modalities for communication and a group identity'. It would be difficult to claim that such consistently shared goals or identity existed in many of the Castleside schools. On the other hand, there was evidence of some of these factors for some of the time.

Nevertheless, as we have illustrated, there were examples of where, as a result of engaging with evidence, staff reconsidered their assumptions and, as a result, were able to develop new ways of working. As we have illustrated, in some cases this led to significant changes in the way problems were defined and addressed. We see these as examples of the way norms of teaching are socially negotiated within the everyday context of the communities of practice within the schools. In this sense, they were evidence of how the culture of the workplace impacts upon how teachers see their work and, indeed, their pupils.

Schein (1992) suggests that cultures are about the deeper levels of basic assumptions and beliefs that are shared by members of an organisation, operating unconsciously to define how they view themselves and their working contexts. Similarly, Hargreaves (1991) argues that cultures may be seen as having a reality-defining function, enabling those within an institution to make sense of themselves, their actions and their environment. A current reality-defining function of culture, he suggests, is often a problem-solving function inherited from the past. In this way, today's cultural form created to solve an emergent problem often becomes tomorrow's taken-for-granted recipe for dealing with matters shorn of their novelty.

Changing the norms that exist within a school is difficult to achieve, particularly within a context that is faced with so many competing pressures and where practitioners tend to work alone in addressing the problems they face. On the other hand, as we have illustrated, the presence of children who are not suited to the existing 'menu' of the school can provide some encouragement to explore a more collaborative culture within which teachers support one another in experimenting with new teaching responses. In this way, **problem-solving activities gradually become the reality-defining, taken-for-granted functions that are the culture of a school which is more geared to fostering inclusive ways of working**.

Hargreaves goes on to argue that organisational cultures stand in a dialectic relationship with what he calls their 'underlying architecture'; that is, the social structures and patterns of social relationships that exist within a particular community. He argues that a structural change often has cultural consequences and that, in a similar way, a shift in culture may alter social structures. This draws our attention to possibilities for making greater sense of the way organisational factors influenced and constrained developments in the network schools.

Crossing boundaries

There was evidence of the effects of what may be described as social boundaries that existed within schools, and between schools and their wider communities. Interestingly, many of these boundaries seemed to be unseen by those who were most affected by them. The work of Bellah *et al.* (cited in Lambert *et al.*, 1995) is relevant to our understanding of the nature of these social boundaries. They suggest that groups are, in important ways, constituted by their past. Schools in this sense are 'communities of memories' which in their practices, relationships, mores and ethos 'retell' that story. This is, we believe, where the potential for development lies, in finding new meanings in that history. It is also a useful reminder to researchers that, as visitors to schools, we have to engage with these histories, and to take their stories seriously if we are going to contribute to institutional development. This is, of course, one of the reasons why this sort of development work takes so much time.

Returning to the schools in Castleside, it was noticeable how some histories proved more of a barrier than others; for example, where some staff avoided all associations with the work of the network due to ongoing tensions among colleagues or with the headteacher. In one school, the head asked a member of the Manchester team to lead a staff meeting on the network. She explained: 'We have one or two booked up, but not many. I usually have them all sorted out before the start of term.' It was clear that these 'bookings' took the form of presentations, usually led by outsiders.

Staff responses during the particular meeting were illuminating, to say the least. Although everyone attended, one teacher did not look at the television during a video screening, reminding us that there is more than one way of not 'joining in'. Others at the meeting were more obviously engaged, but also insisted that what was being suggested could not be done properly without the allocation of additional time.

It seemed clear that in this context the network was seen as being an 'add-on', a new burden in a climate of multiple demands. Such external pressures meant that staff in the schools faced many dilemmas and tensions as they attempted to move practice forward. Involvement in the network was just one part of what happened in each school and had to be seen as one more demand on staff time. In particular, it was evident how systems of audit, and other mechanisms aimed at increasing accountability and quality assurance, resulted in an additional layer of demands on individual heads, teachers and pupils, as we saw in the account of developments in Southminster LEA. However, tensions were also evident at the personal and institutional level that we are concentrating on here. It was clear, for example, during the first meeting of the network in Castleside that factors such as testing, the need to meet performance targets and the publication of results combined to make many of the heads and teachers appear to prioritise the measurable outcomes of schooling. Although, as we saw in the previous chapter, these measurable outcomes were not necessarily seen to be in contradiction with the development of inclusive practices, there were occasions on which the influence of competing agendas was much less positive. Several of the teachers lamented the fact that they could not measure inclusion in the same sorts of ways and struggled with the idea that they could not prove the value of what they were doing in the same 'objective' fashion. Part of the challenge, then, involved finding ways of gathering, interpreting and valuing qualitative data.

There were many occasions on which tensions created by assessment appeared to create potential barriers to participation and learning. Often these tensions arose due to the way in which aspects of learning were 'technologised' as a consequence of the audit culture. So, for example, in their desire to support children in the achievement of high test scores in the area of creative writing, teachers in some primary schools tried to identify and teach the key components of a 'good story', and, in so doing, appeared to reduce the notion of creativity to a formula. There were occasions, too, on which this sort of focus on 'end-points' made attention to *processes* less likely, and added to the frustrations associated with developing inclusive practices.

A further manifestation of what has been referred to as the 'audit culture' (Strathern, 2000) was the way many staff adopted the language of this culture to measure themselves, their pupils and their institutions in the same terms that external agencies were using. Thus it was commonplace to hear teachers refer to 'level four children'. Similarly, headteachers would be heard talking about their 'best teachers' being the ones that 'raised the standards of our Year 6 children beyond what we could imagine'. And, of course, at the same time, schools themselves were being labelled as being 'beacon' or 'failing'. The implication of all of this is that as winners are defined, so losers are created. Inevitably, such a climate brings with it particular challenges to the development of inclusive practices.

The members of the research team were not themselves invested with any powers to intervene in ways that might straightforwardly challenge these circumstances. Meanwhile, their experience suggested that the schools were sites where the micropolitics of power, authority and status made working together a complex business, even in the most collegial and non-hierarchical of the settings. This focused their attention on how the tensions that are created around social structures within schools are often the locations where the marginalisation of certain groups begins and develops. For example, in Chapter 1 we pointed out one strand of thinking about inclusion in education related solely to issues of 'special educational needs'. This formulation may be seen as marking one particular boundary among many that can exist within the social contexts of schools. So, in one primary school in Castleside, the opening of a new unit for children seen as having moderate learning difficulties divided the staff broadly into two groups: those who welcomed the possibility of new resources and additional diversity into their classes; and those who resisted such a change. Delegated funding for the children categorised as 'having learning difficulties' strengthened the sense of boundary, leading to the decision to construct a separate classroom and to employ a specialist teacher. Interestingly, the headteacher, having taken part in a review of network-related developments during the previous twelve months, announced that her priority for the school during the coming year would be inclusion. When pressed, she explained that this meant the opening of the new unit.

Within the schools, boundaries such as this appeared and grew, and, in so doing, created further barriers to the development of more inclusive practices. At the same time, the evidence was that such boundaries could also be crossed, and the more they were crossed, the weaker they became. Seen in this light, the *interruptions* produced by collaborative action research on inclusion have the potential to draw attention to and disrupt some of the existing boundaries and the assumptions behind them. As a result, new connections may be made, as information, time, status, materials or people are used in new ways within schools. But we were also aware that our work in this area could sometimes give rise to, or strengthen, boundaries. So, for example, we saw how positive changes in one direction sometimes led to unfortunate consequences in another.

Challenges for researchers

Attention to new boundaries, then, and how to alleviate their negative effects provided a series of challenges to the research teams as their work proceeded. An example of this involved the written accounts provided for each of the schools. Responding to such an account about developments in her school, one of the heads in Castleside provided a challenge to its authors when she commented:

> This was a far more complicated picture than appears here and the motivations behind the behaviour of the child and the adults are difficult to encapsulate . . . whilst integrating [this child] into the life of the school made us think a great deal about inclusion, the details, motives and reasonings associated with this are difficult to write about so that they accurately reflect the realities. This was an opportunity to explore thinking without committing it to paper – and the outcomes of the thought processes would have been more valuable than recording actual events.

This sort of reflection on the difficulties associated with portrayal in such a complex field parallels another challenge faced by the research teams: how best to communicate the complex interplay of factors through which they were trying to understand and promote the development of inclusion. At the same time, such reactions to written accounts underline the high value headteachers attached to the opportunity to talk about questions and issues of inclusion, to consider options out loud, and to talk to researchers who were both involved in their school and detached from it, without necessarily committing themselves to particular outcomes. Indeed, often the most valued 'outcome' was the very opportunity to talk frankly without particular consequences. This outcome was closely guarded and was seen as vulnerable to other pressures.

So, for example, a meeting in Castleside at which members of the Manchester team attempted to forge better connections between the network schools and staff from LEA support services proved to be particularly uncomfortable. Afterwards there was a useful opportunity to talk about why the meeting had been so tense. One headteacher commented:

> The premise of introspection in one's own school shared by only Manchester University – i.e. you – was one we all bought into. And whilst I agree that inclusion needs the backing of the movers and shakers, we are still grappling with our own research and feelings, and we don't all *want* to go public yet. You and others probably see it from a different standpoint, but I am concerned that too many cooks will spoil the broth.

Headteachers had, it seems, 'bought into' *introspection*, rather than inspection; they valued conversations about issues, but not written accounts or other public processes, which they saw as closing down their exploration, and threatening them with a need to 'account' for their actions, in the sense of justifying them within a regime of external accountability. At a time when schools were increasingly subject to written judgements by outsiders, it was noteworthy that **many head-teachers in the network came to appreciate opportunities to talk about the problems they faced, just as they valued control over the direction of change**.

There is something very significant in this opposition between writing as closure and conversation as exploratory and valuable. It is, we have found, these sorts of opportunities for open exploration that heads and teachers frequently lack. The emphasis does not need to be placed on concrete outcomes, on certainties, but rather on the productive elements of uncertainty. This is why in conversations with schools, a crucial element of the work of the research teams was to keep open the 'both/and' of contradiction, and thereby support schools in negotiating the complex and often contradictory aims they tried to meet. A crucial element in all of this was about making it easier for actors in schools to say 'I don't know' and to see the potential benefit of working out where to go next.

In this sense, an analysis of the barriers experienced by both pupils and adults can in itself be productive, in that it can provide the spur to thought and action, as in the case of a Castleside school where the perspectives of teaching assistants were gathered through an anonymous questionnaire. It was clear that these members of staff did not always feel able to share the knowledge they had about the participation and learning of particular children with whom they worked. Discussion of this evidence by teachers helped them see how their own behaviour might be limiting the willingness of teaching assistants to talk to them. In addition, discussion among the group of teaching assistants helped them to think about the assumptions they held about teachers and how these were part of the problem. In this way, it became clearer to those involved that establishing the practice of exchanging perspectives required a change of behaviour on the part of both teachers and teaching assistants.

In a number of other schools, parallel understandings were gained in relation to the voice of students. When presented not as complaint or problem, but as interesting and surprising perspectives, teachers were reminded of the value of students' views and set about gathering and considering them on a much more systematic basis. One form of 'divide' between teachers and students was thereby weakened as a boundary was crossed and recrossed.

Talking about inclusion

The implication of all of this is that **becoming more inclusive is a matter of thinking and talking, reviewing and refining practice, and making attempts to develop a more inclusive culture.** Such a conceptualisation means that we cannot divorce inclusion from the contexts within which it is developing, nor the social relations that might sustain or limit that development. Within the network schools, evidence of inclusive practices was available in the talk and action (and the talk as action) that we saw and recorded. In this sense, as Adger (2002) puts it, 'Professional talk is not the icing on the cake of professional development. It *is* the cake.' And conceiving of learning as a social practice means that the processes – the thinking and the talking – in crucial ways comprise the 'product' (McLaughlin and Zarrow, 2001, p. 99).

In describing aspects of the process of change in the schools, we saw how relationships between researchers and school staff made it possible to use data to bring about small but significant changes in thinking and practice. Our explorations have convinced us that it is in the complex interplay between individuals, and between groups and individuals, that shared beliefs and values exist and change, and that it is impossible to separate those beliefs from the relationships in which they are embodied. Nias (1989) describes a 'culture of collaboration' developing as both the product and the cause of shared social and moral beliefs. Our work would suggest that what happened as a consequence of the schools' involvement in the network, with the opportunity it provided to work with outsiders committed to promoting inclusion, is that it provoked discussion about social and moral beliefs. In turn, consideration of these beliefs and values, and their connections with curricular and extra-curricular activities, then contributed to a growing commitment to inclusion.

We therefore see *ongoing* conversations, with a commitment to inclusion, as one of the elements that will help to sustain the process of development. Within the developing and changing relationships that this sort of conversation can bring about, it became possible for university and school staff to challenge each other in an acceptable and useful way, and for staff to cross previously unseen boundaries. In turn, these conversations sometimes helped to change a shared history, with a developing emphasis on active participation in a community with inclusive values. This was particularly critical at points of tension, for example, when researchers made inappropriate interventions, misjudging the reactions of individuals or groups. But we have also learned that mistakes such as this can have a value: they can make boundaries visible and in the process help us to consider how we might cross or diminish them.

Our work suggests that there are other features of conversation that are significant to the development of inclusive practices. Conversation allows people under pressure from different sources to shift their position as they try to make sense of contradictory demands. At the same time, conversation also allows the gradual explicit development of a position informed by particular values. In conversation, boundaries may be crossed and recrossed. In many conversations, school and research staff moved backwards and forwards across boundaries, taking steps towards and away from inclusive change. In this way, members of the research teams accompanied school staff in the juggling of priorities they faced as they brought more areas of school life into their inclusive thinking.

School-to-school links

A key factor in maintaining this possibility was the development of the programme of school-to-school visits. While the general idea of schools working together was an assumption within the work of the network, the idea of mutual visits had not been part of the original plan. Rather, it emerged from the suggestion of the Canterbury research team that colleagues might visit host schools during one of the national conferences being held. As a result of these experiences, the groups in all three LEAs made a separate decision to carry out similar visits within their local districts.

It was very evident that many of the staff involved found these occasions both enjoyable and fruitful. We were interested in why this was so and, at the same time, we wanted to explore its potential as a way of maintaining the work of the network in the absence of the resources of a research team.

The visits were not always so successful, however. This seemed to be particularly the case when the host teachers interpreted the visits solely as opportunities for the visitors to learn. On these occasions, the hosts positioned themselves as teachers rather than learners. Typically, the visit then consisted of a demonstration or performance of various teaching strategies that had been judged to be successful. A detailed exposition of the strategies and a short classroom visit was then usually followed by a brief question-and-answer session. On these occasions, those receiving the visit might merely rehearse what they already knew and responded to questions beyond the procedural as if they were challenges, rather than openings for debate.

On the other hand, successful visits were usually characterised by a sense of mutual learning among hosts and visitors. It was noticeable, too, that the focus for these visits often took some time to identify and clarify. Indeed, the preliminary negotiations that took place were in themselves a key aspect of the process. So, for example, during one such visit, the visitors were each invited to observe two children. A simple observation framework, designed by the host school with the assistance of the research team, focused on children's interactions with peers and teachers. The children to be observed were chosen by the class teacher, who was the deputy head of the school. They were chosen on the basis that they were the children he knew *least* about in his class. In addition to observations, the visiting teachers were asked to interview the children. Again, a loose structure was devised but the main emphasis was on the visiting teachers following up what they had seen during observations.

Afterwards, one of the visiting teachers said that the day had been 'absolutely fascinating'. He added: 'There is no way in your own school you could do this.' The host headteacher commented more specifically on the interviews the visitors had carried out with pupils: 'It's so different to what they're like in the school . . . pupils say things to outsiders that they just wouldn't say to us.'

This seemed to be borne out by some of the imagery used by pupils about their teachers in interviews that day. For example, one commented: 'He's like a piranha looking round the class. He knows when I'm not listening.' Another pupil remarked: 'He could be a really good teacher if he could explain but he gets too frustrated.' The joking response by the class teacher to such statements was: 'I want to go home! I've had enough now!'

The personal nature of these observations, and the teacher's willingness to listen to this feedback with colleagues from his own and another school present, illustrate the extent of the challenge that was sometimes involved in this sort of collaboration. Indeed, our experience was that such visits were not 'cosy', nor did they always result in a rosy glow. The key factor seemed to be that of mutual challenge, and this is, we believe, more likely under the sorts of conditions we have outlined above. In the particular example we have described, the teacher's seniority and the fact that he had volunteered for this degree of scrutiny may have been factors in creating a climate within which he felt able to enter into such a challenging dialogue with colleagues from another school. It is also worth reiterating that those visiting the school framed their observations in ways that made it more likely that everyone involved proceeded to ask questions about why these children felt as they did, and how teachers' behaviour could be modified in ways which might alleviate students' concerns. There was, in other words, a mutual desire to think about and try to understand the students' comments, rather than to attribute blame in relation to them. It is also important to reiterate that this incident occurred over two years after the establishment of the network.

Many other themes were raised during the conversation as a direct result of the observations and conversations the teachers had with students. Some of these focused on matters of fine detail that, in our experience, have implications for the extent to which class members participate in lesson activities. For example, one visitor commented:

> One of the interesting findings for me is the extent to which pupils can use eye contact to get picked or not . . . manipulating the lesson and the teacher. . . . One pupil said that he puts his hand up in maths because he knows Mr C will think he knows the answer and *won't* pick him!

The reaction of the host teachers to these observations was again one of considerable surprise. It seemed that the pupil concerned had been seen as passive and that this evidence represented a revelation. This led the teachers to reflect on how the actions of pupils are critical to inclusion – not because pupils are to blame for their underachievement, but that assumptions about their passivity can lead to mistaken beliefs about what is needed to encourage their active and confident participation in lessons. Other important themes that were raised included student views about being asked to work with other students and their fear of making mistakes, which one host teacher found 'revealing and worrying'.

In general, the process appeared to deepen significantly the questioning of the host school staff, who, as a result, wanted to broaden their ways of judging progress. The headteacher suggested that the process had also raised important questions about what was the main cause of different experiences for pupils: '[It was] very useful to hear what the pupils had to say . . . really interesting – things you've no idea about . . . so much to get hold of.' In a subsequent network meeting, where some of this experience was shared more widely, the head stressed how she and the other teachers had 'put themselves on the line'. Her comment was a reminder that this was a risky process, one that depended on a significant level of trust between participants.

In deriving lessons from this example, it is important to emphasise the variety of reasons why participants were able to frame the event as one from which everyone might learn. This was connected to the fact that the evidence that was generated, and the ways in which it was responded to, opened up further questions. The participants also had the time necessary, not just for the event itself, but for formulating the agenda for the visit and for quite lengthy discussion afterwards. Further, they had a wider forum – the LEA network meeting – in which they felt comfortable enough to talk about quite 'risky' findings. In this forum they also knew they had established the sorts of relationships where others were more likely to congratulate them on their work and be intrigued by what had happened, rather than to pass judgement. The atmosphere and nature of the network meetings by this point was significantly different from earlier meetings. They were much more open-ended, there was more unstructured conversation, and there was a sense that people felt they were 'among friends'. This allowed different sorts of exchanges to take place whereby the participants felt able to 'think aloud', trying to make sense of what had happened as a consequence of their involvement in the network.

Summary and conclusions

In this chapter we have looked closely at the experience and outcomes of the collaborative action research in the Castleside schools. In so doing, we have drawn attention to certain ways of engaging with evidence that seem to be helpful in encouraging such developments. We characterise this approach as 'evidence-stimulated reflection'. Our observation is that this can help to create space for reappraisal and rethinking by interrupting existing discourses, and by focusing attention on overlooked possibilities for moving practice forward. As we have seen, under certain conditions this can help to make the familiar unfamiliar in ways that stimulate self-questioning, creativity and action.

The work of the network has also demonstrated the potential power of collaboration between practitioners and academics as a means of fostering more inclusive practices, although the learning that is necessary in order to take advantage of this potential should not be underestimated. Our own experience suggests that successful practitioner/researcher partnerships involve a complex social process within which colleagues with very different experiences, beliefs and methodological assumptions learn how to learn from these differences. This is why it is important to be clear that the members of the academic team are both the instruments of research, gathering and reporting evidence about developments in the LEA and schools, but also a focus of research, as their own thinking and practices are opened to view. In this way, as we have seen, in engaging freely with data about the work of practitioners in their schools, they are constantly challenged to think through their own practice as researchers.

Part III

What are the overall implications?

Chapter 7

Making school improvement inclusive

In earlier chapters we offered a definition of inclusion as being about putting into action values concerned with equity, participation, community, compassion, respect for diversity, sustainability and entitlement. Given that this was our starting point, in this chapter we consider what we have learned as a result of working with our colleagues in the schools as they attempted to move in a more inclusive direction. In particular, we ask: When *does* change become inclusive development? What *is* the role of external intervention? How *do* schools respond to their contexts as they seek to become more inclusive?

Inclusion is, for us, a principled approach to education and society. By implication, therefore, exclusion involves practice which opposes or moves away from these concerns. In Chapter 1 we argued that in the literature, in policy texts and in professional usage, inclusion and exclusion are frequently defined in terms other than these. In particular, they are often used to refer to increasing and decreasing the participation of particular groups of students. We see inclusion in education much more broadly as embodying a set of values applying to all students, and to all the policies, plans and actions through which schools and other educational institutions seek to educate their students. Such values imply the embedding of schools within their communities, and a concern to provide education that is responsive to the diversity of all children and young people within their communities.

This broader view gave rise to the guiding questions for our research: When and how do improvements in schools become inclusive development? And, how can inclusive school development be best supported? We pointed out that putting values into action requires knowledge and skill, as well as commitment. We acknowledged that there might be legitimate disputes about what inclusive values meant in particular contexts and that there might be difficult choices to make between equally attractive (or unattractive) alternatives. In particular, we argued that the current policy context in England, as in many other countries, was not based on inclusive principles and might in many ways be hostile to the development of actions based on such principles, despite the prevalence of policies apparently concerned with these issues. In the accounts of our work in the three LEAs, therefore, we have tracked the extent to which schools attempted to act in accordance with inclusive values and what happened when they did so.

Working with the schools

As we explained in Chapter 1, our reading of the literature on inclusion in schools suggests that it is mainly focused on accounts of schools which had been identified as being especially advanced in one respect or other with their development of inclusion. Some of these stood out from other schools due to the principles-based stances adopted by their staff, frequently led by headteachers for whom inclusion was a powerful driving force. Such accounts may be very valuable in telling us what it means to shift a school towards inclusion when a number of people within the school have already made such a commitment, but on closer examination these schools often adopted a narrow view of inclusion concerned with issues of disability and 'special educational needs', or operated separate and conflicting approaches to inclusion. Further, as we made clear in our earlier account of 'Lovell High School', an in-depth study of a school soon reveals a complex interplay of inclusionary and exclusionary pressures (Booth *et al.*, 1998).

As we argued, we are reluctant to designate any school as 'inclusive', since this implies that inclusion is a realisable end-state rather than a continuous engagement with overcoming barriers to learning and participation at all levels of the system inside and beyond schools. If we use the notion of an inclusive school at all, it is to depict a community that is making an explicit attempt to put inclusive values into action; that is, on an inclusive journey, whatever its current position on that journey, rather than at a destination.

The temptation of some to set up and try to locate schools that are already 'inclusive' in order to provide models for others conforms to a popular belief that development in schools proceeds through the identification and copying of 'good' or 'best' practice. Such a view was behind the designation of some schools in England as 'beacon schools' or, more recently, 'leading-edge schools', whose task was to support the improvement of other schools. This is precisely the error which was made by those in the school effectiveness movement who argued that we might learn how schools could 'improve' simply by studying schools which were already 'effective' (Reynolds *et al.*, 2000; Teddlie and Reynolds, 2000). Apart from the simplistic notion of 'value-neutral effectiveness' that such studies convey, the copying principle, while fine for a machine, is far from straightforward in social contexts, such as schools or classrooms, where human perceptions and other contextual factors influence the way ideas are interpreted.

We were therefore interested in understanding what it meant to try to put inclusive principles into action in schools struggling with all the dilemmas and difficulties which the majority of their counterparts face. In general, all our schools had in common was that they were sufficiently interested in the agenda of the network to be prepared to take part. Beyond that, as we have seen, their conceptualisations of inclusion, the extent to which they acted on explicit values and the sense in which those values permeated their actions varied considerably. Although, in a couple of the schools, many or even most of the staff already expressed an explicit commitment to some of the inclusive values we have identified, in none could it be said that they had resolved all the contradictions between such values and the practices in which they engaged. Most were indistinguishable from thousands of other schools across the country in being committed in general terms to doing their best by their students but not, until the advent of the network at least, much given to thinking explicitly in terms of the discourse of inclusion. These were all schools that had to grapple with the very real contexts within which they found themselves, formed by local and national policies, the demographics and economics of the areas they served, the historical accretions of structures, practices and staffing, and the characteristics of their student populations. However clear these schools might be, or become, about what they meant by inclusive principles, and however committed to turning those principles into action, they could not do so other than within the powerful constraints imposed by these contexts.

Our interest in understanding these ordinary processes was why we stayed with these schools for three years and why we observed, entered into dialogues about and supported their development, rather than attempted to direct it. We did not prescribe a set of practices in which they had to engage in the manner of some school improvement projects; yet neither did we try to pretend that we had not engaged with similar issues in many schools previously. However, we were clear that, while we may know a considerable amount about the possible barriers to learning and participation and the resources that can be mobilised to support learning and participation in schools in general, we could not know what these are in any particular school, nor how actions should be prioritised strategically to push practice in an inclusive direction. So, we tracked the attempts of schools to reconcile the principles of inclusion with their own particular daily realities and tried to learn with them rather than impose our own views upon them, about what they should do next.

Sometimes our interventions took the form of gentle questions, sometimes they involved robust critiques. Most of all, we encouraged the schools to think critically and learn about their own practice by engaging in activities of self-enquiry. We were interested in the process schools must engage in order to realise and sustain the principles of inclusion – but we were also interested in the ways in which that process might be stimulated and supported.

Revisiting the three accounts

As we have seen, there was evidence of significant progress in developing more inclusive practices in many of the network schools. Such developments also seemed to be associated with progress in relation to the schools' performances on national tests and examinations, although, with a generally upward trend within the three LEAs, it was impossible to say that this was directly due to the interventions that were made as a result of their involvement in the network. It is encouraging, however, that over two years after the formal period of the network's funding many of these developments are continuing under local leadership. Separately, members of our team have produced a guidance booklet that is intended to provide practical support for such initiatives (Howes, forthcoming).

The way our work progressed in the LEAs was shaped by three interconnected sets of factors: the stances we adopted as researcher-developers; the local policy and demographic contexts; and the characteristics of the schools, school leaders and teachers and other staff with whom we worked. In what follows we attempt to throw light on what these interconnections reveal.

The Southminster account presents in its starkest form the conflicts between a values-based approach to education and the challenging contexts formed by local circumstances and national policies. In terms of both LEA and school policies, it was Southminster where there was the most explicit use of the discourse of inclusion, an understanding of inclusion as an issue for the organisation and practice of all schools and all students, and a series of initiatives emanating from the LEA that were designed to develop inclusive practices. The Index for Inclusion was seen as a key document for pushing forward inclusion policy and this was used to reflect both on LEA, as well as school, cultures, policies and practices. However, as in the other branches of the network, there was great pressure from within this LEA to be 'on-message' about the importance of raising standards according to the government agenda. In this context, only a few of those involved made specific mention of a conflict between ways of thinking about achievement and other aspects of school life according to their own values and those underlying government policy. Nevertheless, the Canterbury team could point to many examples where the attempts to put in place inclusive values seemed at odds with features of the standards and accountability agendas. Equally, other aspects of the policy environment to do with its fragmentation and incoherence, and its lack of attention to the conditions for teaching and learning, were reproduced within this LEA, and created tensions for the operation of schools and their attempts to bring order and consistency to their own development.

So, the explicit expression of a commitment to inclusion did not mean that supporting the inclusive development of schools was any easier in Southminster than in the other areas. Indeed, the acute pressures of the area and their position in the London spotlight meant that, in many ways, it was even more problematic. This was particularly exacerbated by the strict interpretation of their role by the LEA school development advisers.

The Canterbury team had hoped to be able to connect their work to ongoing processes of development in the schools, bringing to bear an external critical perspective on the basis of values that were broadly shared by the researchers, teachers and the LEA. In practice, this was far from straightforward. Development there certainly was, and much of it consistent to some extent with inclusion. However, since the schools and the LEA were often driven by ways of thinking that were not inclusive in the sense understood by the researchers, the team, like others in the network, found themselves in a position of observing practice and, where possible, opening up dialogues about it and the possibilities for inclusive alternatives. Such interventions might well be heeded. However, although this process was conducted with striking openness at times, there were also examples where schools resisted engagement with information which contradicted the course on which they were already set, or along which they were already being driven. The Northfields account has much in common with what happened in Southminster. Here too we saw schools, LEA and teachers caught between competing agendas and displaying considerable ambiguities in their own thinking. However, there are some important differences. Northfields was an LEA in which the discourse of inclusion was much less explicit. The district is also less socially and economically polarised than Southminster, as indicated in Chapter 3, and the schools face challenges that are a little less acute. If there was not an exactly unequivocal welcome for current national policy directions, there was, at any rate, less evidence of overt resistance, and a view that raising standards in the way specified by government, and promoting inclusion, were often one and the same.

Since the discussion of a broad view of inclusion as an approach to education was less prevalent in Northfields, the initiatives taken by the schools were often more narrowly focused on attainments than in Southminster, and less likely to relate to issues of social relationships within or between schools, or between schools and their communities. There were striking exceptions to this, with one school seizing on the Index for Inclusion as the way to rebuild deteriorating relationships with the community surrounding the school. However, in general, there was also a significant difference in the role played by the LEA, which appeared to have strong influence on the schools, as it took a firm leading position in orchestrating the inclusion network. This allowed the Newcastle research team to adopt a different stance to that of the Canterbury team. Certainly, they offered schools a critical perspective on their actions when the opportunity arose, but they tended to prioritise the promotion of developmental processes *within* the schools based on a particular form of action research. In a situation where the commitment to inclusion was a little less explicit (though not necessarily less real), they took the view that the structured engagement by schools with evidence about the impacts of their actions, in the context of an inclusion project however loosely defined, would be enough to stimulate inclusive development.

The Manchester team too placed a great deal of emphasis on the power of evidence. In some senses, the Castleside situation seemed to be midway between those in Southminster and Northfields. There may have been less of a historical and explicit use of the discourse of inclusion than in Southminster, but none the less, inclusion had become a policy priority and the issue of ethnic segregation was inescapable. As in Southminster, schools varied dramatically in their ethnic composition and this was linked, too, to the position of faith schools within the Borough, which were more ethnically divided than other schools.

Castleside schools, like their Northfields counterparts, were happy to look at issues related to learning outcomes, sometimes quite narrowly focused and rooted in fairly traditional concepts of ability and special educational needs. However, the Manchester team were able to rely on what they call 'evidence-stimulated reflection' and 'social learning'. In contrast to the rather structured process favoured by the Newcastle team, the engagement with evidence in Castleside schools was more opportunistic in its creation of principled interruptions to existing practice, its occurrence more dependent on particular events and its direction dependent on social relations within the school.

Not surprisingly, the Manchester approach was no more straight-forwardly successful than those in Southminster or Northfields. Developments were fragile and perhaps unspectacular in certain cases, and sometimes schools and teachers felt threatened. One school dropped out early on, and at times there seemed to be a retrenchment rather than a development of views. Yet, in all three LEAs, we could point to inclusive developments in the schools that were initiated as a result of the network, that had a degree of permanence, and some of these were quite profound.

We were generally less successful at addressing the inclusive development of the LEAs themselves. In Southminster there had been much discussion in the LEA inclusion strategy group about ways of drawing together disparate agendas to do with 'special educational needs', ethnicity, behaviour and school development. However, actually coordinating the activities between those responsible for these areas was less successful outside of such meetings. It was striking that inclusion conferences persisted in attracting primarily white audiences in a borough with a relatively large non-white population. We saw this as a consequence of the separation of government strands of policy but also as indicating the persistence of local cultures and vested interests. In the other LEAs, even discussions about unifying the strands of the inclusion agenda were much less marked.

Towards a common theory

None of the three accounts from the university teams offers a complete answer to our questions. **Inclusive development seemed to mean something different in each LEA and the processes used to support such development were themselves different.** None the less, the accounts, taken together, point us towards some convincing answers. For instance, the Southminster account emphasises the role played by inclusive values and policy tensions. The Castleside account offers us concepts of communities of practice, social learning and the use of evidence to create interruptions. The Northfields account suggests that it may be possible to identify a structured development process. Throughout all of these accounts, moreover, we can trace (and in many cases are confronted by) the impact of national and local contexts, while the different routes taken by different schools begin to help to identify the within-school factors which shape inclusive development. The puzzle for us has been how we put these different ideas together. How do we explain the interaction between external imperatives, within-school factors generating different trajectories, the more or less explicit pursuit of inclusive values, and the different interventions of the university teams?

As we argued in Chapter 6, the concept of *communities of practice* provides a useful starting point. This notion leads us to challenge the understanding of improvements in practice as the implementation of 'mere' techniques, such as those introduced as part of the national strategies in England, or Success for All (and many similar schemes) in the USA, which are designed centrally and then implemented in more or less identical fashion in groups of schools. Instead, it sees practice as the product of a particular group of practitioners who continuously negotiate and renegotiate practice on the basis of meanings, beliefs and values which are broadly shared but within which conflicts and disagreements can arise. Centrally designed techniques and programmes are, of course, implemented through such communities, but in their implementation they are imbued with the particular meanings given to them by each community and may therefore be changed beyond recognition.

The notion of communities of practice is one of a family of approaches to understanding organised human endeavour that have arisen in reaction to functionalist views of organisations (Burrell and Morgan, 1979). Such approaches counter the idea of organisations as rationally designed responses to self-evident problems and tasks. Instead, they stress the ways in which organisations emerge within particular sets of social conditions, and reflect the assumptions, values and power relations that characterise those conditions. The tasks which social groups set themselves, the problems they identify, the means they devise to carry our their work, the forms and structures within which they organise themselves are all shaped by the social conditions within which they live. These post-functionalist approaches have played a powerful role in the development of thinking about inclusion, since they call into question the inevitability and rationality of traditional forms of schooling which result in exclusive practices. One strand of work has challenged the idea that schools cannot escape from their role in reproducing inequalities and exclusions in society. Skrtic (1991a), for instance, has argued that it is the bureaucratic configuration of schools which generally sustains excluding practices and this can be changed. Skidmore (1999a, 1999b) has suggested that members of school communities adhere to different 'discourses' about learning difficulty, and that tensions and conflicts between these discourses can be explored as a means to construct more inclusive practices. These ideas are consistent with our own earlier work.

Such research involves the use of sociocultural perspectives (Engestrom *et al.*, 1999; Wenger, 1998). What these perspectives add is an analysis of the way in which purposeful activity is shaped by the cultural resources (understandings, values, methods and so on) which particular social groups can bring to bear on their tasks, but also of the social processes through which such resources are developed and deployed. The implication is that if we are to understand how our twenty-five schools responded to the invitation to develop inclusive practices, we need to be aware of the cultural resources available in those schools, the social relations between members of the school communities, and the wider relations and structures of society as a whole.

Thinking about schools in this way is helpful in explaining the divergence in how they responded to the challenge of inclusion in the three local authorities. It means that inclusion can only be understood in context (Artiles and Dyson, 2004). While there might be broad principles of inclusion that may claim to be 'universal', they will be interpreted differently in different contexts. Further, the particular barriers and resources will be those that exist within a particular area and the schools within it for the reasons of history, culture and circumstance that we have identified. Schools, and the education systems of which they are a part, may emphasise the exclusion of different groups, understand the nature and causes of exclusion differently, and devise different strategies for promoting inclusion. For the Southminster schools, for instance, working with the resources of a multi-ethnic context, there is naturally an emphasis on developing cohesive social relations, not least between different ethnic groups. For the Northfields schools, on the other hand, working in a largely mono-ethnic but economically poor area, inclusion may be seen as more about raising the attainments of 'working-class' children in order to enhance their life chances.

We would not wish to overstate such differences, for within Southminster it is acknowledged that it is working-class boys who have the lowest attainments, and there is a concern to ensure that the identities and cultures of white working-class children and their families are valued alongside all other groups. Equally, if inclusion is seen as preparing children and young people for world citizenship, then this colours the perception of children in Northfield as part of a multi-ethnic world as much as those in any other area. Where there are fewer students who are seen as ethnically different within a school it may be even more important that such schools learn to be responsive to and welcoming of such diversity. In addition, it can be seen that resistance to the recognition of diversity acts as an excluding pressure that creates discrimination against any individual or group seen as being different.

We also see the impact of cultural resources in our accounts. For example, all three report the pervasive influence of deficit thinking, in which the source of difficulties in schools is seen to be located in limitations and flaws in the children themselves, or in their families and communities. The schools then develop practices to make good these deficits as far as they think is possible. Less emphasis is placed on alternative understanding as to *why* students might be experiencing difficulties, which attend to the role of other aspects of the schools in creating and reducing barriers to learning and participation. Such alternatives would, of course, be additional cultural resources on which schools might draw. Indeed, one way to understand the interventions of the university teams, of the other 'outsiders' working with the schools, and of the structured interaction between schools as part of the network, is as attempts to provide these additional resources – an issue to which we shall return.

Finally, we see the impact of social relations and processes both at the school level, and between schools and the wider society. These take many forms and include the strength of collaboration that was evident in many of our schools, and is taken up again in Chapter 8. The power of headteachers was also evident in all three accounts, not only in making decisions about action, but also in determining how the tasks of the school will be understood, what values will inform its work and how issues of inclusion and exclusion will be construed. In other words, heads are usually powerful in determining which cultural resources will be deployed, how this will happen, and whether or not the wider resources of staff, children and young people, families and communities will be brought to bear on the development of the school.

However, headteachers were seen to be locked into a wider set of external policy imperatives. Partly, these imperatives come from their LEAs, arising from local history, culture and circumstances. Largely, however, these imperatives come from national policies in the form of the 'standards agenda' and 'accountability culture', the fragmented educational strands of the inclusion agenda, and the multiplicity of initiatives which land on their desks. Some headteachers appear to resist these imperatives. Others seem to internalise them as a way of understanding what they and their schools are about. We observed how the external pressures could distort the role of headteachers so that they became concerned with managed perceptions of the schools and lost sight of, and to some extent influence over, the reality of day-to-day practice.

Organisational learning

The account of developments in Castleside uses the notion of 'communities of practice' to reflect on the detail of processes which can change the non-inclusive practices of a school into more inclusive ones. As we have seen, the communities of practice created within schools can have some elements of stability. Through shared experiences they establish understandings and practices which become fixed into accepted structures, formal procedures and policies, as well as approaches to teaching and learning. However, they are constantly challenged by changing contexts and new members whose understandings may be different from those of existing participants.

Under these circumstances, it makes sense to talk about two kinds of learning. One is the learning which may occur as new members access a community's cultural resources – to learn 'how we do things around here'. The other is the learning which goes on across the community as a whole, as meanings are negotiated and renegotiated. This is in some ways akin to the notion of 'organisational learning', in that it promises to describe processes through which organisations may in some sense learn to do things 'better' (see e.g. Boreham and Morgan, 2004; Brown and Duguid, 1991; Cousins, 1998; Voogt *et al.*, 1998).

Senge (1990) suggests that knowledge within organisations takes two forms – the explicit and the tacit. Explicit knowledge (which will embrace established wisdom) is relatively easy to transfer, but is likely to be generalised rather than specific. On the other hand, tacit knowledge is caught rather than deliberately passed on, but can only be caught if the right circumstances exist. Certainly, in our three accounts, we have many examples of schools which change their practices. Sometimes this was in response to a crisis, or through diktat from a headteacher or external policy requirement. But there were times when new forms of practice were deliberately created to better reflect deeply held values about the conduct of schools.

However, our accounts also present us with a problem. We have examples of schools which changed their practice and did so as a result of some deliberation, but in ways which, in our view at least, left untouched excluding assumptions on which the school was operating and therefore made things no more inclusive or even increased exclusion. Indeed, the accounts emphasise that many of the developments in schools were highly ambiguous, in that they were effectively compliant responses to some of the excluding elements of the standards agenda. In these situations, were those in schools 'learning' how *not* to be inclusive?

An analysis which is helpful at this point – not least because it is closely concerned with issues of inclusion and exclusion (though not using those terms) – is Skrtic's account of how schools operate as 'bureaucracies' (Skrtic, 1991a, 1991b, 1991c, 1995). He argues that schools deal with the complex tasks with which they are faced by dividing them between specialists (teachers with different sorts of expertise, for instance) who operate in largely separate sub-units (classes, departments and so on). When they encounter a challenge which existing practices cannot meet, they tend to create a new sub-unit which deals with the problem without disturbing the established order of the organisation as a whole. Here, then, we have an example of a kind of 'learning' which in effect takes the form of solving a problem in such a way as to avoid learning much at all. An example from our accounts might be the secondary school in Northfields which established a unit to deal with the problems of disruptive behaviour and non-attendance but then felt it had no need to examine the ways in which its own practices helped to generate these problems.

Skrtic's analysis goes on to make a distinction between organisational responses of this kind and those which take the form of a more

fundamental rethinking of understandings and practices. He characterises the realisation that there is a mismatch between those
understandings and the realities with which the organisation is faced
as the recognition of an 'anomaly':

> Given the functionalist grounding of the professional culture of
> education and the bureaucratic work conditions and activities
> of school organizations, most often the value orientation of the
> organization and its members is bureaucratic. On occasion, how-
> ever, some group, or some event introduces or uncovers anomalies
> in the bureaucratic paradigm of practice that, because they violate
> the paradigm-induced expectations of the organization's members,
> increase the inherent ambiguity enough to cast doubt on the
> prevailing paradigm. . . . Under this condition of heightened
> uncertainty, in which the prevailing paradigm loses some of its
> ability to maintain its allegiances, someone or some group, acting
> on a different set of values, manages to convince itself and others
> to see things in a different way.
>
> (Skrtic, 1991a, p. 206)

Likewise, Engestrom, writing from a sociocultural perspective, draws a
distinction between the problem-solving and conflict-resolution activities in which groups may routinely engage, and a more fundamental
encounter with deep-seated contradictions:

> contradictions play a central role as sources of change and devel-
> opment. Contradictions are not the same as problems or conflicts.
> Contradictions are historically accumulating structural tensions
> within and between activity systems. The activity system is
> constantly working through tensions and contradictions within
> and between its elements. Contradictions manifest themselves
> in disturbances and innovative solutions. In this sense, an activity
> system is a virtual disturbance- and innovation-producing machine.
>
> (Engestrom, n.d., pp. 7–8)

We could, of course, look to other fields for similar analyses – Thomas
Kuhn's classic analysis of the structure of scientific 'revolutions', for
instance; or Argyris and Schon's distinction in the field of organisational
learning between 'single-' and 'double-loop' learning (Argyris and
Schon, 1978, 1996). In each case, the assumption is that practice is
based on some more or less deep-seated sets of assumptions and values.
For the most part, routine problems can be overcome within the

framework (for Kuhn and Skrtic, the 'paradigm') provided by these assumptions and values. However, from time to time something, or someone, or perhaps a group with a clearly thought-through plan of action (an 'anomaly' or a 'disturbance'), throws the underlying paradigm into doubt. What follows is not simply new practice, but new ways of thinking about practice – new sets of assumptions and newly configured sets of values.

Such accounts are particularly important for understanding how schools might develop inclusive practices. If inclusion is, as we have asserted throughout this book, an attempt to embody particular values rather than a particular form of school organisation, or a particular set of school and classroom practices, we should expect the development of inclusive schools to involve some fairly fundamental transformations of the sort outlined above. In particular, we should expect to see schools which fail to engage in such transformations also failing to adopt inclusive practices, while schools which do become more inclusive should do so through experiencing and responding to a series of 'disturbances'.

Arguably, this is precisely what our accounts show us. All of the twenty-five schools experienced more or less turbulent situations as they struggled with one or more of external policy imperatives, teacher shortages, community tensions, changing intakes and recalcitrant students. All of them, therefore, had to find ways of changing their practice to meet these difficulties. In some cases we find them doing so in ways which seem to protect their own vested interests, taking the line of least resistance by complying with external requirements, or adjusting teaching methods to improve measured attainments; or, like the secondary school cited above, finding ways to marginalise problematic students – perhaps, even, by excluding them altogether. On the other hand, we also find examples of schools engaging in what resembles very much a fundamental rethinking. We saw, for instance, schools where established notions of ability were called into question, where new, and what had seemed previously to the staff, dangerous forms of pedagogy were embraced, or where a wide range of practices were reconstructed in line with inclusive values. At some points we catch moments of transformation – the intervention of the advisory teacher in Northfields, for instance, or the impact of the inter-LEA visits. At others, we get a sense of the struggle teachers undergo as they face difficult evidence, or negotiate difficult meetings, or feel the need to close ranks against threatening interventions.

Where our experience accords less well with the literature is in the extent to which we were able to see a sharp distinction between more superficial and more fundamental organisational responses. As the accounts make clear, many of the changes in schools were small-scale and restricted to only limited aspects of practice. Moreover, many of them were highly ambiguous in terms of whether they denoted radical rethinking, or simply a radical rhetoric obscuring somewhat traditional aims. These ambiguities are highly problematic if, like Skrtic, we think in terms of paradigmatic shifts or fundamental organisational reconfigurations (see Dyson and Millward, 2000), or, like Argyris and Schon, we think in terms of two distinct types of learning. However, Engestrom's notion that 'The activity system [we might say, the school] is constantly working through tensions and contradictions within and between its elements' suggests a more continuous, low-key process. If we accept that social groups are complex and often conflictual, that activities are undertaken in a wider context that may itself be ambiguous, and that complex activities (such as schooling) may have multiple components which are only loosely coordinated with each other, it is not too difficult to see why development might be neither unidirectional nor uniformly transformatory. Inevitably, what our accounts show us, therefore, is not a single moment of transformation where schools abandon their non-inclusive understandings in favour of inclusive ones. Rather, we see a more complex, even organic process in which there is a mixture of fundamental questioning, conservative practice, defensive responses and open enquiry.

Factors supporting inclusive development

Our accounts suggest that there are factors which make schools more rather than less likely to engage in fundamental rethinking. These are of two main types: the relationships, and attitudes and dominant values within the school; and the sorts of 'disturbances' to which the school is subject.

With the first of these, we are on familiar territory as far as the inclusive schools literature is concerned. As we have explained, there is a recurrent strand in that literature which suggests that schools committed to moving towards inclusion are characterised by particular kinds of 'culture' – usually understood in terms of deeply held institutional values, deeply embedded sets of adult-to-adult and adult-to-child relationships, and deeply ingrained ways of making sense of the educational task (Carrington, 1999; Dyson et al., 2002; Kugelmass, 2001). In this view, the development of inclusive practices is effectively dependent on the development of inclusive cultures, frequently in response to the advent of a headteacher able to energise staff, students and parents of the school around an explicit set of principles (Kugelmass and Ainscow, 2003).

Our three accounts lend some support to this view. We see, for instance, examples of positive outcomes where headteachers took principled stands on inclusive values, but did so in ways which engaged their staff and which encouraged them to work together in maintaining an enquiring stance towards their own practice. Equally, we saw the negative outcomes when headteachers failed to engage their staff, or closed down enquiry, or were frustrated by the ingrained attitudes of their teachers, or saw their role as a quick fix to get the school through a difficult inspection report. However, our accounts also suggest a more complex process than those often described in the literature. The aspects of school culture which seem important to us are not simply the commitment to inclusive values, consensus around inclusive practices and mutually supportive relationships which often emerge as significant in the literature – important as each of these undoubtedly is. We also wish to emphasise the cultural resources which are available to the school community, such as the impact of deficit explanations of difficulty and the need for alternatives, and those aspects of culture which determine how schools will respond to the 'disturbances' and 'anomalies' they encounter. The latter are characterised by Boreham and Morgan as 'relational practices, the kind of practice by which people connect with other people in their world, and which direct them to interact in particular ways'.

However, their significance is not simply that they embody the principles of acceptance and valuing of difference, but that they promote organisational learning,

> because engaging in these practices enables co-workers to co-ordinate different subjectivities with different perspectives and experiences in relation to what then becomes, for the participants, the common object of their activity.
>
> (Boreham and Morgan, 2004, p. 315)

As we have seen, it is the ability of the headteacher and staff to maintain an enquiring stance towards their situation which determines how deeply they will think and rethink their practices. In addition, if they are to develop inclusively, such enquiries will lead them to be concerned with the participation of all staff and governors, children and young people, their families and carers, and members of the surrounding communities.

This brings us to the second set of factors which our accounts suggest are important in development. Within the inclusive values and socio-cultural perspectives we have explored here, development cannot be externally imposed. We argue that change should only be regarded as development when it reflects particular values. If these are inclusive values, then development can only be created around the shared commitments of those who are centrally involved.

We have seen how approaching schools with a commitment to dialogue leads to an emphasis on processes of negotiation, and the recognition or creation of 'disturbance' or interruptions, to established ways of thinking and working. Indeed, externally generated attempts to 'impose' change, whether through the action of change agents or the impact of external policy initiatives, may only be taken up in limited and superficial ways, unless they are mediated through these internal processes. Hence Fullan's (1992) well-known argument that pro-grammes of change have different 'meanings' for different actors and the increasing awareness among scholars that national policy is not so much formulated at the centre for implementation in schools, as formed and re-formed in each arena it enters (Ozga, 2000). This view, of course, accords well with the basic design of the network, in which schools – though they may have been supported externally – were effectively free to determine their own actions and understandings of what 'developing inclusive practices' might mean.

Yet, rather than waiting for disturbances to happen, the university teams deliberately set out to create them. The Manchester team, for instance, describe a series of 'conversations' both within schools, and between themselves and the teachers. These conversations tended to focus on evidence about the nature of practice in the school and the impacts of that practice. The Canterbury team produced accounts of what they had observed in schools and discussed these with the school teams. The Newcastle team produced similar accounts but also encouraged schools to set up their own research processes which would centre on collecting and interpreting evidence. In each case, the aim was to create 'principled interruptions' that would encourage schools to re-examine their established practices and understandings in the light of evidence and a consideration of their value assumptions.

Just as the practice of others can provide opportunities for reflection and learning without being especially valued, interruptions could provoke a re-evaluation of practice in the direction of inclusion without necessarily having that intent. Thus the standards agenda, with its powerful enforcement mechanisms, impinged heavily on how schools understood the educational task and what they saw as appropriate practices for undertaking that task. But it could also create tensions, either through highlighting difficulties in meeting its demands, or in stretching to rethinking point what teachers came to see as distortions of their preferred ways of working. Other disturbances were provided by the work of LEA personnel, by planned encounters with other schools in the network, by changes in school intake and so on. It is clear therefore, although internal processes may be important to the generation of and response to 'disturbances', that there is also considerable scope for them to be provoked externally, either directly or indirectly.

The complexity of values

The network schools had opted into a process which was based on inclusive values (however loosely specified), where there was an expectation that their participation would result in the adoption of more inclusive cultures, policies and practices, and where they were continually encouraged in this direction by the research teams and, to varying extents, LEA staff. While the network did not specify any practices that should be adopted within any particular school, it did involve a continuing assessment of practice and development in the schools within a framework of inclusive values.

Although involvement in the project was a temporary and atypical state of affairs, it is clear that some of the schools engaged in similar processes of challenge and assessment outside of its confines. As the Southminster account makes clear, the discourse of inclusion was already familiar to schools in that LEA and there was, at both the school and authority levels, a conscious attempt in some respects to base practice and the development of practice on inclusive principles. In Northfields and Castleside, however, the discourse was different. There, commitments were more likely to be expressed in general terms of 'doing the best by all children'. None the less, it was clear that to some extent all the schools made such commitments and tended to judge their work on the basis of values as well as on concerns to conform to other agendas. It was also clear that, as the project progressed, the idea of evaluating practice in the light of clearly expressed values became increasingly prevalent. It was as if this had been a dormant possibility for evaluating practice and guiding action that was stimulated within the network.

It is important not to romanticise these commitments. As we saw in the account of developments in Southminster, even the most explicit and – apparently – sincerely meant commitment to inclusive values does not mean that those values will necessarily be realised in practice, nor that other concerns will not also shape practice. However, in the network schools, we can identify at least three sets of cultural resources related to values. One is the explicit articulation of value positions in which most participants – including the university teams – to some extent engaged. It seems clear that, whatever other purposes this served, it was an important means whereby some headteachers in particular could attempt to design and develop their school's practices so that they would embody what they regarded as important values. However, it is also clear that practice was shaped by taken-for-granted 'understandings', and that these too implied values which may or may not have been made explicit. These understandings – of the educational task, the nature and reasons for children's difficulties, what practices were effective and appropriate, and so on – inevitably involved values in relation to what, and who, was more and less worthwhile. The prevalence of deficit thinking referred to above, for example, seems to imply a valuing of particular learning styles and learning outcomes, of particular attitudes to schooling, and, ultimately, of particular people. The third set of resources were the means and methods which schools had available to help them do their work – curricula, organisational structures, established practices and so on. These tools themselves, of course, embodied values in terms of who and what mattered.

It is clear that there could be and were disjunctures between these resources, that the articulated, implied and embodied values in a school might not be synonymous. It is also evident that these three sets of resources interacted with each other. Some schools tried to change their understandings and design their methods to reflect their inclusive values. Others adopted practices from outside (such as the problem-solving approach promulgated by the advisory teacher in Northfields) which began to change their understandings. When we say, therefore, that development becomes inclusive when inclusive values are brought to bear, we need to realise that this implies a complex and difficult process.

Within the network, the university teams often attempted to make implied and embodied values more explicit, and to set these alongside values of inclusion in order to create 'disturbances'. However, the effectiveness of this strategy depended not on how clearly or forcefully we articulated those values, but on how those disturbances played out amidst schools' complex cultural resources and processes. That is, perhaps, why some of the greatest changes occurred in schools where values were least explicit, and why some of the greatest resistance to intervention in schools was where the commitment to inclusion was apparently most fully articulated.

A further factor which might lead to a more rather than a less inclusive response also at first seems self-evident. Schools are in the business of teaching children and young people; these children and young people are diverse and unpredictable – indeed, human; therefore, whatever understandings and practices schools develop, it is always likely that any routine way of organising teaching and learning will be challenged by this diversity and unpredictability. As we put it in Chapter 5, a major prompt to the rethinking of practice in schools is a perception that some children do not 'fit' with the approach to teaching and learning within a school. We mentioned there that this might simply reinforce a deficit model whereby some groups of students come to be perceived as deficient and needing some form of compensation to overcome their difficulties. However, it is also possible that the perception of a child or children as a cause for concern can illuminate barriers to learning and participation within the school that, when reduced, contribute to the learning and relationships of wider groups of children. We have drawn attention to examples of just such a process. This phenomenon may have been especially salient in the course of the network due to the imperative for schools to implement centrally prescribed practices and to achieve specified outcomes. Under these circumstances, the lack of 'fit' between practices and children seems to have become particularly evident.

Not all responses to a perception of a 'lack of fit' were, of course, inclusive; in some cases, for example, schools excluded children for disciplinary reasons without considering the precursors of such exclusions in teaching, learning and social relationships so that they might be better prevented in the future. However, in those instances where schools engaged more deeply with the disturbance caused by such perceptions, they reshaped their understandings and practices around a heightened awareness of the characteristics of all the children they taught. Arguably, then, this encounter with the human realities of students provides a basis for inclusive development. While it cannot alone guarantee such development, if we set it within the context of a broad commitment to equity, and other inclusive values, and the sorts of supportive conditions outlined above, it is not too difficult to see how it might lead schools in a more inclusive direction.

Such developments remain, no doubt, rather fragile, and we would not wish to claim that a process we saw occurring so haltingly in a few schools is an inevitable direction of travel for *all* schools. None the less, it does seem to us that part of the process leading to greater inclusion is not something which has to be introduced to schools from outside, but is part of their inherent dynamic. This raises the possibility, at least, that a move towards greater inclusion is a realistic aim, not just for a few exceptional schools, but for every school. This is an issue to which we will return below.

Standards and understandings

We suggested earlier that when external imperatives enter the arena of schools, they are given meaning by the communities of practice in those schools and hence may take on very different meanings in different contexts. In this sense, external policies are formed and re-formed as they enter each school. We can now take this argument a stage further in order to understand the meaning of the dominant policy imperative – the 'standards agenda' – which impinged on the schools in our three LEAs.

Clearly, for all of these schools, the standards agenda was perceived as inescapable. However else they may have responded, no school could break free of the requirement to raise attainments to target levels, or to teach in ways that were prescribed in the national strategies, and therefore likely to win approval from Ofsted. However, the standards agenda was more than simply a set of neutral requirements with which they had to comply. Instead, it implied an understanding of what the educational task might be, a set of values about what was important within that task, and a set of more or less specified practices which embodied those understandings and values. In this sense, it constituted what we have called a 'disturbance' to the schools by challenging their own understandings and practices in ways which, unlike our own interventions, could not be ignored.

As we argued early on in this book, the standards agenda is itself more complex than is sometimes suggested. Alongside a rather instrumental focus on setting and meeting targets through a prescribed pedagogy, there is also more than a hint of a social justice strand, embodied, among other things, in the assertion that children who have historically performed 'below average' can, in fact, achieve at much higher levels. For a number of schools, it would appear that this strand gave shape to their own commitment to social justice and, within the context of the network, to their commitment to inclusion. Moreover, the practices associated with the standards agenda sometimes offered them what we have referred to as 'alternatives' to their existing practices.

At the same time, schools did not simply import the understandings and practices of the standards agenda. Even in the most favourably disposed schools, there tended to be some unease about swallowing external imperatives whole and some agonising about how to reconcile them with the values and practices which had dominated the school community previously. At the same time, therefore, as schools drew on the standards agenda, they also tended to set it in the context of a broader, more holistic view of the educational task and to embed its prescribed practices in the context of practices designed to achieve these broader goals.

This tendency became particularly evident at the final national conference of the network, where teachers from the three LEAs met to review the outcomes they believed their work had generated for students. There was much debate over the relationship between the outcomes required within the standards agenda and the broader outcomes at which many teachers felt they were aiming. By and large, this particular group of teachers saw little difficulty with the idea that part of their task was to produce the 'observables' demanded by the standards agenda. However, they felt that they were unlikely to be successful in this if all they did was to follow the practices prescribed within that agenda. The students who were failing to meet targets were, they felt, precisely those students who did not learn effectively from such practices. Instead, these teachers believed that they had to work more holistically with such students, nurturing their engagement with learning and developing their self-esteem as learners. The danger was that where this altered approach was confined to an identified group it could be seen as an extension of special education to children not previously categorised, but whose deficits were newly apparent. This meant, in turn, that they had to find ways of making their schools responsive to all students as individuals, even if they could only assess the effectiveness of their efforts through what have been called 'soft measures' rather than the quantifiable data on which they were assessed in performance tables. However, we are inclined to see as 'soft' the adoption of simple quantifiable measures to evaluate schools, rather than the harder attempt to engage with the conditions for deep and sustainable development.

What we have here, then, may be more complex than either a straightforward acceptance or rejection of 'the standards agenda'. Instead, it might be seen that the imperatives of the standards agenda have been combined with the dominant values of school communities, and with teachers' understandings of the characteristics and entitlements of their students, to form a distinctive definition of the educational task out of which new practices can emerge. Insofar as this definition and these practices embody the principles of inclusion, the standards agenda may indeed appear to have acted as a provocation for school communities to refine and elaborate their own understandings and practices. However, this could be seen less as implying a developmental role for national policy, but rather as evidence of the way such polices have constrained or even caused practice to regress. Without such influences, it may be argued, schools might be more widely inclusive in their responses to diversity already.

Inclusive school development

The central task we set ourselves in embarking on this study was to try to understand how inclusive practices could best be developed and sustained in schools. Our thinking was that there was already a considerable body of literature on school improvement. Even a brief acquaintance with our schools showed headteachers and LEA officers working within a prescriptive national policy framework implementing many of the strategies mandated by this literature. However, as others have pointed out (see e.g. Slee *et al.*, 1998), school improvement in this sense tends to aim at narrow goals in terms of measured attainments and other easily quantifiable aspects of schools, such as attendance figures. Our concern was with a much broader notion of development where the aim would be the fuller realisation of the broad principles of inclusion in schools.

In this sense we were building on earlier work with the Index for Inclusion. The Index is taken up by schools when they are at the point where they want to think about what inclusion might mean for aspects of the development of their school, or where they wish to give a greater degree of coherence to their plans for development. It does not require that schools already have a clear idea of what they mean by inclusion but, as we saw our role in the network, it supports staff in schools to refine their views as they engage with materials in which the variety of ways in which actions might be connected to inclusive values are spelt out. The Index materials are strategically structured to draw attention to the development of cultures as well as policies and practices, and then further divided into areas to which schools might need to pay attention if they are not to undermine their efforts to create sustainable development. Schools are encouraged to consider all the resources that may be found in staff, students, families and communities, and how these could be used more fully. They are encouraged to engage in a review of all aspects of a setting, so that the hitherto unconsidered knowledge of staff, children and young people, their families and communities about barriers to learning and participation and resources to support learning and participation may inform the setting of priorities for inclusive development planning. In this way, the process reflects the idea of principled interruptions to development analysed in this chapter.

However, the widespread use of the Index in England and other countries has thrown up many of the same gaps in our understanding of the development of schools that this research set out to explore. We need to know more about how development can be initiated, how it can become a shared responsibility among the participants in schools, and how it can be best supported and sustained. It seems to us that we are now in a position to draw together what the three LEA accounts tell us about these concerns, so as to build on previous understandings of inclusive school development.

We understand schools as comprising communities of practice, where the educational task is given meaning through more or less shared understandings embodied in common activities. It follows, then, that actions in schools are embedded within understandings and cannot simply be imported into a school unless and until they have an appropriate place in the system of meanings and values within that school community. **The development of inclusive practices, which embody a distinctive set of values, cannot be a merely technical exercise.**

We argue that schools create stability through their established practices and artefacts, but at the same time the process of meaning-making is never static, as those involved respond to changing situations and to the dynamic interplay of the individuals and groups of which they are composed. It follows that change is inherent in school communities. In particular they may be 'disturbed' when confronted with situations which cannot be dealt with through established practices or understood within the established system of meanings.

Under these circumstances, schools may be able to preserve stability by accommodating and adapting to the new situation. However, they may also engage in a more fundamental rethinking of some of their basic understandings, out of which new practices may emerge. Certain conditions within the school community – particular leadership styles, an open attitude towards enquiry, a supportive and collaborative set of relationships among staff – increase the likelihood that fundamental rethinking of this kind will occur.

Where this is the case, inclusive development is possible but by no means certain. The fact that school communities are constantly confronted by the complex realities of the students whom they teach may create a weak but inherent dynamic towards more inclusive understandings and practices. However, an acceptance of inclusive values – even if only broadly specified – is also essential. Even then, however, development is likely to be halting, partial and ambiguous.

In this situation, the interactions between schools and the local and national policy environment are complex. On the one hand, externally generated policies set limits on schools' actions and create imperatives which they cannot ignore. On the other hand, because policy has to be given meaning by school communities, and because it embodies particular understandings of the educational task, it can also act as a resource for those communities through which they may clarify and elaborate their own understandings. It can, therefore, constitute a powerful 'provocation' in its own right.

Summary and conclusions

There are two features of the theory of inclusive development developed in this chapter to which we wish to draw particular attention. First, it is derived from a study of *typical* rather than *exceptional* schools. The history of inclusive education has shown that exceptional schools with exceptional leaders can become exceptionally, though not unambiguously, inclusive. The challenge, however, is not to create a few schools in which a tiny fraction of the nation's children get a good deal.

Schools are inevitably characterised by complexity, ambiguity and contradiction, and their achievements are inherently unstable. On the other hand, the potential for inclusive practices to emerge in schools is, by the same token, *not* exceptional. Provided that we are prepared to accept that inclusive development will indeed be halting, partial and ambiguous, there is every reason to believe that conditions may be created where widespread movements in this direction begin to emerge.

Second, our theory sees schools not only as internally dynamic, but also – and for that very reason – as permeable. Negatively, they can, as we have seen, be influenced by exclusionary pressures from national policy. More positively, however, their permeability means that 'interruptions' from external sources are always likely to generate internal disturbances. National policy may reinforce whatever exclusionary tendencies are present in schools; equally, however, national policy of particular kinds might increase the likelihood of interruptions and, moreover, of interruptions with more inclusive outcomes. We therefore see real potential for inclusive education to be widely developed within schools. In the final chapter, we consider some of the practical steps that may be needed for this possibility to become a reality.

Chapter 8

Towards an inclusive education system

In this final chapter, we reflect further on our experiences in the network schools and LEAs in order to consider how the processes we have identified might be shaped in order to move a school system as a whole towards more inclusive practices. We address this question in terms of actions at the levels of the school, inter-school collaboration and national policy. We also comment on the implications of our view of school development for the role of research and researchers. While the conclusions we draw are directly related to our English context, we believe that the lessons have implications for those in other countries addressing similar concerns.

The view of inclusive development developed in Chapter 8 emphasises the complex dynamics which characterise communities of practice in schools, the potential for those communities to be disturbed by externally or internally generated 'interruptions' to established understandings, and the crucial role of values in shaping the responses to those interruptions. It draws attention both to the inherent possibility of inclusive practices in schools and the permeability of schools to external interventions – not least in the form of national policy.

We found that one of the most powerful forms of interruption involved the exposure of teachers to different ways of teaching, and to opportunities to reflect on the difference between what they are doing and what they aspire to do. Our experience in the network supports the findings of earlier research that developments in practice are far more likely to occur with such interventions (e.g. Ainscow, 1999; Huberman, 1993; Little and McLaughlin, 1993). At the heart of such processes is the development of a common language with which colleagues can talk to one another and, indeed, think about detailed aspects of their practice. Without such a language teachers find it very difficult to experiment with new possibilities. However, much of what teachers do in classrooms is largely automatic and intuitive. Furthermore, there is little time to stop and think. This is why having the opportunity to see colleagues at work is so crucial to the success of attempts to develop practice. Mutual observation and critical friendship between professionals can help teachers to articulate what they currently do and to define what they might like to do (Hiebert et al., 2002). They are also the means whereby taken-for-granted assumptions about particular groups of students may be subjected to mutual critique.

Our research has shown how engaging with various types of evidence can be helpful in encouraging such dialogue. As we have seen, evidence can help to create space for reappraisal and rethinking by interrupting existing discourses, and by focusing attention on overlooked possibilities for moving practice forward in an inclusive direction. Listening to the perceptions of students about teaching and learning provides a particularly important source of evidence. Mutual observation and the attention to usually unheard voices can provide interruptions that help to 'make the familiar unfamiliar' in ways that stimulate self-questioning, creativity and action. We have also shown how the roles of headteachers and other senior staff are crucial in encouraging such activities.

However, our accounts show that, **while an engagement with evidence can create space for reviewing thinking and practice, it is not in itself a straightforward mechanism for the development of inclusion.** The space that is created by searching for evidence may be filled by conflicting agendas. This is why a fundamental role has to be given to making explicit the values that practitioners want to see enacted in their schools and the values which underlie alternative courses of action.

We are acutely aware that where the prompt for action in a school starts from a concern about the progress of particular students there is a default position or ideology which frequently shapes the response. It is very easy for educational difficulties to be pathologised as difficulties inherent within students or their families. This is true not only of students with disabilities and those defined as 'having special educational needs', but also of those whose socioeconomic status, race, language and gender are seen as problematic by particular teachers in particular schools. This is why it is so important to develop the capacity of those within schools to reveal and challenge deeply entrenched deficit views of 'difference'.

Writing about similar processes, Timperley and Robinson (2001) explain how teachers' existing understandings influence the way evidence is interpreted, such that they perceive what they expect to perceive. Consequently, new meanings are only likely to emerge when evidence creates 'surprises'. It can be helpful, therefore, to have an external perspective that uses moments of surprise to challenge accepted meanings and take teachers beyond their existing understanding, but it is more important that staff in schools develop cultures which value challenges to existing ways of thinking and, indeed, seek them out from each other, their students, families, communities and others.

Stimulating change beyond the school

It seems, then, that engaging in systematic enquiries, prompted by challenges from outside or inside a school, can foster developments and encourage responsibility for them to be shared. As Copland (2003) suggests, such shared enquiry can be the 'engine' to enable the distribution of leadership, and the 'glue' that can bind a school community together around a common purpose. Turning these successes into processes that make a deeper and more sustainable impact on the cultures of schools is, however, much more difficult. This necessitates longer term, persistent strategies for capacity-building at the school level. It also requires new thinking and, indeed, new relationships at the systems level. In other words, **efforts to foster inclusive school development are more likely to be effective when they are part of a wider, systemic strategy.**

In working closely with schools we experienced some of the pain that practitioners feel within the current policy context. In particular, we saw many examples of how this left teachers addressing personal dilemmas as they wrestled between their desire to do their best for their students in a way that squared with the values that brought them into teaching, and the requirements of the standards and accountability agendas. These difficulties drew our attention yet again to the barriers created by the national reform policies that were restated within the plans of the New Labour government beginning its third term of office in 2005. We summarised these policy tensions created within schools and LEAs in Chapter 4, and these are reproduced in Box 8.1.

Our experience was that the combination of these tensions created profound barriers to the development of the strategies we were

---

BOX 8.1

Policy tensions in schools and LEAs

- Integrated vs. separated strands of inclusion
- An inclusive vs. 'standards agenda' approach to achievement
- Teaching and supporting diversity vs. special needs education
- Emphasising reality vs. attention to image
- Long-term and sustainable change vs. short-term meeting of targets
- Attending to conditions for teaching and learning vs. attending to outcomes
- Rational vs. reactive planning
- Commitment to inclusive values vs. compliance to directives
- Shared vs. charismatic leadership
- Coordination of schools vs. LEAs 'pared to the bone'
- A new framework for education vs. responding to initiatives.

---

exploring within the network. Even more worrying, they seemed to have their most damaging impact in schools facing challenging circumstances, where teachers were struggling to respond to children from more deprived backgrounds. In such highly stressed contexts particularly, but also in schools throughout the network, we saw how competing national policies can foster a lack of trust and confidence within a school community, making it difficult to create an authentic strategy for development.

The policy context pushes schools towards short-term strategies and encourages opportunistic and reactive planning as each new initiative, or even research project, comes into view. It also encourages the reality of the school to be spun to some extent for outside and even internal consumption. In such circumstances long-term sustainable inclusive development is extremely difficult. That they continue to pursue it with such determination is a considerable tribute to those within the schools.

Consequently, we feel that it is important to consider what policy changes are needed in order to replicate the experiences and findings of the network more widely across the education system. Our aim is to identify opportunities to foster the kind of dialogue about policy and practice that may be used to stimulate education systems to move in a more inclusive direction, and to challenge or mitigate those aspects of the policy environment which impede such progress.

Senge (1990) uses the metaphor of 'levers' to depict those points of the system from which influence can be most significant. We see the use of such a term as having limitations, since it implies a mechanistic view of education: that it can be changed with the right tools without engaging fully the participants in the system. We see the discussion of inclusion as a way of critiquing such a view, including the way it permeates government thinking. In our work, we have been painstaking in constructing dialogues with, and respecting the involvement in their own development of participants in schools. In fact, we argue that further wider participation of students, their families and others can provide powerful ideas and resources for school development. Further, we have stressed the importance of the development of an inclusive language for talking and thinking about teaching, and this applies equally to our own research.

Nevertheless, Senge's work is helpful in encouraging us to think strategically about how development might be encouraged, and how it is conceived, particularly in market-imitating systems. He suggests that too often, approaches used to bring about large-scale changes in organisations tend to change the way things look without bringing about any deeper, long-term, coherent revision. Possible examples of such activities in the education field include policy documents, conferences and in-service courses. While such initiatives may make a contribution, they tend not to lead to significant changes in thinking and practice (Fullan, 1992). We are concerned to locate more subtle and powerful ways to encourage the inclusive development of schools.

In our research we have placed schools at the centre of the analysis in order to consider how to increase the capacity of neighbourhood mainstream schools to support the participation and learning of the diversity of learners within their communities. At the same time, we have considered the range of contextual influences on schools that can either provide support and encouragement for the inclusive development of schools, or act as barriers to progress. Such influences include national and local policies, and the principles that guide them, the views and actions of staff in LEAs and members of the wider communities served by schools, and the criteria that are used to evaluate the performance of schools. They also involve global ideological and economic pressures.

Moving policy towards inclusion

Our collaborative action research points to factors that have the potential to either facilitate or inhibit the promotion of inclusive practices in schools and across LEAs. Some of these factors seem to be potentially more potent. Two factors, particularly when they are closely linked, seem to be particularly important. These are to do with clarity of purpose and the forms of evidence that are used to measure educational success.

As we noted in Chapter 1, there is still considerable confusion about what 'inclusion' means. In England, this lack of clarity frequently emanates from the sheer number of, as well as disparities between, central government policy documents. Such multiple and contradictory initiatives undermine efforts to develop inclusion. There is a need, therefore, to strive for a common understanding throughout the education system of inclusion as a principled approach to education. In other words, inclusion should not be seen as a separate policy but rather as a principle, emerging out of a more fundamental set of values, that informs all policies and actions.

The work of the network was based very much on orchestrating a debate around the principles that ought to inform practice and the principles that practice actually embodied. Teachers, LEA officers and academics spent considerable time asking themselves and each other not 'Is this practice effective?' (i.e. in terms of raising attainment), but 'Is this practice inclusive?'

We do not wish to romanticise the nature of such discussions, nor to exaggerate their outcomes. However, the developments we have reported here suggest that a well-orchestrated debate can lead to a wider understanding of the principle of inclusion within and between schools. We have also found that such a debate, though by its nature slow and never-ending, can help to foster the conditions within which schools may feel encouraged to move in a more inclusive direction. However, to have a real impact, we suggest, such a debate must involve all stakeholders within the local community, including political and community leaders, and the media. Of course, it must also involve those within local education authorities.

How should schools be evaluated? It is clear that within education systems, measurement and inspection are powerful ways of shaping the activities of schools. As we have seen, England is a particularly interesting case in this respect, due to the emphasis that has been placed on data and target setting as the basis for realising the government's goals. This is double-edged precisely because it is such a potent controller of school actions. On the one hand, data are required in order to monitor the progress of children, evaluate the impact of interventions, and review the effects of policies and processes. On the other hand, where schools are evaluated on the basis of narrow, even inappropriate, performance indicators, the impact can be deeply damaging. While appearing to promote the causes of accountability and transparency, the use of data can, in practice, conceal more than they reveal; invite misinterpretation or misrepresentation; and, worse of all, have a perverse effect on the behaviour of professionals. This has led the current 'audit culture' to be described as a 'tyranny of transparency' (Strathern, 2000).

This is arguably the most troubling aspect of our own research. It has revealed the processes by which a national context that values narrowly conceived criteria for determining success can act as a barrier to the development of more inclusive cultures, policies and practices within schools. All of this suggests that great care needs to be exercised in deciding what evidence is collected and, indeed, how it is used.

English LEAs are required by government to collect particular data. Given national policies, they cannot opt out of collecting such data on the grounds that their publication might be misinterpreted, or that they may influence practice in an unhelpful way. On the other hand, LEAs can collect additional evidence to evaluate the extent to which their own policy and practice encourages inclusion. The challenge for LEAs is therefore to harness the potential of evidence to promote reflection, planning and implementation, while avoiding exacerbating the problems created by simplistic approaches to measurement.

In our view, it is fine to think of ways to assess and review what we value, but absurd to value only what can be simply measured to create headlines for governments. Much of the most powerful evidence to which schools had access in our work, and which made the most difference to their practice, was in the form of careful observation of each other's practice, and the gathering of views to which they may not have been previously exposed within and beyond their schools, rather than quantitative data. This means that we need to find ways to support schools to review their progress in relation to the presence, participation and achievement of all children and young people, the building of relationships between all participants in schools, and evidence of the nurturing of inclusive cultures through which development is prompted and sustained.

Fostering interdependence

In early 2005, the then Secretary of State for Education, Ruth Kelly, was quoted as saying:

> In the future I think cooperation will become not only the norm, it will probably be the only way of delivering a decent all-round education for all pupils. . . . We have to get schools to operate as part of a network to deliver a fully comprehensive education.
>
> (*New Statesman*, 14 February 2005, pp. 26–27)

Given the experience of our network, we are in sympathy with this suggestion, although there is an irony in the choice of the words 'fully comprehensive education'. It perhaps means something like 'an all-encompassing system', rather than a system of comprehensive community nursery, primary and secondary schools of the sort we discussed in Chapter 1.

Inclusion implies the development of school-to-school cooperation, as illustrated by what happened within our network. **Collaboration between schools can help to reduce the polarisation within the education system, to the particular benefit of those students who are on the edges of the system and performing relatively poorly.** Equally important, however, collaboration creates the opportunity to extend communities of practice beyond the boundary of individual schools and increases the possibilities for principled interruptions of established practices and understandings. This being the case, a key question is: How can schools be encouraged to collaborate within a system that places an emphasis on competition and choice?

In the English context, the work of schools and LEAs has to be seen in relation to structures and relationships that have been fundamentally changed over the past few years. We have seen a decrease in the power of LEAs to influence schools and a corresponding increase in the power over them of central government. While some see the system as also characterised by greater independence of schools, this is debatable. Schools can make their own decisions about who they employ and how they relate to in their external world, including those working within universities, but the control over the detail of their lives from regulation and inspection has increased dramatically over the past twenty-five years. Perhaps their situation is best indicated by the term 'earned autonomy', used to describe schools which have successfully proved that they are sufficiently developed to be allowed to make their own decisions, as mentioned in Chapter 2.

However, the analysis presented in this book confirms that, despite the policy changes which have taken place, LEAs can still have a significant role to play in supporting school development, particularly where they are creative with their role. It is easy to assume that what we have called the 'permeability' of schools relates only to the direct and powerful impacts of central government policy. However, this may lead to an underestimation of the more subtle impacts of locally generated policy, the dense networks of relationships between school staff and LEA staff – officers, services, educators and inspectors – and the even denser network of relationships between schools and school staff in the same LEA. Certainly, for all three groups of schools in our study, the LEA was a significant presence. If the LEAs were no longer able to control 'their' schools, they none the less played a major part in shaping priorities and discourse in their areas, mediating government policy to schools in the light of local conditions and understandings. They exercised what Peter Housden – then a LEA chief education officer and subsequently the government's Director General for Schools – once called the 'moral authority of the LEA' in promoting inclusion (Housden, 1993).

However, our work indicated how LEAs struggled to make an impact on schools within the current overall policy context. While, again, this was often due to the way government policies constrained their actions, there was still considerable room for them to impose greater coherence on such policies through the way they implemented them. We noted that much of what goes on within organisations, such as LEAs and schools, is largely taken for granted, and therefore rarely discussed. In other words, practices are manifestations of organisational cultures (Schein, 1992). Therefore, significant progress in relation to the development of inclusive thinking and practice requires an engagement with questions of purpose and values at all levels of the education system. This suggests that the way forward is for LEAs to engage their various 'communities of practice' in a process of infusing concerns with participation, social justice and the building of community into debates about quality and achievement in education. It also implies the negotiation of new, interdependent relationships among schools, and between schools, LEAs and their wider communities.

Fielding's (1999) distinction between 'collaboration' and 'collegiality' is helpful in exploring such relationships. He characterises 'collaboration' as being driven by a set of common concerns, narrowly functional, and focused strongly on intended gains. In such contexts, the partners in a collaborative activity are regarded as a resource or a source of information. Fielding goes on to suggest that collaboration is a plural form of individualism in which participants are typically intolerant of time spent on anything other than the task in hand, or the core purposes of the business. He argues that once the driving force behind collaboration is weakened, the task has been completed or priorities have changed, such collaborative working arrangements may dissipate, disappear or become more tenuous. 'Collegiality', on the other hand, is characterised as being much more robust. It is overridingly communal, and is rooted in shared ideals, aspirations and valued social ends. Collegiality is therefore by definition, less reliant upon narrowly defined and predictable gains.

In practice, instances of schools working together often do not seem to fall neatly into either collaborative or collegial activity. When the schools first came together as part of the network, there was little sense that they were developing a shared agenda or a shared language. At first, their collaboration was based on the need to solve essentially practical issues about the direction of the project in meetings. Only later did they begin to discuss more fundamental issues with each other, share experiences and visit each other's schools and classrooms. In other words, our research suggests that collaboration may need to be a forerunner to collegiality. Thus, stakeholders may experience the practical benefits of collaborating when the outcomes are clearly defined, while seeking to develop a common language and shared aspirations that might, in the longer term, provide a basis for collegiality.

Introducing such an approach in the current English context, with its cocktail of competing agendas and confusion about forms of governance, is fraught with difficulties. We recall, for example, a meeting called to discuss the proposal to establish the network in one of the partner LEAs. Eventually, one secondary headteacher, while acknowledging that he had enjoyed the debate, commented: 'OK, but, what's in this for me and my school?' He went on to argue that the idea of collaboration in the network would only 'take off' if the key stakeholders could see that there would be significant, practical benefits for their own school or organisation. He wanted to be convinced that the network would support his school to move forward in a direction that he and his staff could support, and that it would also help in the complex positioning of his school in relation to other schools. However, during the life of the network there were striking examples of schools supporting others when there was no apparent advantage to themselves. Thus, for example, the staff in one school were prepared to give considerable time and effort to helping those in a neighbouring school prepare for an inspection, despite the fact that according to the values of government policy this was a competitor.

Collaboration, collegiality and leadership

The way in which staff can work together and with others to create a common purpose in the face of contradictory pressures is critical for bringing about sustained development in schools. As we explained in Chapter 7, unusual and challenging factors, emanating as they did from both outside and inside schools, sometimes created a sense of disturbance and ambiguity. The collaborative arrangements introduced by some headteachers helped to resolve these, and, as a result, they were able to draw their staffs together gradually behind broadly similar principles.

Ambiguity in organisations may be used to increase the extent to which action is consciously guided by values (Weick, 1985); but it matters *how* ambiguity is resolved. We encountered school leaders who resolved ambiguity by closing down debate and others who were content with superficial adjustments of practice in pursuit of narrow goals. However, we also encountered leaders who tried to sustain a more open and profound process of enquiry. In these cases, ambiguity set the scene for a school to learn about itself and its environment, allowing it to emerge from its struggles with uncertainty. In this way, schools can become what Senge (1990) calls 'learning organisations', continually expanding their capacity to create their futures. Or, to borrow a useful phrase from Rosenholtz (1989), they can become 'moving schools', seeking continually to develop and refine their responses to the challenges they meet.

It seems, therefore, that **the perspective and skills of headteachers and other senior staff are central to an understanding of what needs to happen in order that the potential power of collaboration and collegiality can be mobilised.** Their aspirations for their schools, their beliefs about how they can foster the learning of all of their students, and their commitment to the power of interdependent learning, appear to be key influences. Following an extensive review of research literature, Riehl (2000) comes to a similar set of conclusions. This leads her to recommend that school leaders need to attend to three broad types of task: fostering new meanings about diversity; promoting inclusive practices within schools; and building connections between schools and communities. She concludes:

When wedded to a relentless commitment to equity, voice, and social justice, administrators' efforts in the tasks of sensemaking, promoting inclusive cultures and practices in schools, and building positive relationships outside of the school may indeed foster a new form of practice.

(Riehl, 2000, p. 71)

In this respect, the role of school leaders *vis-à-vis* their staff is analogous to the role of LEAs *vis-à-vis* schools – except that, in the English system, headteachers are in a much more powerful position of control. However, this emphasis on school-level leadership has very significant implications for the roles of LEA staff. It means that they have to rethink their priorities and ways of working in response to collaborative arrangements that are led from within schools. Indeed, such rethinking is being mandated nationally. From the latter part of the 1980s onward the role and even existence of LEAs has been increasingly discussed. Although there had already been some such cases, the Children Act 2004 provided a fresh impetus for the merger of local authority Education and Social Services. Indeed, government documents began to refer only to 'local authorities' rather than to 'local education authorities'. In some places, inevitably, the leadership of these new organisations has passed to people with social care rather than educational backgrounds. At the same time, the government is developing a 'new relationship with schools', placing greater emphasis on school-to-school development work, reducing multiple interactions to a 'single conversation' and replacing (effectively) LEA link advisers with nationally accredited 'school improvement partners' (DfES, 2005b). It is therefore certain that the relationship between LEAs and schools will continue to change, and possible that it will disappear altogether.

Having said that, **we cannot conceive of a way for collegial collaboration to continue as a central element of inclusive school development strategies without local coordination.** As we have seen, the contributions of LEA officers were sometimes very significant in the development of the work of schools in the network. Specifically, LEA staff were supported and challenged schools in relation to an agreed set of purposes, while headteachers and their school colleagues shared the overall management of improvement efforts in their schools. Even if 'old-style' LEAs were to disappear, or 'new-style' local authorities were to turn out to be very different organisations, we believe there will still be a need for *some* intermediary body that can mediate national policy, facilitate school-to-school collaboration and, crucially, have the potential (however partially realised) to 'interrupt' established practices and understandings on the basis of inclusive values.

This points towards the roles that staff from LEAs (or, perhaps, their successor bodies) need to take on: not managing and leading change, but rather working in partnership with senior people in schools to diffuse leadership and to strengthen collaborative and collegial ways of working. In such contexts they can bring specific challenges which derive from their knowledge of the bigger picture across their authority and a clarity of purpose. At the same time, they can help to broker the sharing of resources and expertise.

Beyond the collaboration within and between schools, there is a need to reach out to others who have an interest in the education of children and young people. In particular, it is important to ensure that parents/carers, elected members, governors and local community agencies and organisations are aware of, and feel confident about, moves towards a more inclusive education system. In this respect, the integration of support staff from different agencies within district structures in response to the Children Act 2004 should create further disturbance that could be used to encourage the development of inclusive practices among staff in all children's services.

Such proposals for greater collaboration sit uneasily with the widespread development of 'independent specialist' or 'trust' schools, alongside the expansion of academies. Our view is that such developments could further isolate schools from one another in ways that would disadvantage schools and groups of learners who are already seen to be underachieving. While it is true that, by and large, schools develop as a result of leadership from the inside, the wider context influences the progress of such efforts, for good or ill. This is why 'interdependence' can be so powerful. It leads us to argue that, in order to develop more inclusive cultures, policies and practices, schools have both to take the initiative for their own development and create permeable boundaries so that they seek common purpose with their communities and neighbouring schools.

We believe that **it will be helpful to those at the local level who are encouraging schools to collaborate, if national policy initiatives continue to emphasise the principle of collaboration as being a fundamental element of efforts to develop an inclusive education system.** Recent initiatives such as the Leadership Incentive Grant are very encouraging in this respect. Introduced in April 2003, the grant provided additional financial resources (i.e. £125,000 per school annually, for three years) to schools facing challenging circumstances that commit themselves to working together on joint strategies for improving standards and increasing leadership capacity. However, the implications for the government's own inspection frameworks have not yet begun to be addressed, not least in relation to how to build a notion of communal responsibility into a system in which schools are seen to succeed and fail on their own.

The role of research

What, then, does this imply for the role of research and researchers in relation to the development of inclusive practices in the field? There are, we believe, some important lessons to be drawn from our experience within the network, although some of these lessons are uncomfortable. As we have shown in our accounts, members of our team were sometimes faced with tactical dilemmas in their relationships with their school and LEA partners between their roles as observers and as participants in action. Indeed, on some occasions we were tempted to think that the stance of traditional researchers may have been safer and more comfortable. Nevertheless, we remain convinced that by attempting to create a common agenda with our school and LEA partners we were able to gain greater insights into possible avenues for the inclusive development of practice.

At the current time, there is much debate about the relationship between education research, policy-making and practice. Some years ago, the 'Hillage Report' into the state of education research captured a widespread view that research fails to meet the need of policy-makers and practitioners for robust and relevant evidence on which to base their work (Hillage et al., 1998). This invites the question, of course, as to whether the fault lies with self-indulgent researchers confined to their ivory towers, or with short-sighted policy-makers and practitioners unwilling to accept any evidence which does not accord with their assumptions and immediate experiences. More importantly, it requires us to consider whether the provision of evidence for policy and practice is a proper role for research and, if not, precisely what it is that research is supposed to achieve.

Our study enables us to make an important contribution to this debate. Early on in the life of the network we tried to map out the positions and relationships within the partnerships we were establishing between practitioners and local policy-makers on the one hand and researchers on the other (see Figure 8.1). We saw these as involving two interlinked cycles of action research carried out by practitioners and

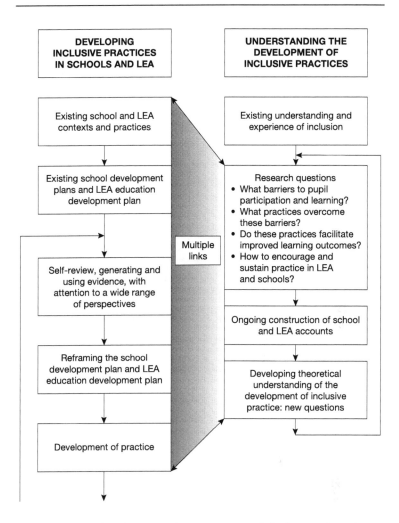

Figure 8.1 Mapping the research strategy – two linked research cycles.

researchers. The first of these cycles was driven by the agendas of the partner LEAs and schools, and set out to use existing knowledge within these contexts, supplemented by further research evidence, as the means of fostering developments in the field. The second cycle attempted to scrutinise these developments in order to address the overall agenda of the network, using existing theory and previous research, including our own work, as a basis for pursuing deeper understandings. Between the two cycles was a set of boundaries that had to be crossed in order for the two driving agendas to be synchronised.

Of course, as the accounts in this book show, we learned much about the difficulties that can occur as researchers attempt to negotiate these boundaries with practitioners. However, the major omission in our starting model was not detail about the practicalities of managing researcher–practitioner relationships, but a failure to think through the nature of the knowledge each possessed and the ways in which such knowledge might be shared and used by each group. The matter was particularly confused given that we encouraged practitioners to undertake their own research, while we as researchers involved ourselves in discussions about the detail of practice and policy.

However, the theory of inclusive school development we proposed in Chapter 7 seems to us to be helpful in clarifying these issues. The theory does not differentiate between research-based and practice-based knowledge, much less between researcher and practitioner knowledge. It does, however, differentiate between the sorts of 'understandings' which sustain ongoing practice (and in this we include the practice of policy-making) and the 'principled interruptions' which can 'disturb' such understandings. Moreover, it is clear that somehow the interruptions have to come from 'outside' current understandings, not in the sense that they must be generated beyond the classroom or school, but that they must start from different assumptions. We see how interruptions in this sense can take many forms – encounters with students who do not respond well to established approaches to teaching and learning, or with teachers who do things differently, or with schools with different value systems.

We also see, however, that research evidence can serve the same function and that research processes can create the capacity for practitioners to step outside their current understandings. This is not, we suggest, because research-based knowledge is in some sense superior to practice-based knowledge – and certainly not because researchers somehow know more than practitioners. Rather, it is because research-based knowledge and practice-based knowledge are built from different assumptions and according to different rules. There is always the potential, therefore, that they will lead to different understandings. In many cases, it seems likely and proper that research will aim at providing evidence *for* practice and policy. In other words, the understandings generated by each will be similar, and the findings of research will readily become practitioner knowledge. However, research-based and practice-based knowledge may also stand in a critical relationship to each other.

This has implications for the relationship between researchers, policy-makers and practitioners. The critical relationship of their different kinds of knowledge has to be embodied in real encounters between these groups. This may involve close engagement, as in our network, or it may involve more distant encounters. In either event, we need new forms of relationship between practitioners and researchers, in the way that is outlined by Hiebert *et al.* (2002). They suggest that fruitful forms of collaboration require a reorientation of values and goals among both groups. So, they argue, teachers need to move away from the dominant view that teaching is a 'personal and private activity'. Rather, teachers have to adopt the 'more risky view' that it is an activity that can be continuously improved, provided it is made public and examined openly. At the same time, they argue that researchers must stop undervaluing the knowledge which teachers acquire in their own classrooms. In this way researchers will be able to recognise the potential of 'personal knowledge as it becomes transformed into professional knowledge' (p.13).

Our own experience suggests that **successful practitioner/ researcher partnerships involve a complex social process within which colleagues with very different experiences, beliefs and methodological assumptions learn how to live with one another's differences and, even more difficult, learn how to learn from these differences.** This is why it is important to be clear, as we suggested in Chapter 3, that the members of our research team both conducted and were the subjects of research, as their thinking and practices were examined by themselves and others. As we engaged with data about the work of practitioners in a different context, we too were constantly challenged to think through our own practice as researchers. In the network, many teachers themselves engaged in enquiries, just as academics had to struggle with the meaning of their findings for practice and had to interrogate their own assumptions in the light of practitioners' sometimes very different understandings.

In other words, the way forward for developing the relationship between research, policy-making and practice may not lie in engineering encounters between different groups of professionals – useful as this may be in certain cases. Rather, it requires a broadening of the repertoire of knowledge-generating strategies to which professional groups have access. In terms of what this means for teachers, all we have said about the sorts of conditions and processes for development in and between schools is likely to be relevant to this expansion of repertoires. However, we will need to replace approaches to initial teacher education and continuing development which has become increasingly routinised and technicised with models which emphasise participation and dialogue.

Summary and conclusions

We have made reference to a contradiction between an 'optimistic' view, which sees inclusive practices as likely to emerge under appropriate organisational conditions, and a 'pessimistic' view, which sees such school-level developments as vulnerable to a hostile and non-inclusive policy environment. How do the ideas in this book relate to these two positions?

We have set out a process of development that can encourage the emergence of inclusive practices. This is a process whose essential dynamic is present in every school, but it is enhanced by factors which can increase the likelihood of the occurrence of principled interruptions. These include the opportunites created for constructive dialogue by the strength of the school's communities of practice; the management style of the headteacher and the distribution of leadership in the school; an engagement with evidence and critical perspectives; and an opportunity to analyse and reflect on the relationship between values and actions. It also requires those seeking to work with schools to understand that real dialogue depends on a consideration of perspectives that may not be their own in a situation where differences in power must be removed or suspended.

We have seen how, where the process is enhanced in these ways, it can enable groups of teachers in schools to reinterpret external imperatives so that they can be made more compatible with inclusive aspirations for development. On the other hand, we have also seen examples where the absence of additional conditions of this sort means that schools are unable to reconsider their practices. While there are events and experiences which challenge all schools, it is far from inevitable that these will provoke a critical interrogation of practice and its underpinning assumptions. Moreover, in the context of a powerfully enforced external policy environment, the problems which schools identify and the aims which they set themselves will inevitably owe much to national agendas, even when these contain exclusionary pressures.

We recognise that all schools contain a wealth of resources to support inclusive development but the conditions to encourage them to initiate such change are by no means universal. Crucially, we see the core of these processes as residing not in optional enhancements, but in the very nature of teaching. Ultimately, the question of the inclusiveness of practice is not one that has to be injected into schools from outside by, for instance, the appearance of a charismatic headteacher, or the work of a consultant, or a transformation of national agendas. Rather, that question is already there in every school, just as processes are present for creating collaborative adjustments of practice in response to it.

The significance of this realisation, as we understand it, is that **the development of inclusive practices, particularly on a national basis, might best be achieved not by seeking an improbable transformation of schools, but by an incremental enhancement of the processes which make the existing dynamic more inclusive**. This has implications for how headteachers are selected and trained, for how staff teams work together, and for how schools collect and use evidence about their practice. It also has implications for the sorts of critical and alternative perspectives to which schools have access and, therefore, for their relationships with other schools, LEAs, researchers and consultants.

Throughout our study we have found indications that an understanding of the way real schools develop is missing from those who frame the complex web of national policy directives and initiatives, and that this has distracted many schools from paying attention to the conditions for their sustained development.

Changes made within schools, we have argued, are frequently reactive and may last as long as a particular initiative or project is placed in the foreground of thinking. Yet we have seen how a reconnection with the underlying values of practitioners can provide a fresh impetus for coherence in planning that is more rational and persistent over time. We received a helpful reminder of such possibilities when, over a year after the end of our project, one of us was approached by a member of the coordinating group of one of the schools in the network. He said that as a result of the project he and other schools in his area had got together to support each other to establish school councils which would give students a real voice in reviewing practices in the schools and planning for change.

Finally, there are also implications for the national policy framework. Our assessment is that a radical shift in national policy, however desirable, is unlikely until the contradictions become even more evident between market-driven ideologies and the desire of large sections of the population for an equitable high-quality education in decent neighbourhoods for all children. At the moment such marketisation of education is still expanding its influence around the world. However, we reiterate the argument that has emerged from our work in the network: that amidst the apparently non-inclusive aspects of 'the standards agenda' there is also a strand that may be used in the service of the development of inclusion, and which may be linked to the broader strands of the government's inclusion agenda. We can now add to this that in the course of implementing and adapting policies on 'standards', schools have been prompted to look closely at groups of students who may otherwise be overlooked and at the practices which are apparently failing such students. Teachers within our network, whether or not they voiced an explicit commitment to values they identified as 'inclusive', retained the deep values of fairness and public service that had brought most into the profession, and these values surfaced when they found themselves engaging in actions and practices prompted by external pressures with which they felt themselves to be in conflict.

We suggest, therefore, that the efforts of those concerned to put inclusive values into action must not only be directed at the radical critique of educational policies, important as such critiques will continue to be. Rather, we must also concentrate on trying to expand the inclusive aspects of current policy and support teachers in taking greater control over their own development. In reframing ideas about achievements so that they are underpinned by inclusive values, we can get past the unhelpful idea that standards and inclusion are in opposition to each other. We conclude that such measured attempts to take control of a 'comprehensive' agenda for the development of participation and learning in schools offers the best hope of moving beyond the achievements of a few exceptional schools towards a school system that is more genuinely and sustainably inclusive.

Appendix

How was the research carried out?

The development of an effective methodology for addressing the network's agenda represented a major challenge and was therefore an important strand within the research programme. We took the view that barriers to learning and participation and the action needed to address them might differ from context to context. We saw the way practitioners understand their own contexts as a privileged source of insights. We also saw it as central both to the creation of barriers and to the development of actions to overcome those barriers.

Rather than handing practitioners a 'blueprint' for action, we sought to work collaboratively with them to explore how their contexts could be understood and what actions might be possible therein. As 'outsiders', our role was to stimulate and support practitioners' exploration, to engage with them in the mutual problematisation of the taken-for-granted assumptions of 'insiders', and to lead the theorisation and generalisation from particular contexts.

We were therefore involved in stimulating and monitoring a series of initiatives to improve the educational experiences of students in schools. However, our approach was closer to one of critical collaborative action research (Macpherson et al., 1998), rather than of quasi-experiment or school improvement, as is usually understood. This is important for understanding how the study progressed and for the ways in which we collected, analysed and used data.

Procedures

In practical terms, the network involved the three teams of researchers in working with practitioner-researchers in twenty-five schools, in three LEAs serving urban contexts. At the start of the initiative, in the summer of 2000, workshops were held in each LEA for groups of teachers in the partner schools. The school teams were invited, in discussion with their LEAs and the university teams, to identify barriers to learning and participation in their contexts and the actions which might be taken to address these barriers. Each school made their participation in the network a part of their development plans, and a core team of practitioners attended regular local meetings and four national seminars.

Members of the university teams visited the schools on a regular basis to support these core teams in collecting and engaging with evidence in order to take their development initiatives forward. The school teams were encouraged to investigate their own practices and monitor the impacts of their actions systematically, while the university teams gave them technical assistance and undertook independent investigations in ways that were negotiated with the schools. Ultimately, however, control over the focus of enquiry in the schools, the direction of action and access to data in relation to that action belonged with the schools themselves. Consequently, although some schools carried out relatively robust evaluations, our data about schools and classrooms served principally to catalyse and illuminate teachers' questioning and development of their practices. On the other hand, we were able to gather rich data on the nature of this questioning and development process, and, specifically, on how practitioners in different institutional contexts conceptualise barriers and the action needed to overcome them.

The approaches used by practitioners to explore their practice and monitor action generated evidence in a wide variety of forms, including records of observations, examples of children's work, performance and attainment statistics, specimen teaching plans, interview notes, questionnaire returns and video recordings. The university researchers used similar techniques and in addition kept detailed field notes of all their involvements with the schools and school teams.

Collaborative enquiry

The approaches used were intended to lead to the development of improved policies and practices within the specific contexts, while, at the same time, providing theoretical understandings of what these practices involved that would be of interest to wider practitioner and research communities. Our earlier research had led to a commitment to the use of collaborative forms of enquiry that emphasise practitioner research as a means of understanding the development of inclusive practices. Specifically it led us to believe that greater understandings of how educational contexts can be developed in order to foster the learning of all children are most likely to emerge from studies in which 'outsiders', such as ourselves, work alongside teachers, students, parents and local authority staff, as they attempt to explore ways of overcoming barriers to participation and learning in schools.

Such an orientation is intended to overcome the traditional gap between research and practice. It has generally been assumed that this gap has resulted from inadequate dissemination strategies, the implication being that educational research does speak to issues of practice, if only the right people would listen (Robinson, 1998). What is proposed here is an alternative explanation, one which suggests that research findings may well continue to be ignored, regardless of how well they are communicated, if they bypass the ways in which practitioners formulate the problems they face and the constraints within which they have to work (Poplin and Weeres, 1992).

Of course, participatory research is fraught with difficulties, not least in terms of developing ways of making it happen that lead to findings that have relevance to a wider audience. There is also the problem of 'false consciousness', i.e. the formulation of problems by practitioners may be constrained by their professional intuition and/or may be contrary to the interests of their students.

The potential benefits of a process of collaborative enquiry through which an open dialogue can develop are enormous. The ideal we aspired to was a process through which critical appraisal leads to understandings which can have an immediate and direct impact on the development of thinking and practice in the field.

The role of academics

The participation of university staff in the schools' action research was intended to strengthen these activities by providing research training and support, while at the same time helping to overcome some of the reported limitations of action research, such as the failure to provide adequate explanations as to how new insights come to be generated through the research process (Adelman, 1989) and problems regarding generalisability of findings (Hammersley, 1992). A central strategy in this respect was the use of 'group interpretive processes' as a means of analysing and interpreting evidence. These involved an engagement with the different perspectives of practitioners, students and academics in ways that encourage critical reflection, collaborative learning and mutual critique (Wasser and Bresler, 1996). In this context, the use of statistical evidence regarding student participation and achievement, and feedback from students regarding their experiences of current practice, were seen as being essential elements in providing challenges to practitioners about their existing approaches (Ainscow et al., 1999). The varied theoretical perspectives of members of the research team also provided a valuable means of questioning taken-for-granted assumptions and helping teachers to reconsider neglected possibilities for moving practice forward.

As these developments occurred, the research teams collected additional data from staff and students in order to map the process of change in schools (Ainscow et al., 1995). At the same time, they analysed what happened to levels of participation and achievement in the schools as they attempted to develop more inclusive practices. In this way the research was able to provide deeper theoretical insights into the impact of practitioner research as a means of increasing student participation and learning.

The strategy involved the teams in developing positions in each LEA and school that were responsive to their particular contexts. Because they were starting from their own perceptions of critical issues, the commitment in these institutions was relatively deep and involved not just the headteacher but also a wider group of staff in thinking about their practices. Through this process, the research teams learned more about these institutions so that they were able to present and in some cases confront them with a critique of their practice from an informed position.

The research teams explored different strategies for this purpose. These involved the use of three overlapping approaches to practitioner–researcher cooperation. Each of these approaches emphasises a different way of setting the agenda for enquiry and a different relationship between practitioners and academics (Wagner, 1997). Together, they were intended to enable those within the network to develop deeper and richer understandings of what is involved in creating inclusive practices.

The three approaches are as follows:

- *Research into school practices in relation to the agendas of practitioners.* This involved a process of collecting evidence of school development in a way that is separate from, and complementary to, the review and development processes used within the school. It involved the university research teams in collecting evidence about developments in the school and feeding this information back in a way that was intended to foster and deepen the engagement of practitioners.

- *Research into school practices and the practices of researchers in relation to the agendas of practitioners and researchers.* This involved an ongoing mutual dialogue between 'outsiders' and 'insiders', as evidence is collected and discussed during visits, or through e-mails and phone calls, to discuss progress and priorities. It included an engagement with the thinking and actions of researchers as well as practitioners.

- *Research into school practices in relation to the agendas of researchers.* In order to analyse school practices in relation to wider policy and theoretical contexts, the research teams also found it necessary sometimes to adopt a more detached perspective.

Trustworthiness

The issue of trustworthiness was a particular challenge to research that involved such a high degree of participation among stakeholders. In particular, it was important to be clear about what constituted rigour within such an approach. Commenting on this issue, Schon (1991) argues that without a serious effort to make clear what is meant by rigour, participatory research 'becomes an open sesame to woolly-headedness, a never-never land where anything goes'. He goes on to suggest that appropriate rigour in the study of practice should focus on validity (e.g. how do we know what we claim to know?) and, utility (e.g. how useful is the research to practitioners?).

With this in mind, we used three forms of triangulation, supporting our observations and reports from a number of viewpoints. These involved comparing and contrasting evidence about the same actions and activities from different people (e.g., teachers, support staff and students); scrutinising events from different angles by making use of a variety of methods for collecting information; and using 'outsiders' in the research teams as observers.

Influenced by the ideas of Karl Popper, Schon (1991) argues that the fundamental test for validity in participatory enquiry is through 'competitive resistance to refutation'. This involves juxtaposing alternate plausible accounts of the phenomenon in question. Schon notes: 'In the absence of an alternate hypothesis, one is likely to be overwhelmed by the obviousness of what one already knows' (p. x). With this advice in mind, the teams discussed with their practitioner partners, and with one another, written accounts of the work carried out in their schools, including alternative explanations as to what lessons could be drawn from these experiences. In this way conclusions were reached which we believe to be both valid and relevant.

A further challenge was to analyse the multiplicity of data in a coherent and trustworthy manner. Our response was to build levels of explanation and theorising by encouraging triangulation between different kinds of data and dialogue between different perspectives. Dialogue between the three university teams' emerging interpretations was built into the research process. Regular meetings of the group of ten academic staff were held, including occasional residential events. The university teams presented working papers to each other and we were particularly careful to challenge each other to be explicit about the assumptions underlying their work. At the same time, a strong sub-network was established between the three research associates, who met, were in regular contact through telephone and e-mail, and were able to contribute their own distinctive perspective based on extended contact with the schools.

The database about what was happening within the partner LEAs and schools was accessible to all members of the three university teams through a 'closed' website. In addition, an 'open' website was developed that encouraged wider involvement in the activities of the network.

In addition, we held four national conferences in which all university, school and LEA participants in the network had the opportunity to discuss their work and share findings. The first conference focused on sharing plans and early developments. The other three conferences included school visits, where practitioners from other LEAs visited the host LEA's schools and carried out small-scale research activities (interviewing students, observing lessons and so on) which were then discussed with the host school. This process proved so powerful for participants that they requested – and undertook – similar research visits within LEAs, and maintained some of their inter-LEA contacts long after the conferences. At each conference, the university teams discussed interim findings with participants. The final conference focused on participants making explicit what they saw as the outcomes of their work, particularly in terms of students' achievements broadly understood.

Crucially, then, the network was not simply a loose collection of studies with different foci and methods. Rather, it was a collaborative effort by academic and practitioner-researchers, working on common issues in a range of settings. The multi-site and multi-perspective nature of the network means that we were better able to address these common issues 'in the round' than if this had been either an isolated study or a collection of separate studies.

Bibliography

Abberley, P. (1987) The concept of oppression and the development of a social theory of disability, *Disability, Handicap and Society* 2 (1), pp. 5–19.

Adger, C.T. (2002) Professional conversation and teacher learning, *Educational Researcher* 31 (9), pp. 26–28.

Adelman, C. (1989) The practical ethic takes priority over methodology. In W. Carr (ed.) *Quality in Teaching*, London: Falmer.

Ainscow, M. (1994) *Special Needs in the Classroom: A Teacher Education Guide*, London: Jessica Kingsley/UNESCO.

Ainscow, M. (1995) Education for all: making it happen, *Support for Learning*, 10 (2), pp. 147–157.

Ainscow, M. (1999) *Understanding the Development of Inclusive Schools*, London: Falmer.

Ainscow, M. (2000) The next step for special education: supporting the development of inclusive practices, *British Journal of Special Education*, June, pp. 76–80.

Ainscow, M. and Brown, D. (2000) *Improving Teaching*, Lewisham: Lewisham LEA.

Ainscow, M. and Haile-Giorgis, M. (1999) Educational arrangements for children categorised as having special needs in Central and Eastern Europe, *European Journal of Special Needs Education* 14 (2), pp. 103–121.

Ainscow, M. and Howes, A. (2001) LEAs and school improvement: what is it that makes the difference? Paper presented at the British Education Research Association Conference, Leeds.

Ainscow, M. and Tweddle, D.A. (2003) Understanding the changing role of English local education authorities in promoting inclusion. In J. Allan (ed.) *Inclusion, Participation and Democracy: What is the Purpose?* Dordrecht: Kluwer Academic, pp. 165–177.

Ainscow, M., Barrs, D. and Martin. J. (1998) Taking school improvement into the classroom. Paper presented at the International Conference on School Effectiveness and Improvement, Manchester, January.

Ainscow, M., Booth, T. and Dyson, A. (1999) Inclusion and exclusion: listening to some hidden voices. In K. Ballard (ed.) *Inclusion and Exclusion in Education and Society*, London: Falmer.

Ainscow, M., Farrell, P. and Tweddle, D.A. (1998) *Effective Practice in Inclusion and in Special and Mainstream Schools Working Together*, London: Department for Education and Employment.

Ainscow, M., Farrell, P. and Tweddle, D.A. (2000) Developing policies for inclusive education: a study of the role of local education authorities, *International Journal of Inclusive Education* 4 (3), pp. 211–229.

Ainscow, M., Fox, S. and O'Kane, J. (2003) *Leadership and Management in Special Schools: A Review of the Literature*, London: National College for School Leadership.

Ainscow, M., Hargreaves, D.H. and Hopkins, D. (1995) Mapping the process of change in schools: the development of six new research techniques, *Evaluation and Research in Education* 9 (2), pp. 75–89.

Ainscow, M., Howes, A. and Tweddle, D.A. (2006) Moving practice forward at the district level. In M. Ainscow and M. West (eds) *Improving Urban Schools: Leadership and Collaboration*, Buckingham: Open University Press.

Ainscow, M., Hopkins, D., Southworth, G. and West, M. (1994) *Creating the Conditions for School Improvement*, London: Fulton.

Ainscow, M., Howes, A., Farrell, P. and Frankham, J. (2003) Making sense of the development of inclusive practices, *European Journal of Special Needs Education* 18 (2), pp. 227–242.

Alur M. (1999) *Invisible Children, a Study of Policy Exclusion*, New Delhi: Viva Books.

Argyris, C. and Schon, D.A. (1978) *Organisational Learning*, Reading, MA: Addison-Wesley.

Argyris, C. and Schon, D.A. (1996) *Organisational Learning II: Theory, Method and Practice*, Reading, MA: Addison-Wesley.

Artiles, A. and Dyson, A. (2004) Inclusion, education and culture in developed and developing countries. In D. Mitchell (ed.) *Contextualising Inclusive Education*, London: Routledge Falmer.

Ball, S.J. (2001) Labour, learning and the economy: a 'policy sociology' perspective. In M. Fielding (ed.) *Taking Education Seriously: Four Years' Hard Labour*, London: Routledge.

Balshaw, M. (1999) *Help in the Classroom*, London: David Fulton.

Bartolome, L.I. (1994) Beyond the methods fetish: towards a humanising pedagogy, *Harvard Education Review* 54 (2), pp. 173–194.

Bastiani, J. (2003) *Parental Involvement in Children's Learning: A Practical Framework for the Review and Development of Home-school Work*, London: London Borough of Tower Hamlets.

Bell, D. (2003) Speech to the City of York Council Education Conference, February 2003, *Guardian*, 28 February.

Benn, C. and Simon, B. (1972) *Half Way There: Report on the British Comprehensive School Reform*, Harmondsworth: Penguin Books.

Blair, M. (2001) *Why Pick on Me? School Exclusion and Black Youth*, Stoke-on-Trent: Trentham Books.

Blunkett, D. (1999) Excellence for the many, not just the few: raising standards and extending opportunities in our schools, *The CBI President's Reception Address by the Rt. Hon. David Blunkett MP 19 July 1999*, London: DfEE.

Bonal, X. (2002) Plus ça change: the World Bank global education policy and the post-Washington consensus, *International Studies in Sociology of Education* 12 (1), pp. 3–21.

Booth, T. (1981a) Demystifying integration. In W. Swann (ed.) *The Practice of Special Education*, Oxford: Blackwell.

Booth, T. (1981b) *Special Biographies, Units 1/2 Special Needs in Education*, Milton Keynes: Open University Press.

Booth, T. (1983) Integration and participation in comprehensive schools, *Forum* 25 (2), pp. 40–42.

Booth, T. (1988) Challenging conceptions of integration. In L. Barton (ed.) *The Politics of Special Educational Needs*, London: Falmer.

Booth, T. (1995) Mapping inclusion and exclusion: concepts for all? In C. Clark, A. Dyson and A. Millward (eds) *Towards Inclusive Schools?* London: David Fulton.

Booth, T. (1996a) A perspective on inclusion from England, *Cambridge Review of Education* 26 (1), pp. 87–99.

Booth, T. (1996b) Stories of exclusion: natural and unnatural selection. In E. Blyth and J. Milner (eds) *Exclusion from School; Inter-professional Issues for Policy and Practice*, London: Routledge.

Booth, T. (1999) Controlling the agenda: policies on inclusion and exclusion in England, in D. Armstrong, F. Armstrong and L. Barton (eds) *Inclusive Education, Policy, Contexts and Comparative Perspectives*, London: David Fulton.

Booth, T. (2003a) Inclusion and exclusion in the city, concepts and contexts. In P. Potts (ed.) *Inclusion in the City*, London: Routledge.

Booth, T. (2003b) Embracing the faith, including the community. In P. Potts (ed.) *Inclusion in the City*, London: Routledge.

Booth, T. and Ainscow, M. (eds) (1998) *From Them to Us: An International Study of Inclusion in Education*, London:. Routledge.

Booth, T. and Ainscow, M. (2002) *The Index for Inclusion; Developing Learning and Participation in Schools* (2nd edn), Bristol: Centre for Studies on Inclusive Education.

Booth, T. and Coulby, D. (eds) (1987) *Curricula for All:Producing and Reducing Disaffection*, Milton Keynes: Open University Press.

Booth, T. and Potts, P. (eds) (1983) *Integrating Special Education*, Oxford: Blackwell.

Booth, T. and Swann, W. (eds) (1987) *Curricula for All: Including Pupils with Disabilities*, Milton Keynes: Open University Press.

Booth, T., Ainscow, M. and Dyson, A. (1997) Understanding inclusion and exclusion in the English competitive education system, *International Journal of Inclusive Education* 1 (40), pp. 337–356.

Booth, T., Ainscow, M. and Dyson, A. (1998) Inclusion and exclusion in a competitive system. In T. Booth and M. Ainscow (eds) *From Them to Us: An International Study of Inclusion in Education*, London: Routledge.

Booth, T., Ainscow, M. and Kingston, D. (2004; revised edn 2006) *The Index for Inclusion; Developing Learning Participation and Play in Early Years and Childcare*, Bristol: Centre for Studies on Inclusive Education.

Booth, T., Potts, P. and Swann, W. (eds) (1987) *Curricula for All: Preventing Difficulties in Learning*, Milton Keynes: Open University Press.

Booth, T., Swann, W., Masterson, M. and Potts, P. (eds) (1992a) *Learning for All: Curricula for Diversity in Education*, London: Routledge.

Booth, T., Swann, W., Masterson, M. and Potts, P. (eds) (1992b) *Learning for All: Policies for Diversity in Education*, London: Routledge.

Boreham, N. and Morgan, C. (2004) A sociocultural analysis of organisational learning, *Oxford Review of Education* 30 (3), pp. 307–325

Brown, J.S. and Duguid, P. (1991) Organizational learning and communities of practice: toward a unifying view of working, learning and innovation. In M.D. Cohen and L.S. Sproull (eds) *Organizational Learning*, London: Sage.

Burrell, G. and Morgan, G. (1979) *Sociological Paradigms and Organisational Analysis*, Aldershot: Gower.

Campbell, C. (ed.) (2002) *Developing Inclusive Schooling: Perspectives, Policies and Practices*, London: Institute of Education University of London.

Carrington, S. (1999) Inclusion needs a different school culture, *International Journal of Inclusive Education* 3 (3), pp. 257–268.

Carvita, S. and Hallden, O. (1994) Reframing the problem of conceptual change, *Learning and Instruction*, p. 4.

Clark, C., Dyson, A. and Millward, A. (1998) Theorising special education: time to move on? In C. Clark, A. Dyson and A. Millward (eds) *Theorising Special Education*, London: Routledge.

Clark, C., Dyson, A., Millward, A. and Skidmore, D. (1995a) Dialectical analysis, special needs and schools as organisations. In C. Clark, A. Dyson and A. Millward (eds) *Towards Inclusive Schooling?* London: David Fulton.

Clark, C., Dyson, A., Millward, A. and Skidmore, D. (1995b) *Innovatory Practice in Mainstream Schools for Special Educational Needs*, London: HMSO.

Clark, C., Dyson, A., Millward, A. and Skidmore, D. (1997) *New Directions in Special Needs: Innovations in Mainstream Schools*, London: Cassell.

Clark, C., Dyson, A., Millward, A. and Robson, S. (1999) Theories of inclusion, theories of schools: deconstructing and reconstructing the 'inclusive school', *British Educational Research Journal* 25(2), pp. 157–177.

Commission for Racial Equality (2000) *Learning for All*, London: CRE.

Commission for Racial Equality (2002) *Preparing a Race Equality Policy for Schools*, London: CRC.

Copland, M.A. (2003) Leadership of inquiry: building and sustaining capacity for school improvement, *Educational Evaluation and Policy Analysis* 25 (4), pp. 375–395.

Corbett, J. (1995) *Badmouthing: The Language of Special Educational Needs*, London: Taylor & Francis.

Corbett, J. (2001) *Supporting Inclusive Education: A Connective Pedagogy*, London: Routledge.

Corbett, J. and Slee, R. (2000) An international conversation on inclusive education. In F. Armstrong, D. Armstrong and L. Barton (eds) *Inclusive Education: Policy Contexts and Comparative Perspectives*, London: David Fulton.

Cousins, J.B. (1998) Intellectual roots of organisational learning. In K. Leithwood and K.S. Louis (eds) *Organisational Learning in Schools*, Lisse: Swets & Zeitlinger.

Department for Education and Employment (DfEE) (1997) *Excellence for All Children: Meeting Special Educational Needs*, London: HM Stationery Office.

DfEE (1998a) *School Standards and Framework Act*, London: DfEE.

DfEE (1998b) *Meeting Special Educational Needs: A Programme of Action*, London: DfEE.

DfEE (1999a) *Excellence in Cities*, London: DfEE.

DfEE (1999b) *Circular 11/99: Social Inclusion: Pupil Support*, London: DfEE.

DfEE (1999c) *Code of Practice on LEA–School Relations*, London: DfEE.

DfEE (2000a) *Bullying: Don't Suffer in Silence*, London: DfEE.

DfEE (2000b) *Working with Teaching Assistants: A good practice guide*, London: DfEE.

DfEE/Qualifications and Curriculum Authority (1999) *Inclusion Statement, The National Curriculum: Handbook for Primary Teachers in England*, London: DfEE/QCA.

Department for education and skills (DfES) (2001a) *The Special Educational Needs Code of Practice*, London: DfES.

DfES (2001b) *Inclusive Schooling: Children with Special Educational Needs*, London: DfES.

DfES (2002) *The Education Act*, London: HM Stationery Office.

DfES (2003) *Every Child Matters. Cm. 5860*, London: HM Stationery Office.

DfES (2004) *Five Year Strategy for Children and Learners*, London: HM Stationery Office.

DfES (2005a) *Higher Standards, Better Schools for All: More choice for parents and pupils*, (White paper), London: DfES

DfES (2005b) *A New Relationship with Schools: Improving Performance Through Self-evaluation*, London: DfES.

DfES/Department of Health (DfES/DOH) (2004) *Stand up for Us: Challenging Homophobia in Schools*, London: DfES/DOH.

Disability Rights Commission (DRC) (2002) *Code of Practice for Schools*, London: DRC.

Docking, J. (ed.) (2000) *New Labour's Policies for Schools: Raising the Standard?*, London: David Fulton.

Dyson, A. (1990a) Effective learning consultancy: a future role for special needs coordinators?, *Support for Learning* 5 (3), pp. 116–127.

Dyson, A. (1990b) Special educational needs and the concept of change, *Oxford Review of Education* 16 (1), pp. 55–66.

Dyson, A. (1991) Rethinking roles, rethinking concepts: special needs teachers in mainstream schools, *Support for Learning* 6 (2), pp. 51–60.

Dyson, A. and Millward, A. (2000) *Schools and Special Needs: Issues of Innovation and Inclusion*, London: Paul Chapman.

Dyson, A. and Millward, A. (2001) *Schools and Special Needs*, London: Paul Chapman.

Dyson, A., Ainscow, M. and Booth, T. (1999) Processes of inclusion and exclusion in schools. Paper presented at the American Educational Research Association meeting, Montreal, 19–23 April.

Dyson, A., Gallannaugh, F. and Millward, A. (2003) Making space in the standards agenda: developing inclusive practices in schools, *European Educational Research Journal* 2 (2), pp. 228–244.

Dyson, A., Howes, A. and Roberts, B. (2002) A systematic review of the effectiveness of school-level actions for promoting participation by all students, *Inclusive Education Review Group for the EPPI Centre*, Institute of Education, University of London.

Dyson, A., Howes, A. and Roberts, B. (2004) What do we really know about inclusive schools? A systematic review of the research evidence. In D. Mitchell (ed.) *Special Educational Needs and Inclusive Education: Major Themes in Education*, London: Routledge Falmer.

Dyson, A., Millward, A. and Skidmore, D. (1994) Beyond the whole school approach: an emerging model of special needs practice and provision in mainstream secondary schools, *British Educational Research Journal* 20 (3), pp. 301–317.

Engestrom, Y. (n.d.) *Collaborative Intentionality Capital: Object-oriented Interagency in Multiorganizational Fields*, Helsinki: University of Helsinki Centre for Activity Theory and Developmental Work Research.

Engestrom, Y., Miettinen, R., Raija-Leena, P., Pea, R., Seely Brown, J. and Heath, C. (eds) (1999) *Perspectives on Activity Theory (Learning in Doing: Social, Cognitive and Computational Perspectives)*, Cambridge: Cambridge University Press.

Epstein, D., Elwood, J., Hey, V. and Maw, J. (eds) (1998) *Failing Boys? Issues in Gender and Education*, Buckingham: Open University Press.

Fielding, M. (1999) Radical collegiality: affirming teaching as an inclusive professional practice. *Australian Educational Researcher* 26 (2), pp. 1–34.

Finkelstein, N.D. and Grubb. W.N. (2000) Making sense of education and training markets, *American Educational Research Journal* 37 (3), pp. 601–633.

Florian, L., Rose, R. and Tilstone, C. (eds) (1998) *Planning Inclusive Practice*, London: Routledge.

Floud, J.E. (1961) Social class factors in educational achievement. In A.H. Halsey (ed.) *Ability and Educational Opportunity*, Paris: OECD.

Floud, J.E., Halsey, A.H. and Martin, F.M. (1956) *Social Class and Educational Opportunity*, London: Heinemann.

Franklin, B.M. (1994) *From 'Backwardness' to 'At-risk': Childhood Learning Difficulties and the Contradictions of School Reform*, Albany, NY: State University of New York Press.

Frost, D., Durrant, J., Head, M. and Holden, G. (2000) *Teacher-led School Improvement*, London: Routledge Falmer.

Fulcher, G. (1989) *Disabling Policies? A Comparative Approach to Education Policy and Disability*, Lewes: Falmer Press.

Fullan, M. (1992) *Successful School Improvement*, Buckingham: Open University Press.

Fullan, M. (2001) *The New Meaning of Educational Reform*, Columbia: Teachers College Press.

Garner, P. and Gains, C. (2001) The debate begins, *Special*, spring, pp. 20–23.

Gillborn, D. and Youdell, D. (1999) *Rationing Education: Policy, Practice Reform and Equity*, Buckingham: Open University Press.

Giroux, H.A. and Schmidt, M. (2004) Closing the achievement gap: a metaphor for children left behind, *Journal of Educational Change* 5, pp. 213–228.

Hammersley, M. (1992) *What's Wrong With Ethnography?* London: Routledge.

Hansen, J. (1992) The development of the Danish Folkeskole: towards a school for all, *European Journal of Special Needs Education* 7(1), pp. 38–46.

Hardman, F., Smith, F. and Wall, K. (2005) Teacher–pupil dialogue with pupils with special educational needs in the National Literacy Strategy. *Educational Review* 57 (3), pp. 17–31.

Hargreaves, D. (1991) Contrived collegiality: the micropolitics of teacher collaboration. In J. Blaséé (ed.) *The Politics of Life in Schools*, Newbury Park, CA: Sage.

Harris, A. (2001) Building the capacity for school improvement, *School Leadership and Management* 21 (3), pp. 261–270.

Harris, J. (2005) *So Now Who Do We Vote For?* London: Faber and Faber.

Hart, S. (1996) *Beyond Special Needs, Enhancing Children's Learning Through Innovative Thinking*, London: Paul Chapman.

Hart, S. (2000) *Thinking Through Teaching*, London: David Fulton.

Hart, S., Dixon, A., Drummond, M.J. and McIntyre, D. (2004) *Learning Without Limits*, Buckingham: Open University Press.

Hatch, T. (2000) *What Happens When Multiple Improvement Initiatives Collide?* Menlo Park: Carnegie Foundation for the Advancement of Teaching.

Hatcher, R. (2002) Popular empowerment and education, participatory democracy in Porto Alegro and Rio Grande do Sul, Brazil. Paper presented at the conference of the British Education Research Association, Exeter.

Haug, P. (2003) Qualifying teachers for the School for All. In T. Booth, K. Nes and M. Stromstad (eds) *Developing Inclusive Teacher Education*, London: Routledge.

Hayton, A. (ed.) (1999) *Tackling Disaffection and Special Exclusion: Education Perspectives and Policies*, London: Kogan Page.

Hiebert, J., Gallimore, R. and Stigler, J.W. (2002) A knowledge base for the teaching profession, *Educational Researcher* 31 (5), pp. 3–15.

Hillage, J., Pearson, R., Anderson, A. and Tamkin, P. (1998) *Excellence in Research on Schools*. DfEE Research Report RR74, London: DfEE.

Home Office (2000) *Race Relations (Amendment) Act*, London: The Home Office.

Home Office (2001a) *Community Cohesion*, a report of the Independent Review Team chaired by Ted Cantle, London: HMSO.

Home Office (2001b) *Building Cohesive Communities*, a report of the Ministerial Group on Public Order and Community Cohesion, London: HMSO.

Honig, M.I. and Hatch, T.C. (2004) Crafting coherence: how schools strategically manage multiple, external demands, *Educational Researcher* 33 (8), pp. 16–30.

Hopkins, D., Ainscow, M. and West, M. (1994) *School Improvement in an Era of Change*, London: Cassell.

Hopkins, D., Ainscow, M. and West, M. (1997a) Unravelling the complexities of school improvement: a case study of the Improving the Quality of Education for All (IQEA) project. In A. Harris, N. Bennett and M. Preedy (eds) *Organisational Effectiveness and Improvement in Education*, Buckingham: Open University Press.

Hopkins, D., West, M. and Ainscow, M. (1997b) *Creating the Conditions for Classroom Improvement*, London: David Fulton.

Housden, P. (1993) *Bucking the Market: LEAs and Special Needs*, Stafford: National Association for Special Educational Needs.

House of Commons (2006) *Equality Act*, London: House of Commons.

House of Lords (2003) *Equality Bill*, London: House of Lords.

Howes, A. (forthcoming) *Becoming More Inclusive*, London: Network Educational Press.

Howes, A., Emanuel, J. and Farrell, P. (2002) Can nurture groups facilitate inclusive practices in primary schools? In P. Farrell and M. Ainscow (eds) *Making Special Education Inclusive*, London: David Fulton.

Huberman, M. (1993) The model of the independent artisan in teachers' professional relationships. In J.W. Little and M.W. McLaughlin (eds) *Teachers' Work: Individuals, Colleagues and Contexts*, New York: Teachers College Press.

Joyce, B., Calhoun, E. and Hopkins, D. (1999) *The New Structure of School Improvement: Inquiring Schools and Achieving Students*, Buckingham: Open University Press.

Kugelmass, J.W. (2001) Collaboration and compromise in creating and sustaining an inclusive school, *Journal of Inclusive Education* 5 (1), pp. 47–65.

Kugelmass, J.W. (2004) *The Inclusive School: Sustaining Equity and Standards*, New York: Teachers College Press.

Kugelmass, J.W. and Ainscow, M. (2003) Leadership for inclusion: a comparison of international practices. Paper presented at the meeting of the American Educational Research Association, Chicago, April.

Lambert, L., Walker, D., Zimmerman, D., Cooper, J., Lambert, M., Gardner, M. and Szabo, M. (1995) *The Constructivist Leader*. New York: Teachers College Press.

Lewin, K. (1946) Action research and minority problems, *Journal of Social Issues* 2 (4), pp. 34–36.

Lipsky, D.K. and Gartner, A. (1997) *Inclusion and School Reform: Transforming America's Classrooms*, Baltimore, MD: Paul H. Brooks.

Little, J.W. and McLaughlin, M.W. (eds) (1993) *Teachers' Work: Individuals, Colleagues and Contexts*, New York: Teachers College Press.

Machin, S., McNally, S. and Rajagopalan, S. (2005) *Tackling the Poverty of Opportunity, Developing 'RBS Enterprise Works' for the Prince's Trust*, London: The Prince's Trust.

Macpherson, I., Aspland, T., Elliott, B., Proudfoot, C., Shaw, L. and Thurlow, G. (1998) A journey into learning partnership: a university and state system working together for curriculum change. In B. Atweh, S. Kemmis and P. Weeks (eds) *Action Research in Practice*, London: Routledge.

Macpherson, W. (1999) *The Stephen Lawrence Inquiry*, London: HM Stationery Office.

McLaughlin, M.W. and Zarrow, J. (2001) Teachers engaged in evidence-based reform: trajectories of teachers' inquiry, analysis and action. In A. Lieberman and L. Miller (eds) *Teachers Caught in the Action. Professional Development that Matters*, New York: Teachers College, pp. 79–101.

Mittler, P. (2000) *Working Towards Inclusive Education: Social Contexts*, London: David Fulton.

Morley, A. (2006) The development of leadership capacity in a school facing challenging circumstances. In M. Ainscow and M. West (eds) *Improving Urban Schools: Leadership and Collaboration*, Buckingham: Open University Press.

Morley, L. and Rassool, N. (1999) *School Effectiveness: Fracturing the Discourse*, London: Falmer Press.

Nias, J. (1989) *Primary Teachers Talking. A Study of Teaching as Work*, London: Routledge.

Norwich, B. (2002) *LEA Inclusion Trends in England 1997–2001. Statistics on Special School Placements and Pupils with Statements in Special Schools*, Bristol: CSIE.

O'Hanlon, C. (ed.) (1995) *Inclusive Education in Europe*, London: David Fulton.

O'Neill, O. (2002) *A Question of Trust: The BBC Reith Lectures 2002*. Cambridge: Cambridge University Press.

Office for Standards in Education (2000a) *Evaluating Educational Inclusion*, London: Ofsted.

Office for Standards in Education (2000b) *Improving City Schools; Strategies to Promote Educational Inclusion*, London: Ofsted.

Office for Standards in Education (2000c) *The Teaching of Writing in Primary Schools: Could do Better – A Discussion Paper by HMI*, London: Ofsted.

Office for Standards in Education (2002a) *Achievement of Black Caribbean Pupils: Three Successful Primary Schools*, London: Ofsted.

Office for Standards in Education (2002b) *Achievement of Black Caribbean Pupils, Good Practice in Secondary Schools*, London: Ofsted.

Ozga, J. (2000) *Policy Research in Educational Settings: Contested Terrain*, Buckingham: Open University Press.

Peters, S. (2003) *Inclusive Education: Achieving Education for All by Including those with Disabilities and Special Needs*, Prepared for the World Bank Disability Group, New York: World Bank.

Poplin, M. and Weeres, J. (1992). *Voices from the Inside: A Report on Schooling from Inside the Classroom. Part One: Naming the Problem*, Claremont, CA: The Institute for Education in Transformation at the Claremont Graduate School.

Potts, P. (ed.) (2003) *Inclusion in the City*, London: Routledge.

Reynolds, D., Teddlie, C., with Hopkins, D. and Stringfield, S. (2000) Linking school effectiveness and school improvement. In C. Teddlie and D. Reynolds (eds) *The International Handbook of School Effectiveness Research*, London: Falmer Press.

Richardson, J.G. (1994) Common, delinquent, and special: on the formalization of common schooling in the American states, *American Educational Research Journal* 31 (4), pp. 695–723.

Riddell, S. and Tett, L. (eds) (2001) *Education, Social Justice and Interagency Working: Joined up or Fractured Policy?*, London: Routledge.

Riehl, C.J. (2000) The principal's role in creating inclusive schools for diverse students: a review of normative, empirical, and critical literature on the practice of educational administration, *Review of Educational Research* 70 (1), pp. 55–81.

Robinson, V.M.J. (1998) Methodology and the research–practice gap, *Educational Researcher* 27, pp. 17–26.

Rosenholtz, S. J. (1989). *Teacher's Workplace: The Social Organization of Schools*, White Plains, NY: Longman.

Rouse, M. and Florian, L. (1997) Inclusive education in the market-place, *International Journal of Inclusive Education* 1 (4), pp. 323–336.

Rustemier, S. and Booth, T. (2005) *Learning about the Index in Use: A Study of the Use of the Index for Inclusion in Schools and LEAs in England*, Bristol: CSIE.

Schein, E. (1992) *Organisation Culture and Leadership* (2nd edn), San Francisco, CA: Jossey-Bass.

Schon, D.A. (ed.) (1991) *The Reflective Turn: Case Studies in and on Educational Practice*, New York: Teachers' College Press.

Sebba, J. with Sachdev, D. (1997) *What Works in Inclusive Education?*, Ilford: Barnardo's.

Senge. P. (1990) *The Fifth Discipline: The Art and Practice of The Learning Organization*, New York: Currency Doubleday.

Skidmore, D. (1999a) Discourses of learning difficulty and the conditions of school development, *Educational Review* 51 (1), pp. 17–28.

Skidmore, D. (1999b) Divergent discourses of learning difficulty, *British Educational Research Journal* 25 (5), pp. 651–663.

Skrtic, T. (1991a) *Behind Special Education: A Critical Analysis of Professional Culture and School Organization*, Denver: Love.

Skrtic, T. (1991b) The special education paradox: equity as the way to excellence, *Harvard Educational Review* 61 (2), pp. 148–206.

Skrtic, T. (1991c) Students with special educational needs: artefacts of the traditional curriculum. In M. Ainscow (ed.) *Effective Schools for All*, London: David Fulton.

Skrtic, T. (ed.) (1995) *Disability and Democracy: Reconstructing (Special) Education for Postmodernity*, New York: Teachers College Press.

Slee, R. (1996) Inclusive education in Australia? Not yet!, *Cambridge Journal of Education* 26 (1), pp. 19–32.

Slee, R., Weiner, G. with Tomlinson, S. (eds) (1998) *School Effectiveness for Whom?* London: Falmer Press.

Smyth, J., Dow, A., Hattam, R., Reid, A. and Shacklock, G. (2000) *Teachers' Work in a Globalising Economy*, London: Falmer Press.

Social Exclusion Unit (1998) *Bringing Britain Together: A National Strategy for Neighbourhood Renewal*, London: HM Stationery Office.

Social Exclusion Unit (2000a) *Minority Ethnic Issues in Social Exclusion and Neighbourhood Renewal*, London: Cabinet Office.

Social Exclusion Unit (2000b) *National Strategy for Neighbourhood Renewal: Policy Action Team Report Summaries: A Compendium*, London: HM Stationery Office.

Social Exclusion Unit (2001) *Preventing Social Exclusion*, London: HM Stationery Office.

Stainback, W. and Stainback, S. (eds) (1990) *Support Networks for Inclusive Schooling*, Baltimore, MD: Paul H. Brookes.

Stigler, J.W. and Hiebert, J. (1999) *The Teaching Gap*, New York: The Free Press.

Strathern, M. (2000) The tyranny of transparency, *British Educational Research Journal* 26 (3), pp. 309–321.

Teddlie, C. and Reynolds, D. (eds) (2000) *The International Handbook of School Effectiveness Research*, London: Falmer Press.

Thomas, G. and Loxley, A. (2001) *Deconstructing Special Education and Constructing Inclusion*, Buckingham: Open University Press.

Thousand, J.S. and Villa, R.A. (1991) Accommodating for greater student variance. In M. Ainscow (ed.) *Effective Schools for All*, London: David Fulton.

Thousand, J.S. and Villa, R.A. (1995) Managing complex change towards inclusive schooling. In R.A. Villa and J.S. Thousand (eds) *Creating an Inclusive School*, Alexandria, VA: Association for Supervision and Curriculum Development.

Thrupp, M. (1999) *Schools Making a Difference: Let's be Realistic!*, Buckingham: Open University Press.

Thrupp, M. (2001) School quasi-markets in England and Wales: best understood as a class strategy? Paper presented at the British Education Research Association Conference, Leeds, 13–15 April.

Timperley, S.H. and Robinson, V.M.J. (2001) Achieving school improvement through challenging and changing teachers' schema, *Journal of Educational Change* 2, pp. 281–300.

Trent, S.C., Artiles, A.J. and Englert, C.S. (1998) From deficit thinking to social constructivism: a review of theory, research and practice in special education, *Review of Research in Education* 23, pp. 277–307.

Udvari-Solner, A. and Thousand, J. (1995) Effective organizational, instructional and curricular practices in inclusive schools and classrooms. In C. Clark, A. Dyson and A. Millward (eds) *Towards Inclusive Schools?*, London: David Fulton.

UNESCO (2000) *Education For All: Meeting Our Collective Commitments*, Paris: UNESCO.

UNESCO (2001) *Open File on Inclusive Education. Support Materials for Managers and Administrators*, Paris: UNESCO.

Villa, R.A. and Thousand, J.S. (1992) Restructuring public school systems: strategies for organizational change and progress. In R.A. Villa, J.S. Thousand, W. Stainback and S. Stainback (eds) *Restructuring for Caring and Effective Education: An Administrative Guide to Creating Heterogeneous Schools*, Baltimore, MD: Paul H. Brookes.

Villa, R.A. and Thousand, J.S. (1995) *Creating an Inclusive School*, Alexandra, VA: Association for Supervision and Curriculum Development.

Villa, R.A., Thousand, J.S., Stainback, W. and Stainback S. (eds) (1992) *Restructuring for Caring and Effective Education: An Administrative Guide to Creating Heterogeneous Schools*, Baltimore, MD: Paul H. Brookes.

Voogt, J.C., Lagerweij, N.A.J. and Seashore Louis, K. (1998) School development and organizational learning: toward an integrative theory. In K. Leithwood and K. Seashore Louis (eds) *Organizational Learning in Schools*, Lisse, NL: Swets & Zeitlinger.

Wagner, J. (1997) The unavoidable intervention of educational research: a framework for reconsidering researcher–practitioner cooperation, *Educational Researcher* 26 (7), pp. 13–22.

Walford, G. (2000) *Policy and Politics in Education*, Aldershot: Ashgate.

Wang, M.C. (1991) Adaptive instruction: an alternative approach to providing for student diversity. In M. Ainscow (ed.) *Effective Schools for All*, London: David Fulton.

Warwick, I. and Douglas, N. (2001) *Safe for All: A Best Practice Guide to Prevent Homophobic Bullying in Secondary Schools*, London: Citizenship 21.

Wasser, J.D. and Bresler, L. (1996) Working in the collaborative zone: conceptualising collaboration in qualitative research teams, *Educational Researcher* 25(5), pp. 5–15.

Weatherley, R. and Lipsky, M. (1977) Street-level bureaucrats and institutional innovation: implementing special education reform, *Harvard Educational Review* 47 (2), pp. 171–197.

Weick, K.E. (1985) Sources of order in underorganized systems: themes in recent organizational theory. In Y.S. Lincoln (ed.) *Organizational Theory and Inquiry: The Paradigm Revolution*, Beverly Hills, CA: Sage.

Wenger, E. (1998) *Communities of Practice: Learning, Meaning and Identity*, Cambridge: Cambridge University Press.

West, M., Ainscow, M. and Stanford, J. (2005) Sustaining improvement in schools in challenging circumstances: a study of successful practice. *School Leadership and Management* 25 (1), pp. 77–93.

Index